New Frontiers for College Education

D1785428

The college sector is facing a growing number of new challenges caused by technological change, globalisation and the growth of mass higher education. *New Frontiers for College Education* considers the impact these changes have had and explores the developing role of college education in countries throughout the world. Whilst analysing the issues associated with providing high quality vocational education and training, the book also reflects on the role of colleges in widening access to both further and higher education.

Drawing together contributions from leading international academics, policymakers and practitioners, the book explores common themes across these diverse societies, as well some of the key challenges experienced within individual countries. It considers the distinctive contributions that colleges can make in responding to these challenges through apprenticeships and other types of vocational education and training. Contributors discuss the growing emphasis on creating more integrated systems of tertiary education, recognising that colleges and universities are now expected to work more closely together and that these diverse demands can be difficult to reconcile.

Providing an authoritative and timely analysis of the changing role of colleges in contemporary society, this book will be of great interest to academics, researchers and postgraduate students in the areas of further and higher education, vocational education and training, lifelong learning, and skills development. It should also be essential reading for policymakers, as well as practitioners working in colleges and other institutions of higher and further education.

Jim Gallacher is Emeritus Professor of Lifelong Learning at Glasgow Caledonian University.

Fiona Reeve is Senior Lecturer in Lifelong Learning at the Open University.

New Frontiers for College Education

International perspectives

Edited by Jim Gallacher and
Fiona Reeve

Routledge
Taylor & Francis Group

LONDON AND NEW YORK

First published 2019 by Routledge

2 Park Square, Milton Park, Abingdon, Oxfordshire OX14 4RN
52 Vanderbilt Avenue, New York, NY 10017

Routledge is an imprint of the Taylor & Francis Group, an informa business

First issued in paperback 2020

British Library Cataloguing-in-Publication Data
A catalogue record for this book is available from the British Library

Library of Congress Cataloguing-in-Publication Data
A catalog record for this book has been requested

ISBN: 978-1-138-30769-8 (hbk)
ISBN: 978-0-367-48891-8 (pbk)

Typeset in Bembo
by Apex CoVantage, LLC

Contents

Conclusions 221

Contributors

Edmund G. Adam, Graduate Assistant, Ontario Institute for Studies in Education, University of Toronto, Canada.

Ann-Marie Bathmaker, Professor of Vocational and Higher Education, School of Education, University of Birmingham, UK.

Adele Bergin, Senior Research Officer, Economic and Social Research Institute, Dublin; Adjunct Associate Professor at the Department of Economics, Trinity College Dublin, Ireland; Research Fellow, IZA Bonn, Germany.

Lucy Hunter Blackburn, PhD student in the Centre for Research in Education Inclusion and Diversity, University of Edinburgh, UK.

Thomas Deissinger, Professor, Konstanz University, Germany.

Martin Doel FETL Chair of Leadership in FE and Skills, University College London, Institute of Education, UK.

Kevin J. Dougherty, Professor of Higher Education and Education Policy and Senior Research Associate, Community College Research Centre, Teachers College, Columbia University, USA.

Jim Gallacher, Emeritus Professor of Lifelong Learning, Glasgow Caledonian University, UK.

Ewart Keep, Chair in Education, Training and Skills and Director of SKOPE, Department of Education, University of Oxford, UK.

Hana Lahr, Research Associate, Community College Research Centre, Teachers College, Columbia University, USA.

Paul Little, Principal and CEO, City of Glasgow College, UK.

Qin Liu, Postdoctoral Fellow, Ontario Institute for Studies in Education, University of Toronto, Canada.

Gavin Moodie, Adjunct Professor in the Department of Leadership, Higher and Adult Education, Ontario Institute for Studies in Education, University of Toronto, Canada.

Vanessa S. Morest, Vice President for Academic Affairs, Westchester Community College, USA.

Ng Cher Pong, Deputy Secretary (SkillsFuture), Ministry of Education, Singapore: Chief Executive, SkillsFuture Singapore Agency.

Fiona Reeve, Senior Lecturer, Faculty of Wellbeing, Education and Language Studies, The Open University, UK.

Sheila Riddell, Professor of Education and Director of the Centre for Research in Education Inclusion and Diversity, University of Edinburgh, UK.

Conor Ryan, Director of Research and Communications (2012–18), The Sutton Trust, UK.

Diane Simpson, Graduate Assistant, Ontario Institute for Studies in Education, University of Toronto, Canada.

Michael L. Skolnik, Professor Emeritus, Ontario Institute for Studies in Education, University of Toronto, Canada.

Emer Smyth, Research Professor, Economic and Social Research Institute, Dublin; Adjunct Professor at the Department of Sociology, Trinity College Dublin, Ireland.

Ni Tang, Assistant Research Fellow at the Central Institute for Vocational & Technical Education at the Ministry of Education, China.

Leesa Wheelahan, William G. Davis Chair in Community College Leadership, Ontario Institute for Studies in Education, University of Toronto, Canada.

Adele Whelan, Research Officer, Economic and Social Research Institute, Dublin; Adjunct Assistant Professor at the Department of Economics, Trinity College Dublin, Ireland.

Dayong Yuan, Senior Researcher, Deputy Director of Institute for Lifelong Learning and ESD at Beijing Academy of Educational Sciences (BAES).

Figures and tables

Figures

Tables

Foreword

As Principal of the City of Glasgow College (CoGC), I was delighted to host an international symposium as part of the launch celebrations for our new super campus in October 2016. This book had its origins in the presentations at the symposium made by the distinguished contributors from a number of countries around the world. We see CoGC, with its two new award-winning and state-of-the-art campuses, as making a statement for the future of college education, not just in Scotland but for the UK and beyond. This is an important time for college sectors as they re-establish their positions in the changing world of tertiary education in general and professional and technical education in particular. The expert contributors to this book raise important questions for the future of colleges across the world and highlight the many challenges we must rise to as we redefine a new era of college education. I hope that this book will inform both policy and practice in college education for the 21st century.

Paul Little
Principal & CEO, City of Glasgow College

Part I

The changing context
for colleges

Chapter 1

New frontiers for college education

The challenges

Jim Gallacher and Fiona Reeve

Introduction

This book is about the challenges and opportunities for college education in the 21st century. We must begin by defining our field of study. The book will focus on the institutions which lie between secondary schools and universities. The nature and type of these institutions differ across the world. In the UK, they include the further education colleges (FECs), although in Scotland, these are now known as Scotland's Colleges, reflecting the relatively high level of higher education-level work in these colleges. In the USA and Canada, they include community colleges, in Australia technical and further education institutes (TAFEs) and in countries such as Germany, a range of vocational colleges. With respect to other countries included in this book, China established a system of vocational schools which has later been augmented by vocational colleges, and Singapore has established Institutes of Technical Education (ITEs) and polytechnics for higher level study. There is therefore a range of different types of institutions across the world. All of them, in their various ways, have important roles in the transition from school to work or to further study at higher levels for many young people and also for older adults returning to study.

However, in many countries, particularly the Anglophone ones, they have often suffered from a lack of status, reflecting the fact that their qualifications are generally at a level below university bachelor's degrees and the vocational character of many of these qualifications. This problem has been exacerbated by changes in the economy and labour markets, as a result of which the skills and vocational qualifications required in contemporary societies are often of a different order from those required in earlier years, and colleges have to respond to these new demands. In addition, higher education has been expanding across the globe, and much higher percentages of young people now proceed directly to university from school rather than undertaking vocational education in the college sector (Gallacher and Parry, 2017; Marginson, 2016). This chapter will aim to set a context for the chapters which follow by exploring the evolving roles of these colleges and the challenges which they must address if they are to have important and central functions in systems of education and training throughout the world in the 21st century.

Three roles for colleges

Three main roles can be identified for the colleges. Firstly, *the provision of vocational education and training*: this has been provided on a part-time basis for those already in employment or apprenticeships and also for those undertaking full-time study, enrolled in programmes at further education or higher education levels. Secondly, colleges have increasingly become providers of general education, and this has contributed to an important role in promoting *social inclusion* and widening access to further and higher education through the provision of 'second chances' for both adults and young people whose achievements in school have been limited. Thirdly, there has been *the provision of higher education* courses which often lead to progression to bachelor's degree level study in universities (sometimes referred to as 'transfer' or 'articulation'). This is linked to the social inclusion role referred to above. In some countries, the emphasis has been less on providing higher education in the colleges and more on 'access' courses which prepare students for entry to higher education. The relative emphasis placed on each of these roles has, of course, differed between countries, and, over time, they have been shaped by wider changes in society.

The impact of wider societal change on the role of colleges

The role which colleges now have in many societies and the functions which they perform are being reshaped by important changes in the economy and in the wider society. Two of these changes will now be considered before returning to a more detailed discussion of these roles.

The changing nature of work

The growth and spread of industrialisation has created the demand for more highly skilled work forces throughout the world, and colleges have emerged to meet the needs for vocational education and training. This can be seen in the UK, where FECs were established to meet this need, a role which continued to be important in the period after the Second World War, when there was a recognised need for training to support the development of the British economy. Provision was mainly part-time and met the needs of a wide range of occupations, including traditional crafts, such as those in the construction industry, as well as those in industry and commerce. The range of provision has included off-the-job education for apprentices and courses at a higher education level thorough Higher National Certificates and Diplomas (HNC/Ds).

In the community colleges in the USA and Canada, there has been an emphasis on the provision of vocational education and training and developing strong links with employers during most of the 20th century. While, at times and in places throughout the century, this vocational focus has had to compete with an emphasis on the 'transfer' function from associate's degrees in the colleges to bachelor's degrees in the four-year universities (Brint and Karabel, 1989), this role in the provision of vocational training has remained strong (Skolnik, 2004; Dougherty and Keinzl, 2006). In Australia, the initial function of TAFEs when they were established in the 1970s was clearly 'to deliver competency-based qualifications designed to meet the needs of industry as part of a broader VET sector' (Wheelahan, 2016, p. 37), and it is only more recently that their role has been extended to include the provision of higher education.

The examples discussed above are all from Anglophone countries. However, in Germany and other countries with similar systems, such as Austria and Switzerland, the need to provide vocational education and training in response to the needs of a developing economy has led to the establishment of the 'dual system'. In these countries, the relationship with employers is much more central. Within this model, there are two 'learning venues' – the company in which an apprentice is employed, and the part-time vocational school (in Germany, the Berufsschulen) which they must attend for a specified number of days per week as part of their apprenticeship programme, the curriculum for which will be established by a State Education Act (Deissinger, 2015). Alongside this dual system, there are also a number of vocational colleges which provide a variety of full-time vocational education programmes (see Deissinger's chapter in this volume for a discussion of the role of these colleges in Germany). Within these systems, vocational education and training have had a much higher status than in the Anglophone countries.

In a very different context of rapid industrialisation and economic development in China, a system of vocational schools was established which expanded rapidly during the 1980s and into the first part of the 21st century. This provided vocational training, including in the rural areas of China, to support the development of industrialisation.

While the skill needs of industrial societies have contributed to the establishment and growth of college sectors and other forms of vocational education and training in societies across the world, the impact of new technological developments is now creating new challenges for colleges. Green and Henseke (2017), in their recent paper on graduate jobs in Europe, conclude that across all countries, job polarisation has increased between 2004 and 2015. They provide evidence that employment has shifted away from intermediate-skilled occupations towards high- and low-skilled occupations. Despite differences across Europe, with significant variations between the countries of southern Europe and the Anglo and Nordic countries, high-skilled occupations have grown in all of Western Europe over this period, while intermediate-skilled ones have declined. Alongside these changes in the occupational structure, the growth of mass systems of higher education now means that much more of the education and training of young people now takes place in universities. However, Green and Henseke also note the growth of graduate underemployment across the OECD countries, although there is a big range, from around 10 per cent in Finland to almost 50 per cent in Japan. They conclude that '. . . the prospects for a successfully employed and contented graduate workforce in the coming decade look far from rosy' (Green and Henseke, 2017, p. 35). This then raises important questions regarding the skills and vocational education and training which will be required to meet the needs of this changing job market.

A rather different focus on the skills and training which are required in this changing labour market is taken by McIntosh in his review of research on the changing nature of work in a number of countries across the world. He concludes that while the impact of technological change and globalisation has had an impact on what has been referred to as the 'hollowing out' of the labour market, with more jobs at the higher level and the lower level, and less at the intermediate levels, this effect should not be over-emphasised. Instead, he suggests that '. . . the changes in the jobs distribution, particularly at intermediate levels, have not been as dramatic as the phrase "hollowing out" implies . . .' (McIntosh, 2013, p. 40). He goes on to suggest that '. . . intermediate jobs still exist in large numbers, and will continue to exist' (p. 40). He suggests that a vitally important policy implication is that we must continue to invest in education and training for people who will enter jobs at that level, both because that level of education continues to be needed and because it provides the people involved with the opportunity to enter these occupations and possibly proceed to further education and training which will provide them with new opportunities as the occupational structure continues to change.

These changes in the nature of work and in labour markets raise important questions regarding the distinctive contribution which colleges can make to the provision of vocational education, an issue which will be considered further below.

The growth of mass higher education

The second major development which has had a significant impact on the colleges, and which has been mentioned briefly above, has been the growth of mass higher education across the world (Gallacher and Parry, 2017; Marginson, 2016). Martin Trow's analysis of the transition from elite to mass higher education has been important in helping us understand the factors which have contributed to this growth. Writing in 1973, he suggested that one of the important driving forces of this development would be the aspirations of middle-class young people and their parents who would see higher education, first of all as a right, and then as an obligation if they were to maintain their more privileged position in society. However, the growth of more democratic and egalitarian values in society would also lead to the recognition of the need to provide opportunities for the sons and daughters of the less privileged social classes to gain access to higher education. All of these demands would create continuing pressures for expansion of the higher education systems:

it seems to me very unlikely that any advanced society can or will be able to stabilize the numbers going on to some form of higher education any time in the near future.

(Trow, 1973, p. 40)

As a result of these drivers, we can see that more and more young people wish to enrol in universities and gain degrees, and there is now clear evidence of the continuing growth in participation in higher education throughout the world. Marginson (2016), in his analysis of what he terms high participation systems (HPS), provides evidence of the very rapid expansion of higher education over the last 20 years, particularly in countries where participation rates have traditionally been much lower than in North America or Western Europe. He refers to this as a 'surge' in higher education participation.

The result of this growth is that on average around 37 per cent of 20-year-olds in OECD countries are enrolled in some form of tertiary education,[1] while four countries have over 50 per cent, most notably South Korea, where 70 per cent of 20-year-olds were enrolled in a tertiary programme in 2013, and 68 per cent of 25–34-year-olds had attained a tertiary-level qualification (OECD, 2015). As a result of these developments, many young people now progress to university, while in the past, they would have gone straight into employment and studied part-time in colleges to gain relevant qualifications. Thus, many workers in the past would have studied for part-time HNCs or other professional qualifications in areas such as accountancy in FECs in the UK. However, over the past 20 years or more, the numbers of part-time students on courses of this kind have been declining. An example of this is that only 16 per cent of HNC/D students in Scotland are now part-time, while the percentage was double that just ten years previously.

Alongside this growth of mass higher education, and the aspirations among many young people to gain a university degree, we have noted the extent of graduate unemployment. These developments raise further questions regarding the types of education and training which are now required in 21st-century societies and the most appropriate and useful roles which colleges can have in responding to these needs.

The three roles of colleges re-examined

We have suggested above that colleges can now have three main roles, although the relative emphasis on these roles may vary from society to society. These three roles will now be considered in greater detail and in light of the wider changes in the economy and society discussed above.

Vocational education and training

It has been noted above that while the demands of industrial societies helped established the need for a vocational education and training sector, the role of colleges in this respect has declined or become more problematic in a number of countries. In the UK the erosion of the manufacturing base in the 1970s and 1980s and the collapse of the youth labour market led to a decline in apprenticeships and other forms of off-the-job training and a diminished role for colleges in vocational education and training. In China the popularity of vocational schools declined, associated with the quality of the education provided and the attraction of a more academic education (Shi, 2012). It has also been suggested that the changing nature of work and the labour market and the growth of mass higher education are creating new challenges for colleges in identifying their role in this area. However, there is also a recognition that modern, 21st-century economies need high quality and appropriate skills training systems, so an important question is – to what extent can the college sector re-engage more effectively with this agenda? Three areas of provision have been identified in recent discussions of this question.

Apprenticeships and similar programmes

The provision of apprenticeship training is an issue which continues to attract a considerable measure of attention in policy discussion and new initiatives. We have noted the decline, until recently, of this type of provision in countries such as the UK, while it has remained a very strong feature of the vocational training system in countries such as Germany, with its dual system (Deissinger, 2015). The value of apprenticeship systems of this kind has attracted considerable interest from many countries throughout the world, as policies are sought which will provide robust and effective skills training systems and also help alleviate problems of youth unemployment. For these reasons, it has been referred to as a 'travelling policy' (Ozga and Jones, 2006). The impact of this renewed interest in apprenticeships in the UK can be seen in that starts rose from around 400,000 in England in the early 2000s to over 800,000 by 2013 (Hupkau and Ventura, 2017). However, it can be noted that while the number of these apprenticeships has grown markedly, the involvement of the college sector has been relatively limited. For example, in Scotland, only about 8 per cent of the apprenticeship programme involves direct contracts with colleges, although this figure will be augmented by sub-contracting some parts of the off-the-job training from other providers to the colleges. In England, about 12 per cent of students in general FE colleges are enrolled in apprenticeships, while 59 per cent of those in private independent training providers are registered on these programmes. This reflects in some measure the decline of a focus on vocational education in these colleges and is associated with more limited levels of relationships between colleges and employers. The problematic relationship with employers can be seen as underlying the very sharp decline in apprenticeship starts in England (around 60 per cent in figures reported in October 2017) associated with the introduction of a new apprenticeship levy by the UK government to support the funding of apprenticeships. It has been suggested that there was an insufficient level of employer engagement in developing this new apprenticeship funding model.

Underlying this are differences in the vocational and training model which exists in a country such as the UK, other Anglophone countries and many others throughout the world, when compared with countries such as Germany, Austria and Switzerland. Commenting on this, Wheelahan and Moodie (2017) have suggested that Germany and a number of other European countries tend to have market economies which are coordinated at a national and regional level by governments and their social partners, including employers and trade unions. Employers and Chambers of Commerce are heavily involved in the design of qualifications. Employers are therefore more confident that these qualifications will meet their needs, and they are happier to invest in vocational training, and work with the schools or colleges which provide this training. By contrast, in the liberal market economies of the Anglophone and other similar countries, there is an absence of this close coordination. There is a greater emphasis on general and employability skills because employers are wary of investing in education and training if it is likely that employees may be poached by other employers. These national differences at a structural and cultural level make it difficult to import the apprenticeship model which has been so successful in some countries, a point noted by Valiente and Scandurra (2017) in their review of the place of apprenticeships in recent policy. In discussing the problems encountered in moving from small scale pilot projects to national systems they reach the following conclusions.

> Scaling up these innovative experiences . . . would require increasing public expenditure in the incentives offered to employers, the development of new regulation and institutional capacity, and the reform of governance structures in order to include social partners in the management of the system. It is not surprising that many countries have not been able or have decided not to scale up exemplar pilot experiences of dual apprenticeships to a systemic level.
>
> (Valiente and Scandurra, 2017, p. 54)

In understanding the underlying nature of these problems, David Raffe's distinction between 'policy learning' and 'policy borrowing' is a helpful one which can guide policy formation. He suggests that policy borrowing is usually unsuccessful because of the failure to recognise differences between countries and the conditions which are required for the successful development of new policies (Raffe and Byrne, 2005). By contrast, he suggests that there is potentially much to be gained by policy learning. This is an approach which it will be useful to consider if colleges are to strengthen their relationships with employers and become more fully involved in apprenticeships and similar programmes in countries where these type of programmes are weak. Cher Pong's chapter provides a brief outline of the ways in which Singapore is seeking to implement such an approach of policy learning in establishing the Earn and Learn Programme (ELP) as their approach to apprenticeship training.

Higher level vocational qualifications

The second area which is of considerable interest is the potentially important role of colleges in the provision of higher level vocational qualifications. This has included associate degrees in community colleges in the USA, HNC/Ds and foundation degrees in the UK and similar qualifications in other parts of the world. These qualifications have often been for semi- or para-professional roles, in a wide range of occupations, including nursing (in the USA), social care, nursery nursing and early years, business, administration and engineering. While they continue to have important roles in many of these areas, we have noted above that the growth of mass higher education and the increased numbers of young people going straight from school to university are creating new challenges for colleges. There is also the question of what kinds of qualifications are required to respond the needs of the changing 21st-century labour markets in a context in which there is also evidence of graduate underemployment.

An earlier attempt to address this question was the introduction of foundation degrees (FDs) in England in the early years of this century (DfEE, 2000; Blunkett, 2001). These programmes largely replaced HNDs in many English colleges, and the numbers on them grew quite rapidly up to 2010. They were designed to be employer-led and work-based and in these ways to be more effective in responding to the skills needed by employers. However, they were also validated by universities when they were first introduced (some colleges now have been awarded power to validate their own FDs), and, consequently, the vocational focus of these programmes was often limited by the need to meet university-quality assurance requirements (Reeve et al., 2007). As a result, they never established themselves as the radical new vocational qualifications which would enable colleges to make a major contribution to addressing the need for high skills in the evolving labour market, and the policy focus has moved away from these qualifications. An alternative which is now attracting considerable interest within the UK policy communities is the development of Degree Apprenticeships, or Graduate Apprenticeships in Scotland. The aim here is to build on the success of the apprenticeship model in countries such as Germany and to establish a range of programmes at a graduate level in which those involved will be employees and will undertake both high quality work-based learning and off-the-job training in colleges or universities (Kelly, 2015; Sutton Trust, 2013). These developments are still at an early stage, and it is notable that in Scotland it is universities, rather than colleges, which have been involved so far. This has led to a concern that they will, like the FDs, be dominated by the demands of the university degree curriculum, rather than vocational needs of the labour market.

In China, the Ministry of Education and other stakeholders have responded to these issues by developing a plan for a more fully developed and enhanced system of technical and vocational education which will link vocational schools, vocational colleges and applied universities in response to perceived shortages of skilled workers and an oversupply of university and college graduates (Tang and Shi, 2017). The chapter by Tang and Yuan in this volume also discusses policies to achieve a much closer integration between enterprise and colleges in China. In Singapore, which has also gone through a rapid process of development to establish itself as one of the leading economies in Asia and beyond, there has been the development not just of an integrated structure of ITEs, polytechnics and applied universities, but also a skills strategy based on lessons learned from other successful nations such as Germany and Switzerland, as Cher Pong outlines in his chapter in this volume.

It is also interesting to note some changes in Germany, as a higher percentage of young people gain the *Abitur* which would enable them to gain entry to university. As a result, more are now combining apprenticeships with degrees, and a range of 'hybrid' qualifications are being developed and provided through universities of applied sciences (Fachhochschule) or universities of cooperative education (*Duale Hochschule*) (Edeling and Pilz, 2017).

Upskilling, reskilling and lifelong learning

A further issue which is raised by the rapidly changing nature of work is the need for reskilling and a return to the idea of lifelong learning which had slipped off the policy agenda in many societies. The argument here is that with the pace of change in technology and the impact of globalisation many people will need to retrain and reskill during their working lives. This has been recognised by the UK government in the Foresight project on the future of skills and lifelong learning and the publications associated with this (Government Office for Science Foresight (GOSF), 2017) Cher Pong also refers to it as a key aspect of the skills strategy which has been developed in Singapore. The role of colleges in responding to the demands of this agenda should also be considered.

The future of vocational education and training in the college sector

We have noted in our discussion that, while the provision of vocational education and training has been an important role for the college sectors across the world, this is a role which has declined in some countries. The changing nature of the economy and the labour markets, and the growth of mass higher education have also created new challenges which must be recognised and addressed. These issues will be discussed further in the chapters by Martin Doel, Ewart Keep, and Reeve and Gallacher with respect to the UK. The rather different responses in countries which are now major players in a globalised economy will be considered in Cher Pong's chapter on Singapore, while Tang and Yuan will discuss recent developments in China.

Social inclusion

The second function, which is now an important one for colleges in a number of countries, is to promote *social inclusion* and provide pathways for students from social and ethnic groups who would otherwise struggle to gain access to educational opportunities. This is often seen as a form of 'second chance education' (Kennedy, 1997).

We have noted above how the decline of manufacturing in the UK and the collapse of the youth labour market led to a decline in apprenticeships and other forms of off-the-job training and a diminished role for colleges in vocational education and training. This then led to colleges seeking other areas of work, one of which has been general education, with a particular focus on providing second chances for both young people and older students who have been less successful at school. This enables students to continue with their education or to return to education later in life. As a result, more colleges have seen making a contribution to a social inclusion agenda, and compensating for failures within the school system as an increasingly important aspect of their work.

Adult students have become a major part of the student group in colleges in the UK. In Scotland, 43 per cent were aged 25 or older in 2015–16 (SFC, 2017), while in England, there were 90,000 students aged 60 or older (AOC, 2017). This work also includes people suffering from a range of disabilities, both physical and mental (17 per cent of students in English colleges in 2016–17), and young people who have been in care as a result of family disruption or other problems. Provision of this kind can include general education as well as various types of vocational education. It is now a major aspect of provision in many colleges. In Scotland, 31 per cent of students are enrolled in courses of a general rather than a vocational nature, most of which are ones which would otherwise be taken in secondary schools (SFC, 2017). We have noted the relatively high percentage of adult students, often involved in 'second chance' education (Kennedy, 1997). Outreach work based in local communities is one important aspect of this second-chance provision, particularly for working class women returning to study after having children. For these women, the more informal ethos of a community learning centre has often eased the transition back into learning (Gallacher et al., 2007). Some indication of the continuing importance of this second-chance provision for women can be seen from data which shows that 48 per cent of all female students in colleges are aged 25 or older (SFC, 2017).

Community colleges in the USA have also had a strong tradition of providing educational opportunities for students from disadvantaged backgrounds of various kinds. Dougherty et al. in their chapter in this book refer to the ethos of social inclusion which these colleges have developed to enable them to be the 'open door college'. Thus, there have been higher percentages of students who are from less socio-economic advantaged backgrounds, are non-white and are older when compared to the four-year colleges.

This role of colleges in providing education and training opportunities for those who have been less successful in the school system can also be seen as being reflected in the more traditional role of vocational and skills training, where they have provided alternative routes to qualifications and employment. A question can, however, be asked regarding the extent to which a focus on social inclusion has weakened a focus on vocational and skills training at a time when it was becoming increasingly difficult to fulfil this role, and is there a possible conflict between these roles. We will return to this question in the concluding section of this chapter.

Higher education and 'transfer' or articulation

The third function which has become increasingly important for colleges in a number of countries is the *provision of HE courses and opportunities for 'transfer'* to bachelor's degree programmes in the universities. While there is considerable variation in the nature and extent of this provision, colleges have become, through this work, important contributors either directly or indirectly to the growth of mass higher education, and their role in that respect must be considered. This has also been associated with their role in promoting social inclusion which has been discussed above. Brint and Karabel (1989) have noted the importance of higher education in community colleges as a means of gaining academic respectability when they were established in the USA in the early years of the 20th century. The chapter by Dougherty et al. in this book confirms the continuing importance of this role, noting that data published in 2017 recorded 6.2 million students enrolled in community colleges, accounting for 30.4 per cent of all students in degree-granting institutions. The 'transfer' function also continues to be important for many students, with 21 per cent of them transferring to a four-year institution to complete a bachelor's degree (Horn and Skomsvold, 2012). In addition, a number of states have now authorised their community colleges to offer bachelor's degrees. While there are differences in the roles of community colleges in Canada between provinces, they have broadly similar roles to those in the USA in the provision of higher education and the opportunities to progress to bachelor's degree study (Skolnik, 2004). The chapter by Moodie et al. also discusses the role which these colleges now have in providing bachelor level degrees, although it can be noted that the numbers involved are small. In Australia, while TAFEs were established with a very strong vocational function, they are now increasingly being encouraged to provide HE courses, although this is still limited and generally involves partnerships with universities (Wheelahan et al., 2009).

HE courses are also an important aspect of work in colleges in the UK, although there are some significant differences between the UK countries (Gallacher, 2017). In Scotland, around 20 per cent of all college students are studying in HE level courses, and this accounts for 22 per cent of all students on HE courses below postgraduate level in colleges and universities. Most of this provision is in the form of HNC/D programmes, and while these courses were originally developed as vocational qualifications, there has been an increasing emphasis on policies to encourage articulation links with universities, facilitating transfer to bachelor's degree programmes (SFC, 2008). In England HE courses are a less significant aspect of the work of the college sector, with students on these courses accounting for around 7 per cent of all FEC students and 11 per cent of all HE level students in England (Parry et al., 2012). Most of the provision is in the form of degrees or foundation degrees franchised from universities. As in the USA, colleges in the UK have an important role in widening access to higher education, with a much higher percentages of students coming from disadvantaged backgrounds when compared with university students (Gallacher, 2017; Hunter Blackburn et al., 2016; Parry et al., 2012). A rather different but related role for colleges with respect to HE is the provision of 'access' courses which prepare students for university study and can provide a 'second chance' route into degrees for the students involved. Bergin et al. discuss this in their chapter in this book.

However, while the role of colleges in widening access to higher education can be seen as a positive contribution, there are also significant challenges which colleges must address. The first set of issues centre around some possible contradictions in their role of promoting social inclusion. They focus on the question which Brint and Karabel raised in their seminal book on community colleges in the USA (Brint and Karabel, 1989) – should the route to higher education through colleges should be seen as a form of 'cooling out' which 'diverts' students from less advantaged backgrounds from gaining access to the more prestigious higher education institutions? The evidence presented in Riddell and Hunter Blackburn's chapter in this volume might provide some support for this, in that since 2006 the differences in entry routes to university in Scotland between the most and least disadvantaged have become more pronounced. The more advantaged are more likely to enter directly into traditional degree courses, often in the most prestigious 'ancient' universities, while the least advantaged are more likely to enter a college course and possibly progress to a post 1992 university (Hunter Blackburn et al., 2016). In the USA Dougherty and Keinzl (2006) note that earlier studies of community college entrants found that 45 per cent had left higher education six years later without a degree, while the comparable figure for entrants to four-year colleges or universities is 24 per cent. They also concluded that those of lower socio-economic status, black or Hispanic and older students are less likely to transfer to a four college or university. Furthermore, there is evidence that less than half of the students in Scotland who progress from colleges to universities gain full credit for their college HNC/Ds qualifications, and, as we have noted, progression opportunities are greatest in the newer 'post-1992' universities and most limited in the most prestigious 'ancient' universities. As a result, a large number of college students can take up to six years to complete a four-year honours degree (Gallacher, 2017). All of this reflects underlying problems regarding the strength of the articulation links between colleges and universities.

It is therefore important to recognise that mass higher education systems are also highly stratified ones (Boliver, 2011), and while colleges have a valuable role in widening access to higher education, there is paradoxically a danger that this may 'divert' socially and economically disadvantaged students from the more prestigious higher education sectors. This may limit the routes into and through higher education which are available to them. If colleges are to play a part in higher education which contributes to fair and equal access, it is important that these problems and challenges are recognised when developing policy and provision.

A second set of issues focus around the possible conflict between this role of enabling 'transfer' or articulation to bachelor's degree study and the other role which these qualifications can have in contributing to vocational education and training. It has been noted above that, while many of these programmes were originally provided on a part-time basis for people in work, a higher proportion of students are now full-time and are using these qualifications as routes to degree-level study, rather than as terminal qualifications which lead directly into employment. While there is no necessary contradiction between these roles, and college qualifications can be seen as stepping stones towards vocationally oriented degrees, there is also a danger that this can weaken a strong vocational focus for these qualifications. It has been suggested above that there is a need to consider whether colleges can develop a stronger focus on higher level vocational qualifications, and this focus on articulation or transfer may lead to tensions with this agenda.

Concluding comments

We have used this introductory chapter to outline what we see as the three main roles which have emerged for colleges in a number of countries across the world. The first of these, the provision of *vocational education and training*, has been seen as a central one in the countries of the UK and in the Australian TAFEs. It has also been an important one in the community colleges in the USA and Canada, although a more contested one, especially in the USA. It has also become an important element in emerging global economies such as China and Singapore. We have, however, suggested that in the UK, this role has been eroded as the economy has changed, and many of the occupations for which colleges provided training have declined. As a result, the apprenticeship system was much reduced, and while recent policy initiatives have sought to reinvigorate it, colleges have struggled to be main players in this field. The growth of mass higher education and the tendency for many young people to progress from school to full-time higher education, rather than employment and part-time vocational training has further weakened the college role in this respect. This has, however, encouraged colleges to place a greater emphasis on other roles. This has led to the emergence of the second main role we have identified for colleges: the promotion of *social inclusion*. This has been associated with the provision of more general education for a wide range of students, including many older adult returners. This provision has often focused on the more socially and economically disadvantaged and has become part of a wider set of policies and provision to promote social inclusion. In many colleges, particularly in the UK, a large part of provision would appear to focus on these issues. The third main role has also been associated with the increasing demand for higher education.

This has seen a greater emphasis on *higher education and the opportunities for 'transfer'* from colleges courses to bachelor's degrees in universities (this was already well-established in American community colleges).

These functions, and their evolution as outlined here, have been most associated with colleges and their development in the Anglophone countries. In other countries, most notably Germany, Austria and Switzerland, there has been a much more coordinated policy of skills development and training, involving governments, social partners and educational providers. This model and the apprenticeship system associated in particular with the German 'dual system' have been seen by many other countries as one that they would wish to emulate. However, we have suggested that there are problems with 'policy borrowing' of this kind when the political and cultural infrastructure which has underpinned it does not exist. In this respect, we have noted Singapore's interest in 'policy learning'. We have also noted that the growth of mass higher education is having an impact on countries such as Germany, where more young people are gaining the *Abitur* which gives them entry to higher education, and more are seeking to combine vocational and academic qualifications, sometimes in the form of new 'hybrid' qualifications.

We would suggest that colleges in countries across the world now have a range of important roles. However, there is the possibility of tension between these roles. There is also a further problem, in part associated with these multiple roles, in that these colleges, sitting between schools and universities, have often lacked a clear identity and the status which other parts of the educational system have enjoyed. This has been exacerbated by the status which academic qualifications have enjoyed by contrast with vocational ones, particularly within the Anglophone countries and in countries with a Confucian tradition, such as China. Given these challenges, how can colleges clarify their roles, and what will be the most effective way forward for these institutions? Should they continue to combine all of these functions in single institutions, as many of them do at present, and, if so, how can they strengthen their roles? An alternative for them might be to focus more clearly on certain aspects of their role and aspire to become centre of excellence to provide the highest quality of provision for their students and the societies in which they are located. There could be problems with either of these alternatives, and there will no doubt be other ways of addressing these issues. We hope that the chapters in this book, contributed by a number of informed authors from around the world, will contribute to a more critical analysis of these issues, and to the debates we need to have, not just within the college communities, but in the wider policy communities if colleges are to make their most effective contributions as we proceed into the 21st century.

Note

1 Tertiary education is the term used by the OECD to refer to post-secondary education. It encompasses the full range of higher education including short-cycle tertiary programmes

at ISCED level 5 (programmes which are at a level below bachelor's degrees and are often involve the equivalent of two years of full-time study), bachelor's degrees, master's and doctoral level study.

References

AOC (2017) *College Key Facts 2017–18* [Online], Association of Colleges. Available at www. aoc.co.uk/sites/default/files/Key%20Facts%202017-18%20.pdf (Accessed 21 November 2017).

Blunkett, D. (2001) *Education into Employability: The Role of the DfEE in the Economy*, London, Department for Education and Employment.

Boliver, V. (2011) 'Expansion, differentiation and persistence of social class inequalities in British higher education', *Higher Education*, vol. 61, pp. 229–242.

Brint, S. G. and Karabel, J. (1989) *The Diverted Dream: Community Colleges and the Promise of Educational Opportunity in America 1900–1985*, Oxford, Oxford University Press.

Deissinger, T. (2015) 'The German dual vocational education and training system as "good practice"?', *Local Economy*, vol. 30, no. 5, pp. 557–567.

DfEE (Department for Education and Employment) (2000) *Foundation Degrees: A Consultation Document*, London, Department for Education and Employment.

Dougherty, K. and Keinzl, G. S. (2006) 'It's not enough to get through the open door: Inequalities by social background in transfer from community colleges to four year colleges', *Teachers College Record*, vol. 108, no. 3, March, pp. 452–487.

Edeling, S. and Pilz, M. (2017) 'Should I stay or should I go?: The additive double qualification in Germany', *Journal of Vocational Education and Training*, vol. 69, no. 1, pp. 81–99.

Gallacher, J. (2017) 'Higher education in the college sector: Widening access or diversion? Questions and challenges from the Scottish experience', *Journal of Education and Work*, vol. 30, no. 7, pp. 1–10.

Gallacher, J., Crossan, B., Mayes, T., Smith, L., and Watson, D. (2007) 'Expanding our understanding of the learning cultures in community based further education', *Educational Review*, vol. 59, no. 4, pp. 501–517.

Gallacher, J. and Parry, G. (2017) 'Student participation in the twenty first century: Mass or universal systems?', in Scott, P., Gallacher, J., and Parry, G. (eds.), *New Languages and Landscapes of Higher Education*, Oxford, Oxford University Press.

Government Office for Science Foresight (2017) *Future of Skills and Lifelong Learning* [Online], London, GOSF. Available at www.gov.uk/government/collections/future-of-skills-and-lifelong-learning (Accessed 30 November 2017).

Green, F. and Henseke, G. (2017) *Graduates and "Graduate Jobs" in Europe: A Picture of Growth and Diversification: Centre for Global Higher Education*, London, UCL Institute of Education.

Horn, L. and Skomsvold, P. (2012) *Community College Student Outcomes, 1994–2009* [Online], Washington, DC, National Center for Education Statistics. Available at https://nces. ed.gov/pubs2012/2012253.pdf (Accessed 17 October 2017).

Hunter Blackburn, L., Kadar-Satat, G., Riddell, S., and Weedon, E. (2016) *Access in Scotland: Access to Higher Education for People from Less Advantaged Backgrounds in Scotland*, CREID University of Edinburgh and The Sutton Trust. Available at www.suttontrust.com/wp-content/uploads/2016/05/Access-in-Scotland_May2016.pdf (Accessed 29 May 2016).

Hupkau, C. and Ventura, G. (2017) *Further Education in England: Learners and Institutions*, LSE, Centre for Vocational Education Research, Briefing Note 001. Available at http://cver.lse. ac.uk/textonly/cver/pubs/cverbrf001.pdf (Accessed 15 November 2017).

Kelly, S. (2015) *Raising Productivity by Improving Higher Technical Education*, Oxford, HEPI.

Kennedy, H. (1997) *Learning Works: Widening Participation in Further Education*, FEFC.

Marginson, S. (2016) 'High participation systems of higher education', *The Journal of Higher Education*, vol. 87, no. 2, pp. 243–270.

McIntosh, S. (2013) 'Hollowing out and the future of the labour market', *Department for Business Innovation and Skills Research Paper* No. 134, London, Department for Business Innovation and Skills.

OECD (2015) *Education at a Glance 2015: OECD Indicators* [Online], Paris, OECD Publications. Available at www.oecd.org/edu/education-at-a-glance-19991487.htm (Accessed 25 January 2016).

Ozga, J. and Jones, R. (2006) 'Travelling and embedded policy: The case of knowledge transfer', *Journal of Education Policy*, vol. 21, no. 1, pp. 1–17.

Parry, G., Callender, C., Scott, P., and Temple, P. (2012) 'Understanding higher education in further education colleges', *BIS Research Paper* No. 69, London, Department for Business, Innovation and Skills.

Raffe, D. and Byrne, D. (2005) *Policy Learning from "Home International" Comparisons*, CES Briefing No. 34, Edinburgh, Centre for Educational Sociology, University of Edinburgh. Available at www.ces.ed.ac.uk/PDF%20Files/Brief034.pdf (Accessed 30 September 2016).

Reeve, F., Gallacher, J., and Ingram, R. (2007) 'A comparative study of HNs in Scotland and foundation degrees in England: Contrast, complexity and continuity', *Journal of Education and Work*, vol. 20, no. 4, pp. 305–318.

Scottish Funding Council (2008) *Articulation for All?* Edinburgh, Scottish Funding Council.

Scottish Funding Council (2017) *Infact Database* [Online]. Available at www.sfc.ac.uk/infact/ (Accessed 30 September 2017).

Shi, W. (2012) 'Development of TVET in China: Issues and challenges', in Pilz, M. (ed.), *The Future of Vocational Education and Training in a Changing World*, Wiesbaden, Springer.

Skolnik, M. L. (2004) 'The relationship of community colleges to other providers of post-secondary and adult education in Canada and implications for policy', *Higher Education Perspectives*, vol. 1, no. 1, pp. 36–58.

Sutton Trust (2013) *Real Apprenticeships: Creating a Revolution in English Skills*, Sutton Trust.

Tang, N. and Shi, W. (2017) 'Youth employment and technical and vocational and training (TVET) in China', in Pilz, M. (ed.), *Vocational Education and Training in Times of Economic Crisis*, Springer.

Trow, M. (1973) *Problems in the Transition from Elite to Mass Higher Education*, Berkeley, CA, Carnegie Commission on Higher Education.

Valiente, O. and Scandurra, R. (2017) 'Challenges to the implementation of dual apprenticeships in OECD countries: A literature review', in Pilz, M. (ed.), *Vocational Education and Training in Times of Economic Crisis*, Springer.

Wheelahan, L. (2016) '"Colleges for all" in Anglophone countries-meritocracy or social inequality? An Australian example', *Research in Post-Compulsory Education*, vol. 21, no. 1–2, pp. 33–48.

Wheelahan, L. and Moodie, G. (2017) 'Vocational education qualifications' roles in pathways to work in liberal market economies', *Journal of Vocational Education & Training*, vol. 69, no. 1, pp. 10–27.

Wheelahan, L., Moodie, G., Billet, S., and Kelly, A. (2009) *HE in TAFEs*, NCVER Monograph Series 01/2009, Adelaide, NCVER.

Chapter 2

Technical and professional education – a defining role for further education colleges?

Martin Doel

With the successive publication of the UK government's Productivity Plan (HM Treasury, 2015), the Sainsbury Panel Report (BIS and DfE, 2016a), the UK Skills Plan (BIS and DfE, 2016b) and, most lately, the UK Industrial Strategy (DBEIS, 2017), the term 'technical education' has increasingly been used as an alternative to 'vocational education'. Internationally, the Organisation for Economic Cooperation and Development (OECD) has similarly mooted the use of the term 'Professional and Technical Education' (PTET) as an alternative to the longer standing acronym TVET (Technical and Vocational Education and Training). In either case, both technical education in the UK, and PTET in the OECD, the terms are not at any point precisely defined; the Sainsbury Panel Report comes closest to an inferential definition by proposing two distinct educational pathways for students from age 16 onwards: an academic route and a technical route, the latter comprising two forms: a work-based route of apprenticeships, and a college-based route with incorporated substantive work placements.

The colleges referred to in the 'college-based' routes can reasonably be presumed to be further education (FE) colleges. FE colleges and FE more generally do not have a singular coalescing mission or purpose. Might technical education become a defining role for FE colleges and for other FE providers, including independent training providers? The prospect of technical education becoming the defining role for FE colleges and other FE providers rests, first, upon an understanding of what is distinctive about technical, or technical and professional education and, second, consideration of its 'fit' with FE providers.

The description of policy reviews and changes that follows in relation to technical and professional education relates almost solely to England, reflecting the fact that education and skills policy is a devolved matter within the United Kingdom. Some comparative remarks are, however, made and the conceptual analysis of what differentiates technical education from other forms of education will hopefully be of wider interest.

Defining technical education

Nowhere in the Sainsbury Panel Report is there a direct definition of technical education. Such definition as there is may be inferred by the Panel's identification of 15 routes into skilled employment and the insistence that content of qualifications associated with the technical pathway – whether work-based or college-based – be determined primarily by the needs of the workplace and employers. The identification of the 15 routes is based upon the grouping of standard occupational codes (SOC), with four likely to be reserved for apprenticeships only.[1] The routes do not encompass all occupations:

> Technical education must require the acquisition of both a substantial body of technical knowledge and a set of skills valued by industry. However, not all occupations require technical training in college or as part of an apprenticeship. Unskilled and very low-skilled occupations do not have sufficiently large knowledge requirements to warrant a technical education route.
>
> (BIS and DfE, 2016a, p. 33)

Quite aside from the tautological nature of this reasoning, with the word *technical* remaining undefined in relation to either *education* or *knowledge*, it also stretches the use of the word technical beyond its everyday use; the inclusion of occupations like child care and hospitality means that the OECD descriptor of technical *and* professional education might be more appropriate. The passage above also clearly implies that technical education sits within a hierarchy and is associated with high- and not low-skilled occupations. It is this juxtaposition that drives the requirement for qualifications within the college-based route, named T-levels in the Skills Plan, at level 3 (the equivalent level to A levels), and that not all young people will be able access them directly at age 16.[2] The intention behind these conditions is that T levels be highly regarded as rigorous and stretching by employers, parents and students. Additionally, and as an aside, it could be inferred that 'vocational', in the lexicon of education and training, has become a damaged word, being associated with lower level provision for the 50 per cent in England who don't or can't follow the more recognised academic pathway.[3]

The restriction of technical (or technical and professional) education to certain occupational groups, to higher achieving students and to levels at or above level 3 is not, however, sufficiently clear a definition to inform curriculum development, pedagogy, quality assurance or assessment methodologies. Each of these considerations are critical in assessing whether technical education and its associated qualifications are a good fit for FE providers as a default, or defining, purpose.

In searching for a more comprehensive characterisation of technical education it may be worth posing some key questions:

- **What** is to be taught in terms of content and skills?
- **Who** should be the teachers?
- **Where** should it be taught?
- **How** should it be taught?
- **How** should it be assessed?

It is only the first of these questions that the Sainsbury Panel Report answers to any significant degree. The content of the curriculum for technical education should be drawn from the workplace with the needs of the occupation being the pre-eminent determinant. It follows that employers should have a leading role in sanctioning the content of the curriculum. In this respect, technical education is avowedly instrumental which at the higher levels, in particular, may make it an uncomfortable fit for higher education institutions that value academic independence and autonomy. But, whilst instrumental, there is a difference between technical education and technical training. Apprentices and full-time technical education students need to develop underlying skills that enable them to learn and re-interpret experience after formal instruction has been completed. The term education could also be taken to imply a need to develop wider competencies and knowledge particularly in the case of younger people such as citizenship, social action and health and well-being. Setting qualifications in such a wider context is entirely consistent with the Wolf[4] Report (2011) on vocational qualifications which introduced programmes of study for young people, within which qualifications are embedded; technical education must be embedded within a developmental programme of study, as well as leading to a discrete qualification.

In identifying what might be required of teachers of high quality technical education, the report of the Commission on Adult Vocational Education and Learning (CAVTL) (2013), though prepared in relation to adults has salience for technical education at all ages. A key conclusion of the Commission was that excellent vocational education was most likely to be delivered by what they termed *dual professionals* – teachers or lecturers who were both expert in their occupational profession or trade **and** as teachers. To be credible with their students, such teachers are most likely to have been recruited from the industry and employment field toward which a technical education course is oriented. To remain credible as teachers of technical education they need also to be continually updated as the state of practice within their trade or profession in a parallel way to lecturers in academic studies who need keep themselves abreast of research.[5]

A further condition of excellent vocational teaching identified by CAVTL was the need for a *clear line of sight* between the learning environment and the work environment. This line of sight was most likely to be engendered by what the Commission called a *two-way street* of continuous engagement between the education provider and its teachers and the industries in which students were being prepared for employment. Through this means the curriculum could be continuously updated to meet emerging needs within the workplace. The *clear line of sight* also benefits from education and training being conducted in industry-standard facilities, or through the use of high quality simulators, enabling the most realistic experience for students, albeit in more closely controlled conditions than might be possible in the actual workplace.

Controlled conditions are important in much technical education since there are consequences of error that are more immediate and unforgiving than in academic education which is most often theoretical in nature. Servicing an aircraft, repairing a braking system on a car, installing an electrical ring main, applying chemicals in a hair salon or cooking a meal for 50 diners must done safely and comply with stringent quality conditions. Fundamentally, at the outset students in technical education must understand that there are right and wrong ways to do things. This does not mean that creativity and innovation have no place in technical education, but they must be based upon sound technique. This then demands that learning through discovery in technical education must be within clearly defined bounds and that an overtly didactic approach to teaching is necessary to a greater degree than in most academic study.[6]

It may too be that the relationship between theory and practice is inverted in technical education when compared to academic study, with practice preceding theory. Rather than being taught concepts and then seeking exemplification in reality, in technical education a more effective approach may be to use theory to interpret experience, to understand why techniques are used and how things work. As an example, learning to fly an aeroplane is first a practical experience achieved through demonstration and application of operating procedures within closely controlled conditions; an understanding of aeronautical principles is then used subsequently to extend and deepen learning, prior to the next practical experience.

The aeronautical example is also instructive when considering essential differences in assessing learning between technical and academic education. It is the decision of a flying instructor that a student can safely permitted to fly solo; this is not a decision that is easily subject to external weighting and oversight. The flying instructor is trusted to make the decision, but that decision-making trust is subject to periodic quality assurance by a peer simulating the behaviour of an ab-initio student. This approach is very much in keeping with the traditional approach to apprenticeships as conceived in the medieval guilds, with a master craftsman signing off the indenture papers of an apprentice, judging the apprentice to be fit to join the guild. Distinctive technical education depends upon the mastery and demonstration of practical skills, not simply upon the completion of written exams or papers. Such a requirement poses considerable challenges to systems of mass education, though use of virtual realities may provide a way forward here, albeit without the jeopardy involved in fully realistic circumstances.

The Sainsbury Panel Report is clear that technical education must continue beyond level 3, particularly encompassing levels 4 and 5. These latter levels are associated with a technical level of expertise that is held to be deficient within the UK skills base (CBI/Pearson, 2015) and a level of educational provision that is more prevalent in other OECD skills education systems than in the UK.(OECD, 2014) This is a domain that broaches the divide between UK universities and colleges of further education, and which in other countries is occupied by a distinct set of institutions such as applied universities and polytechnics. This level of provision receives proportionally less attention in the Sainsbury Panel Report, but recent developments in the form of National

Colleges and Institutes of Technology, identify it as an area of interest in England. Whether technical education at this level will remain distinctive at levels 4 and 5 and above must be a moot point. What I have called elsewhere the 'gravitational pull of the academic' is particularly strong in England and sustained by regulatory and funding incentives that will be difficult to redress. (AoC, 2014)

At levels 6 and above, much has been made of the introduction of degree apprenticeships in England. It remains to be seen, however, whether most degree apprenticeships meet the characteristics of technical education described above, rather than comprising of existing degree provision that is delivered on a part-time basis to employees of levy paying firms. In the latter case, the content of the degrees conferred may not be altered to meet the needs of employers. Nor is off-the-job learning necessarily intimately related to practice and experience from the workplace, providing a means of reflecting upon experience and deepening understanding.

Apprenticeships

The Sainsbury Panel Report is also relatively light in its coverage of apprenticeships below the degree level, despite this mode of technical education being seen as one of the twin bedrocks of a technical education system.[7] That this is so is largely due to that fact that substantive reform to apprenticeships was already underway before the Sainsbury Panel was convened. The initial resurgence in apprenticeships provision in England came in the latter of years of the Labour administration, prior to the election of the coalition government in 2010. This direction of travel was reinforced after 2010 with the adoption of a target of three million apprenticeship starts by 2020. This represented a substantial change of emphasis in vocational provision, but with growth in apprenticeships came concerns over the quality of such provision and the potential for existing short courses, often at lower levels, simply be re-badged as apprenticeships. The initial reaction was to specify that apprenticeships to be at least 12 months in duration. A more extensive review of apprenticeships was conducted by the entrepreneur Doug Richard in 2012. Amongst the key recommendations in the Richard Review was more direct involvement of employers in determining the content of apprenticeships, rather than this work being conducted through intermediate bodies. To carry out this work, so-called Trailblazer groups were formed to propose new standards that would replace the existing apprenticeship frameworks. Critically, these new standards would not necessarily require qualifications to be embedded within the apprenticeship; with the addition of an endpoint assessment in all apprenticeships, the apprenticeship itself would become a qualification in itself.

In its references to apprenticeships, the Sainsbury Panel Report indicated that knowledge, skills and behaviours developed within apprenticeships standards would be broadly similar to those developed in the equivalent college-based route. This equivalence would in turn allow easier transition between the two pathways – the part-time study apprenticeship route and full-time technical education in colleges – as had been observed elsewhere, most particularly in Norway (Sainsbury Panel Report). This apparently common sense recommendation will, however, be difficult to achieve in practice. Quite aside from the fact that it will be difficult for a work placement to replicate the depth of workplace experience to be gained in an apprenticeship, the development of Trailblazer standards has become increasingly job, rather than occupationally related. At the time of writing there were over 200 level 3 Trailblazer standards. Reconciling those standards which have become increasingly narrow and specialised, and which do not have embedded qualifications, with the 15 broad occupational routes recommended by the Sainsbury Panel will be a major task for the newly formed Institute for Apprenticeships and Technical Education.[8] Indeed, in many ways, it would have been preferable for the Sainsbury Panel Report to have preceded the Richard Review of apprenticeships, in the sense that it provides more of a template for the overall reform of technical education in England.

A UK perspective

The preceding paragraphs have been devoted exclusively to the English technical education reform programme. That this is so because education is a policy area which has been devolved to the each of the UK's constituent nations. This said, whilst Scotland, Wales and Northern Ireland have developed their own policies with respect to skills development and tertiary education, the phrase 'technical and professional education' is being used increasingly across the four nations of the UK. It is further suggested that the differentiating principles of technical education identified earlier could be seen to have application not just in the other UK countries, but more widely.

Defining further education

Whether or not technical and professional education as described above may or may not represent a defining mission for FE colleges and other providers regarded as being a part of the FE Sector in England depends to a significant extent on how FE is characterised and how its providers see themselves.

FE has no singular definition. It is more often defined by what it is not, being education or training that is not delivered in a school or a university. It serves a wide age range, most often age 16 and upwards, but, in some cases, from age 14. The FE Sector encompasses education and training providers as diverse as: sixth form colleges primarily meeting the needs of students seeking academic progression to university by means of A levels or a blend of A levels and general applied qualifications; tertiary colleges making similar provision mainly to young people but with a greater vocational focus; general FE colleges covering a mix of age ranges and levels from basic numeracy and literacy to full degrees (most often in association with a validating university); adult education colleges providing residential or community education, local authority providers making similar provision in a defined location; third sector providers making provision for particular communities either locally or nationally and independent training providers, both for profit and not for profit, delivering apprenticeships, as well as other courses direct to students.

Dame Ruth Silver, former Principal of Lewisham College, a large, general FE college in South London, characterised the FE Sector, as the '*adaptive layer*' of education, flexing to meet the needs of localities, communities and students. This characterisation has much in common with that provided by Baroness Sharp as the '*dynamic nucleus*' (Baroness Sharp of Guildford, 2011) in communities, albeit this latter characterisation better fits further education colleges and locally focussed providers, rather than national skills providers. Both characterisations provide for FE evolving in order to meet wider changes in society and in government policy, but in this there is a sense that autonomy in FE is more constrained than in HE, with the sector simply responding to external drivers, rather than setting its own course. Overall, though, the characterisations fail to provide a distinctive mission for further education leading to multiple overlaps and direct competition with the school and university sectors being manifest in England. Interestingly, in Scotland, Wales and Northern Ireland, greater differentiation in roles can be observed, with a distinct 'College Sector' being most visible in Scotland, with colleges delivering a range of qualifications and being the primary providers of levels 4 and 5 vocational higher education in the form of Higher National Diplomas and Certificates.[9]

The diversity of functions covered by the descriptor further education has often led to the sector being seen as being unduly complex or seeking to be all things to all people. During his tenure as Secretary of State for Business, Innovation and Skills, Vince Cable argued that this lack of firm identity was in part responsible for neglect that the sector and its students had suffered in terms of inconstancy of policymaking and inadequate funding. (BIS, 2015) His alternative formulation was to accord the sector what was termed a '*dual mandate*' in:

- Providing vocational education for the workplace with a focus on higher level professional and technical skills
  And
- Providing second chances for those who have not succeeded in the school system.

This formulation comes closer to providing *further education* with more active and defining functions, if not a singular purpose. It was also one of the first occasions upon which the descriptor 'professional and technical' was used in a policy document. It is also useful in combining the social inclusion mission of FE which is close to the heart of many of its leaders and practitioners, and its vocational role. However, the counter argument could be that there is a tension in combining the two functions – one high level and requiring deep technical expertise and facilities, and the other focusing more on student-centred recovery, often with an emphasis on basic skills. (See for instance Lord Lingfield, 2012). Like the 'adaptive layer' characterisation, the formulation also feels like an explanation of what further education had become, rather than a more active and directional definition. Moreover, no doubt due to the division of responsibility for further education, at the time, between the Business and Education Departments, the dual mandate was held only to apply to adult provision and not that made for 14–19-year-olds.

A defining role for further education?

Despite being generally well-received within the FE Sector, the consultation that was launched to test and develop the dual mandate was quietly dropped by the incoming Conservative Government in 2105. It is possible, however, to see some continuity between the 'dual mandate' and the policy that emerged from the incoming Conservative administration in 2015. The focus on apprenticeship growth and technical education has clearly continued and has been combined with an emphasis upon social inclusion and mobility. The former tracks to the first element of the dual mandate, and the latter to the 'second chance' role. On the face of it, the duality of what the term *further education* encompasses seems inescapable, making a single, defining role difficult, if not impossible, to achieve.

The characteristics of technical education explored earlier are, however, a good fit for many, but not all providers, classified as being a part of the FE Sector. Research conducted by the Association of Colleges indicates that each general further education college works with an average of 600 employers. The quality of engagement with employers may vary, but its extent marks out these institutions from schools; the focus on place and employers of all sizes also mark colleges out from most, if not all, universities. So too does the focus on progression from lower levels, through intermediate levels to higher levels of technical education. This engagement provides a sound basis for developing *the two-way street* identified by CAVTL.

Facilities in FE colleges vary, but there is a widespread acceptance of the need and value in providing realistic work environments as an essential element in successful teaching and learning. It is unlikely that schools will be able to reproduce the technical facilities to be found in even the most under-resourced FE college. The concept of dual professionalism is similarly embedded, albeit pressures on funding have constrained opportunities for professional updating of teaching staff, which is likely to represent a serious constraint upon the ability of some colleges to deliver technical education at the higher levels.

When combined with power imbalances between FE and HE in accreditation and quality assessment, pressure on funding has been a material factor in limiting the extent to which many colleges have developed higher technical provision. At the higher levels, there is a premium on staff updating and in cooperative research with employers. Currently, the relative financial well-being of universities confers on them a degree of advantage in developing higher technical education. Likewise, universities gain from having the ability to confer their own qualifications. The distorting effect of this power was arguably most apparent in the provision of foundation degrees. On their introduction, foundation degrees were intended to be primarily employer facing qualifications with a major emphasis upon practical experience. As such, they were intended to embody many of the characteristics of technical education described earlier. Though a few FE colleges eventually achieved foundation degree awarding powers,[10] the great majority of these qualifications were conferred by universities who validated and sometimes franchised provision in FE colleges. When combined with the requirement that all foundation degrees should articulate to an identified bachelor's degree at the conferring university, the content within foundation degrees has become increasingly generic and driven by academic and not employer need. Despite their positional advantages, however, it remains to be seen if a significant number of universities are prepared to adapt to the instrumental nature of technical education, the pedagogical model implied by such education, a staff profile that values industry experience and teaching skills over research activity and a need to rapidly update their curricula and courses to meet the emerging and evolving needs of employers.

Much of what has been said about further education colleges, applies to those independent training providers (ITPs) whose business is integrally based upon employer engagement and the delivery of training in the workplace. ITPs still deliver the majority of apprenticeships in England, either directly, or via subcontracting relationships with colleges.[11] Though not exclusively the case, few ITPs, many of whom are small in comparison to further education colleges, have extensive fixed education facilities and have, instead, optimised their delivery in the workplace. This makes it hard to see that they will be prime providers of T levels or the off-the-job teaching involved in higher level apprenticeships.

But whilst technical education may be a good fit for many FE colleges and for many independent training providers, it will not be a fit for other institutions and providers judged to be a part of the FE Sector. Though many adult education colleges, local authority providers and third sector organisations may count the preparation of their students for work amongst their roles, technical education per se is not at the core of their provision. Nor do the capabilities required to deliver technical education well seem a good fit for many sixth form colleges.

Though technical education may not be a defining role for all FE providers this does not mean it cannot be so for many and most particularly general further education colleges and some independent training providers. Nor does the fact that it is a defining role mean that this should be their role to the exclusion of others. Many colleges rightly value the breadth of their offer and its responsiveness to local communities. Indeed, a breadth of provision and associated agility have been keys to the survival of many colleges and providers in the face of frequently changing government policy and scarce funding.

Rather, technical education could be seen as defining in so far as it is at the core of what such colleges and providers do. It can become what they are known for and what they optimise their structures and processes to deliver. Other roles may be taken on in a contingent way, filing gaps in local provision, or in providing pathways to higher levels of study. In many ways, this feels like a return to the future. The forbears of many of today's colleges, and some universities, were once technical colleges. Perhaps their time has come again.

Notes

1 Protective Services, Sales and Marketing, Social Care, and Transport and Logistics.
2 Students who have not met benchmark standards by age 16 (GCSE maths and English at grade C or above) will be afforded the opportunity to complete a transition year that is aimed at enabling to reach the entry standard to commence studies for A levels or a T level.
3 The reference to the 50% who do not follow the academic route at age 16 or proceed to university is often cited with vocational education providing an alternative route. See, for instance, the 2015 Labour Party Election Manifesto.
4 Baroness Wolf was also a member of the Sainsbury Panel.
5 In the UK Armed Forces, trade instructors are normally required to return to front line duties within five years to ensure their credibility with trainees. In FE circles, the term *triple professional* has been mooted to reflect the need for teachers to be active researchers in their trade or profession in order to ensure continuous updating.
6 Vocational pedagogy is much less researched than traditional pedagogy for school-based or university-based learning, but *How to Teach Vocational Education* by Lucas, Spencer and Claxton (Centre for Real Life Learning University of Winchester 2012) explores these issues, as does *A Practical Guide to Craftsmanship* by Lucas and Spencer (Centre for Real Life Learning University of Winchester 2014). It is also worth reflecting that the observations here apply well within the medical education, which is not generally regarded as technical education.
7 The inclusion of both apprenticeships and college-based routes are represented in graphical form at page 28 of the Sainsbury Panel Report.
8 For a concise and cogent summary of the tasks being placed upon the new Institute, see Parry (2017): www.researchcghe.org/publications/a-new-design-and-regulatory-framework-for-technical-education-in-england/
9 The diversity of providers and the overlaps between them may to some extent be related to the greater degree of marketisation in education in England. The extent that England is an outlier in this regard has become evident through a series of seminars convened by the UCL IOE Post-14 Centre for Education and Work and funded by Edge in 2017/18.
10 Most notably New College Durham and Newcastle College Group.
11 Though it is difficult to compare apprenticeship statistics in each of the four UK nations, the proportion of apprenticeships delivered by independent training providers compared to further education colleges appears even greater in Scotland, Wales and Northern Ireland than in England, i.e. fewer apprenticeships are delivered by colleges who concentrate more fully on full-time student provision.

References

Association of Colleges AoC (2014) *Breaking the Mould* [Online]. Available at www.aoc.co.uk/system/files/Breaking%20the%20Mould%20(web).pdf (Accessed 30 October 2016).
Baroness Sharp of Guildford (2011) *A Dynamic Nucleus: Colleges at the Heart of Local Communities: The Final Report of the Independent Commission on Colleges in Their Communities* [Online].

Available at www.learningandwork.org.uk.gridhosted.co.uk/wp-content/uploads/2017/ 01/dynamic_nucleus_-_full_-final.pdf (Accessed 2 November 2017).

CBI/Pearson (2015) *Inspiring Growth: Education and Skills Survey*, London, Pearson.

Commission for Adult Vocational Teaching and Learning (CAVTL) (2013) *It's about Work . . . Excellent Adult Vocational Teaching and Learning* [Online]. Available at https://cavtl.excel lencegateway.org.uk/commission-news/its-about-work (Accessed 20 October 2017).

Department for Business, Energy and Industrial Strategy (2017) *Industrial Strategy: Building a Britain Fit for the Future*, Cm 9528, London, DBEIS/HMSO.

Department for Business, Innovation and Skills (BIS) (2015) *A Dual Mandate for Adult Vocational Education. A Consultation Paper* [Online]. Available at https://assets.publishing.service.gov.uk/ government/uploads/system/uploads/attachment_data/file/427342/bis-15-145-A-dual-mandate-for-adult-vocational-education.pdf (Accessed 21 October 2017).

Department for Business, Innovation and Skills (BIS) and Department for Education (DfE) (2016a) *Report of the Independent Panel on Technical Education (The Sainsbury Report)* [Online]. Available at www.gov.uk/government/uploads/system/uploads/attachment_data/file/536046/Report_ of_the_Independent_Panel_on_Technical_Education.pdf (Accessed 30 September 2016).

Department for Business, Innovation and Skills (BIS) and Department for Education (DfE) (2016b) *Post-16 Skills Plan*, Cm 9280, London, HMSO.

HM Treasury (2015) *Fixing the Foundations: Creating a More Prosperous Nation*, Cm 9098, London, HM Treasury/HMSO.

Lord Lingfield, et al. (2012) *Professionalism in Further Education Final Report of the Independent Review Panel* [Online]. Available at www.gov.uk/government/uploads/system/uploads/ attachment_data/file/422247/bis-12-1198-professionalism-in-further-education-review-final-report.pdf (Accessed 25 October 2017).

Lucas, B. and Spencer, E. (2014) *A Practical Guide to Craftsmanship*, Centre for Real Life Learning University of Winchester and City and Guilds [Online]. Available at www. cityandguilds.com/~/media/cityandguilds-site/documents/news/a%20practical%20 guide%20to%20craftsmanship%20final%20pdf.ashx (Accessed 20 October 2017).

Lucas, B., Spencer, E., and Claxton, G. (2012) *How to Teach Vocational Education*, Centre for Real Life Learning University of Winchester.

OECD (2014) *Skills beyond the School System: A Synthesis Report*, Paris, OECD.

Parry (2017) *A New Design and Regulatory Framework for Technical Education in England*, UCL IOE Centre for Global Higher Education [Online]. Available at www.researchcghe.org/ publications/a-new-design-and-regulatory-framework-for-technical-education-in-england/ (Accessed 5 December 2017).

Wolf, A. (2011) *Review of Vocational Education: The Wolf Report* [Online]. Available at www. gov.uk/government/uploads/system/uploads/. . ./DFE-00031-2011.pdf (Accessed 20 June 2016).

Chapter 3

Post-Leaving Certificate education in Ireland

Managing different goals

Adele Bergin, Emer Smyth and Adele Whelan

Introduction

Ireland experienced a late development of vocational education largely related to delayed industrialisation, the low status of manual work and the emphasis of Church-run schools on providing an academic education (Coolahan, 1981). Despite some technical education initiatives in the early part of the 20th century, the main framework for vocational education and training (VET) was provided by the 1930 Vocational Education Act which established 38 regionally based Vocational Educational Committees (VECs) whose schools provided two-year full-time 'continuation education', designed to prepare young people for the labour market, along with evening courses ('technical education'), designed initially to improve the practical skills of the employed. This delayed development makes Ireland an interesting case-study in order to examine broader issues in FE provision.

The European Economic Community (EEC) was very influential in shaping vocational education and training in Ireland (Coolahan, 1981; O'Sullivan, 2005), and the European Social Fund (ESF) provided funding for the establishment of pre-employment courses in over 120 schools in 1977. These courses were targeted at post-lower secondary students and aimed to provide social, general and technical education combined with work experience. They were initially confined to vocational and community/comprehensive schools[1] but were redeveloped as Vocational Preparation and Training (VPT) courses, VPT1 and VPT2, in 1984 and were extended to voluntary secondary schools (NESC, 1993). The programmes consisted of vocational studies, work experience and general studies. A second year was added to the courses in 1985 and these VPT2 courses became commonly known as Post-Leaving Certificate (PLC) courses. These courses were primarily designed to provide vocational education in order to facilitate young people's transition to employment. Despite its growing importance, the further education (FE) sector has not been subject to a good deal of policy analysis or empirical research. In contrast, there has been a much greater research focus on higher education, most likely reflecting its dramatic expansion. Therefore, for the purpose of this chapter, the focus will be on PLC Courses, the largest component of FE, that is, post-secondary education for people above school age, in Ireland.

The further education and training (FET) sector in the Irish context has developed to serve multiple roles: as a conduit for the acquisition of vocational skills, as a gateway on to higher education for more disadvantaged groups and as second-chance education for adult learners. In terms of the current overall organisation structure, the Education and Training Boards (ETBs) have overall responsibility for FET provision at a regional level, with SOLAS, the Further Education and Training Authority, being responsible for coordination and over-sight of the sector. In 2017, SOLAS estimates that approximately 323,308 learn-ers will participate in over 30,000 FET programmes with an estimated total annual budget allocation of €638m (SOLAS, 2017).[2] At the same time, FET makes up just 7 per cent of the total education budget (current and capital) and, despite an increase in places, has been dwarfed by the dramatic expansion of higher education (see Figure 3.1).

Irish FET is much more fragmented and is much less focused around voca-tional labour market demand, especially when compared to the German, Dutch and Australian systems (Hannan et al., 1998; McGuinness et al., 2014). A diverse range of courses and programmes are offered through various providers, mostly provided by the regional Education and Training Boards (ETBs) who offer over 30,000 courses across 28 different course titles. The most significant full-time FET programmes provided by the ETBs are the PLC, Vocational Train-ing Opportunities Scheme[3] (VTOS) and Youthreach[4] programmes. The PLC programme is designed to provide specific vocational skills to those who have completed upper secondary education, adults returning to education deemed to

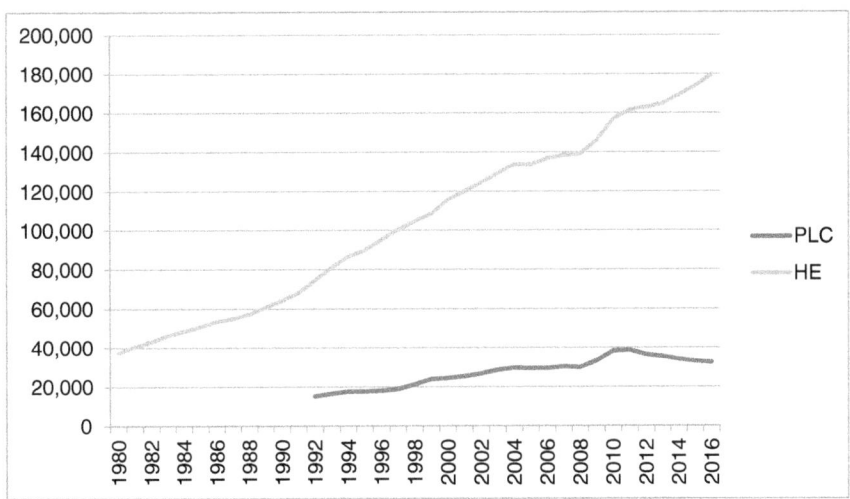

Figure 3.1 Number of PLC and higher education places over time

have the necessary competencies, and those who are unemployed and seeking to upskill.[5] The principal part-time programmes provided by the ETBs are the Back to Education Initiative (BTEI), Community Education, Adult Literacy, Intensive Tuition in Adult Basic Education (ITABE) and English for Speakers of Other Languages (ESOL).

In relation to the apprenticeship model, the scale is currently small, at 3 per cent of total FET provision in 2017. However, the way in which apprenticeship training and education is being provided in Ireland is evolving and broadening. There is currently a target to expand apprenticeship registrations to 9,000 by 2020 (from approximately 3,500 in 2016).[6] There are currently 27 craft apprenticeships in Ireland, in areas such as construction, engineering and, more recently, 13 new programmes have been launched in various sectors such as medical devices, polymer processing, culinary and financial services. However, there still exists a communication challenge to increase awareness and recognition of apprenticeships as a viable training and career path in Ireland.

In 2017, a quarter of places are in full-time FE courses, over half (56%) in part-time FE and a fifth in training. However, taking account of the intensity (hours) of provision (see McGuinness et al., 2014) changes the picture, with the majority of FTE enrolments (70%) being in full-time programmes, predominantly PLCs, and part-time programmes accounting for only 30 per cent of all enrolments.

The remainder of this chapter will focus on PLC courses, given that they represent the largest component of full-time FET provision in Ireland, with over 32,000 new learners enrolled in such courses in 2016/17 (SOLAS, 2017). Furthermore, PLC provision serves as an appropriate example of the multiple roles served by FE in Ireland. In analysing the programme, we draw on two pieces of research: one which used administrative data and in-depth interviews with key policy informants to highlight issues for FET policy development (McGuinness et al., 2014); and an in-depth evaluation of PLC provision, learner experiences and outcomes (McGuinness et al., 2018). As stated previously, the aim of the PLC programme is to provide specific vocational skills for young people who have completed their Leaving Certificate (upper secondary qualification), adults returning to education deemed to have the necessary competencies, and those who are unemployed and seeking to upskill. This multiplicity of functions is not unique to the Irish context, with much international literature on further education discussing potentially competing goals and blurred boundaries between FE and other forms of education provision (see, for example, Gallacher, 2006). PLC participants are disproportionately female, from less educated backgrounds, are more likely to be older and parents and have greater Special Educational Needs (SEN) prevalence rates than their counterparts enrolling directly in higher education.

The multiple goals of PLC provision were echoed in the survey responses of principals (McGuinness et al., 2018) who saw PLC courses in general as fulfilling a range of roles, including progression to employment, progression to higher education, lifelong learning and social inclusion, with principals placing relatively equal weight on each component. However, the views of principals contrasted somewhat with the views of learners who were more likely to indicate a primary rationale for taking a PLC course. This most likely reflects the fact that PLC providers offer multiple courses serving different goals within the same college setting so learners within a particular course may share a common goal (such as progression to employment).

The remainder of the chapter explores how PLC provision serves three distinct roles in the Irish context. Section Two examines the extent to which PLC provision provides learners with vocational skills which are relevant to labour market needs. In exploring the degree of alignment between provision and the labour market, it also draws on survey data from FE colleges to trace variation between providers in the level of engagement with local employers and in the relative emphasis on the promotion of work-related skills within the course. Section Three deals with FE as a route into higher education and the challenges this poses for FE, with new survey data indicating that school leavers often view it as a 'second best' option when they do not achieve the grades to enter university. The tensions in developing a vibrant FE sector are explored in a context where there are few formal links between the education/training system and employers and where higher education has assumed a dominant role in young people's aspirations and in policy discourses more generally. Section Four examines the function of PLC courses as a second-chance education for adult learners and more disadvantaged groups. Section Five concludes by highlighting the way in which Irish FE provision can serve as an interesting case-study in examining the role and purpose of provision.

Vocational skills and labour market alignment

As discussed above, the PLC sector represents the cornerstone of further education and training in Ireland. Its main objective is to provide specific vocational skills to learners, with programmes directly related to areas of labour demand.[7] Many FET stakeholders felt that, although the overall objectives of FET may be broad in nature, its crucial goal centres on providing vocational skills for the labour market. One stakeholder argued its role is primarily to 'provide [the] economy with the skills and expertise, training and education that is needed . . . at national, regional and local level' (Statutory department/body), and others echoed this point: 'It [FET] should be ninety per cent about that. It should be labour market preparation, specific training, skills training for jobs' (Other provider group) (McGuinness et al., 2014)). However, at a broad level, there is not a strong relationship between the labour market and the further education and training system although there is variation within sectors. This section explores the linkages between the labour market and the further education and training sector, particularly in relation to PLC, and investigates how well aligned the structure of provision is to the needs of the labour market and the flexibility and responsiveness of provision in the context of changing labour market conditions.

It also examines the relationship with employers in the provision-planning process and the work experience of learners.

Alignment with labour market

Given the labour market focus of PLC programmes, it is important to assess the extent to which supply from these programmes meets the labour market needs for sub-degree vocational qualifications. Ensuring a supply of vocational labour is important as skill shortages can negatively affect firm-level performance. However, McGuinness et al. (2018) find that it is unclear in many instances that the emphasis of provision coincides with labour demand. They examine administrative data on enrolments in PLC courses by field of study and use it as a proxy for the composition of the inflow of new labour supply. Specifically, they examine subject areas with a direct labour market orientation and limited progression for further study. To estimate demand for newly qualified younger workers educated to sub-degree level, they use Labour Force Survey data to identify occupations where the majority of workers are educated to a sub-degree level. This gives a broad estimate of the number of jobs likely to be available for newly qualified individuals within specific occupations. They find that the annual enrolment levels greatly exceed the number of jobs likely to be available for completers in areas such as early childhood care and education, hairdressing and community and health services. This indicates that provision in the sector is not closely aligned to labour market needs. This is a similar finding to McGuinness et al. (2014), who looked at the labour market-orientated programmes in the overall FET sector. That study was augmented by stakeholder interviews and stakeholders who felt that current FET provision was aligned with the labour market only 'to some extent'.

To assess the employment outcomes for learners, McGuinness et al. (2018) compare PLC leavers to a group of upper secondary school leavers who are similar in terms of characteristics but who directly entered the labour market after leaving school. They find that (after five years, by 2015) PLC participants were 16 per cent more likely to be in employment relative to similar individuals who entered the labour market after leaving school. They also distinguish between more job-specific programmes that tend to be targeted at the labour market (such as engineering and engineering trades and mechanics and metal work) and more general programmes that are not directly targeted at specific occupations (such as arts and foreign languages). They find that the employment effects are stronger for PLC participants in more job-specific, as opposed to general, programmes.

Responsiveness of sector to changing labour market conditions

Concerns have been raised around a lack of responsiveness of FET providers to changing demands in the labour market. Specifically, many see the FET sector as having a 'lack of agility' and being slow to respond to employer needs

(McGuinness et al., 2014). A survey of PLC principals examined the factors that influence their decision to establish new courses (McGuinness et al., 2018). While principals, on average, take a range of factors into account, factors such as being highlighted by occupational forecasts, highlighted as an area of demand by government and requested by employers, all received lower or more neutral rankings in this decision. The results suggest that decisions to establish new courses are more heavily dependent on meeting student demand and existing resources although a relatively high focus is placed on meeting local labour market needs. Similarly, when it comes to discontinuing courses, principals are more responsive to falling enrolments and student perceptions than to labour market issues. These patterns suggest that, student demand (or lack thereof) plays a more important role in course provision than labour market conditions. In fact, McGuinness et al. (2014) find that provision within the FET sector appears to have largely grown organically over time, with national policy not appearing to have played any central role in determining the level, distribution or composition of Irish FET provision.

There is very little evidence that PLC programmes are quick to respond to changing economic conditions. Ireland was hit particularly hard by the global financial crisis and this was intensified by a collapse in property prices and the construction sector, followed by severe difficulties in the banking sector. The crisis had a dramatic effect on employment in all sectors but the largest employment losses were in construction and services (Bergin et al., 2012). Against this backdrop, there was limited change in the proportions enrolled in PLC programmes by broad subject area. McGuinness et al. (2018) examine PLC enrolments by broad subject area in 2008/2009 and 2011/12. They find that overall enrolments rose by 16 per cent over this period. Furthermore, they find that the relative proportions in each broad subject area appear to have remained relatively stable over the period, despite the macroeconomic shock having a big impact on the composition of labour demand. This suggests that PLC provision is not highly responsive to changing labour market conditions and shocks.

McGuinness et al. (2018) argue there is a need for labour market-orientated PLC courses to be more responsive to changing labour market conditions and more flexible in terms of the types of courses offered. Overall, PLC provision is currently constrained by legacy issues, including the skillset of existing staff, with relatively little input of information on skill gaps and employer demand.

Employer engagement in planning and work experience

Employer engagement and work placement help to align FET programmes to the needs of the vocational labour market with FET stakeholders viewing this engagement as crucial (McGuinness et al., 2014). In other countries, employer input into course design and content is seen as important in terms of ensuring FET is able to respond to changing labour market conditions.[8] McGuinness et al. (2014) found that a significant group of FET stakeholders felt that employers were at best only engaged 'to some degree' in providing placements for students and providing training for existing workers. Furthermore, the majority of FET stakeholders felt that employers were not very engaged in providing input into courses. This could reflect the lack of structures to ask for their input; some stakeholders said that often effective engagement with employers does take place at a local level but tends to be based on informal relationships rather than formal structures (McGuinness et al., 2014). The existing evidence for Ireland suggests that employer engagement has been relatively weak to date. However, the National Skills Council and nine Regional Skills Fora were launched in April 2017. The Department of Education and Skills (DES) has stated that this network will aim to provide a cohesive education-led structure for employers and the further and higher education system to work together in building the skills needs of their regions; assist employers to better understand and access the full range of services available across the education and training system; and improve the links between education and training providers in planning and delivering programmes, reduce duplication and inform national funding decisions. Given the recent establishment of this network, it is difficult to evaluate progress at this stage and unclear as to the extent to which it will serve to shape the overall nature of course provision at a national level. The Regional Skills Fora are currently engaging with a broad range of sectors, particularly high-skilled manufacturing and ICT. Furthermore, the DES report that over 60 per cent of the engagement to date in 2017 is with small and medium-sized enterprises (SMEs), which make up the greater proportion of employers in Ireland.

In terms of PLC provision, work experience does not appear to be a universal feature of the programme, with results from a survey of PLC principals showing that only three-quarters of learners took part in work experience (McGuinness et al., 2018). Survey evidence revealed perceptions amongst principals varied with respect to the level of difficulty in learners achieving work placements, with an almost even split of principals describing the process as 'easy' and 'quite difficult' (McGuinness et al., 2018). This may be explained by factors such as differences in local labour market conditions and/or by the level of contact with local employers. The survey results showed a lot of variation in terms of the level of contact with local employers, with just under 50 per cent of principals indicating that staff met with local employers up to once a year, while the remaining 50 per cent reported more than three meetings per year.

FE as a gateway to higher education

The previous sections have highlighted the multiple goals for further education courses indicated by FE college principals, with progression to higher education rated highly as one of these goals. Over two-thirds (68%) of principals strongly agreed that one of the purposes of the PLC programme was to enable progression to higher education, with only 8 per cent disagreeing with this statement.

Providers saw further education as offering learners a 'bridge' into higher education by equipping them with the skills and competencies they needed for that transition:

> [It is an] excellent stepping stone which bridges the gap between second[ary] level and third level. [It] prepares students very well for third level, both in terms of content of programmes, and in helping students to get into the habit of study.
>
> (FE College principal)

This was seen as particularly valuable for young people who might have otherwise struggled to settle into higher education:

> All students are not ready for higher education when they finish second[ary] level. PLC is an excellent transition, learning how to learn, researching and writing assignments and projects as well as developing communication skills.
>
> (FE College principal)

When asked about the outcomes of their students, principals stated that an average of 28 per cent of their cohort progressed on to higher education. Among learners themselves, 39 per cent took their PLC course primarily to progress on to higher education, about the same proportion that wanted to use the course to get a job (see above). Students were more likely to enter STEM subjects as a means of progressing to HE, with those with HE intentions making up 58 per cent of those in STEM courses. Women were much more likely than men to enter FET in order to progress to higher education than to obtain a job, with 57 per cent of females doing so compared with 38 per cent of men. This group was also significantly more likely to be older, by an average of four years, than those taking the course for employment-oriented reasons. Despite differing in gender and age, the two groups did not differ in terms of their family background (measured in terms of parental education).

Analyses compared the actual outcomes of FE participants to a control group of upper secondary leavers with similar characteristics (see above). Compared to the control group, PLC participants were 27 percentage points more likely to have participated in higher education within five years of having finished the course. Not surprisingly, the rate of progression was higher, an additional 38 per cent compared with upper secondary leavers, among those who had taken 'general', or education–oriented, courses. However, it is worth noting that even those who had taken job-specific courses were more likely than the control group to go on to higher education, suggesting that in some cases experience of college education served to reshape learners' longer-term educational plans. The analysis shows that PLC provision acts as an important access platform to higher education for individuals who might not have otherwise have pursued that option.

Despite the impact on progression to higher education, there is some evidence of a lack of articulation between FE colleges and higher education institutions. Learners were asked whether they felt their PLC studies opened up opportunities for further study at a range of alternative institutions. Over 40 per cent of respondents felt that it opened a pathway to Institutes of Technology but only 24 per cent indicated that PLC provided an opportunity to access Irish universities. This pattern parallels findings in systems such as the United States and Scotland where students who enter higher education through FE or community colleges are found to be much less likely to subsequently access élite universities and progression rates are themselves socially differentiated (Dougherty and Kienzl, 2006; Gallacher, 2017).

There have been long-standing concerns about the lack of status of vocational education and training in the Irish context (see, for example, Coolahan, 1981). Recent decades have seen very marked increases in higher education participation among school leavers. This pattern is seen by stakeholders as having established higher education as the cultural norm, with FET seen as a second best option in this context:

> You go to secondary school, you get your Leaving Cert[ificate], you go to university and any kind of deviation from that is seen as second-class education.
>
> (Employer group)

> It's the aspiration of most Irish families for their kids to go to higher education, and apprenticeships and further education, all that kind of thing, are seen almost as a badge of academic failure.
>
> (Employer group)

From this perspective, FE has come to be seen by many as an avenue for those who 'fail' to get into higher education:

> [The] perception is it's something people go in to if they fail to go in to college rather than something people go into to actually give them a qualification that will help them find a job.
>
> (Statutory department/body)

This perception was strongly echoed in the accounts of learners themselves. Less than four in ten of learners who took PLC courses felt they had achieved the plans they held on leaving school. Among those who progressed onto higher education via FET, a quarter felt they did not achieve their goals at all, while a further third felt they had only partially achieved their goals. This contrasts with the 71 per cent of school leavers who went directly into higher education and felt they had achieved their intended goals. The majority of PLC entrants who applied to (but did not enrol in) higher education felt they did not realise their goals, suggesting that FET was seen as a 'second best' option by this group.

Learners were also asked whether they would take the same pathway if they were free to choose again. As with goal realisation, regret was more common among those who had taken FET courses than among those who progressed directly to HE; 43 per cent of those who pursued higher education via FET would not make the same decision over again, while this applied to less than a quarter of direct higher education entrants.

The patterns found pose a dilemma for the system. On the one hand, FET appears to act as an important gateway into higher education for those who would not otherwise access it. At the same time, presenting higher education as a goal of FET progression risks reinforcing its status as a 'second best' option and one that is geared towards reaching the more socially desirable goal of third-level education.

Social inclusion

Social inclusion was seen by policy stakeholders and FE college principals as a key goal of provision. This reflected two complementary dimensions: offering a pathway to young people from more socio-economically disadvantaged backgrounds, who may not have achieved the grades needed for direct access to tertiary education, and second-chance education for adults who had not had the opportunity to pursue education and training when they had first left school.

> Adult learners . . . see it as a way of, you know, undoing some of the missed opportunities that they've had in the past.
>
> (State provider group)

> All of our courses are provided in a fully inclusive way. There are no formal entry requirements, thus removing the barrier to access that is the requirement to have the Leaving Certificate.
>
> (FE College principal)

This was seen as facilitating a more diverse profile of learners than was often the case in other education settings:

> FE provision under the PLC programme is a highly visible, widely understood and valued provision, providing very many opportunities for a broad range of learners.
>
> (FE College principal)

Thus, nine in ten college principals felt that social inclusion was an important goal of FE provision, with only 4 per cent disagreeing with this perspective.

At the same time, the importance of social inclusion as a goal relative to the other goals of employment and higher education progression was not uncontentious in policy circles. Some stakeholders pointed to the complementarity of the different goals in shaping provision:

There are programmes which are primarily economic driven, [in] other words, they have this close relationship with labour market and enterprise needs and there are programmes which are primarily driven by a broader social inclusion approach which could include a personal development within that . . . they are not discrete. Even those programmes which have a prime purpose of social inclusion will have some objectives which are linked to labour market outcomes.

(Statutory department/body)

I actually think it's not an exclusive choice, that you can have both . . . you can maintain both with different cohorts of learners . . . I think there's a danger in seeing it as one or the other.

(State provider group)

However, other stakeholders, while acknowledging the importance of social inclusion within FET, argued that this was secondary and that 'getting the people back to work' (State provider group) should be given priority:

The primary service of FET . . . is to equip people with the skills to compete in the labour market, to acquire income, to determine a future for themselves, their families and their communities. So for . . . the majority of people the way out of poverty is a job . . . every course should have some element of lifelong learning in it but the end game is skills for work and skills for jobs.

(Other provider group)

Survey data on learners provide an opportunity to assess the extent to which those taking FET courses are from more socio-economically disadvantaged backgrounds than other groups. Those who had taken a PLC course were significantly more likely to be from a family with low levels of educational qualifications (lower secondary education or less), with 36 per cent falling into this group compared with 25 per cent of other leavers. Those who used a PLC course to progress to higher education were much more likely to be from a family with lower education levels than those who went into higher education directly (38 per cent compared with 28 per cent). Thus, FET appears to be providing a route to qualifications and a pathway into higher education for more disadvantaged groups. Furthermore, those who had an illness or disability were overrepresented among those who entered higher education via FET rather than directly (26 per cent compared with 14 per cent), highlighting the importance of provision in terms of broader inclusion.

Conclusions

This chapter has shown that, as in many other countries, FE in Ireland attempts to meet multiple objectives, providing vocational skills relevant to labour market demand, offering a gateway into higher education and promoting social inclusion through provision for groups who otherwise would not have accessed education and training. PLC course providers see these multiple goals as fundamental to the nature of the programme and generally seek to meet these goals by providing different types of courses within the same college setting, with some focusing on the transition to employment while other, more general, courses are geared towards progression to higher education. The social inclusion goal appears to be cross-cutting, with the intake to both types of PLC course being more socially diverse and older in profile than those entering higher education. The principals of PLC colleges do not appear to see these goals as competing or contradictory but the findings discussed in this chapter highlight the constraints posed by the broader education/training and labour market systems to the capacity of providers to address these multiple goals. Two dimensions of the institutional context are worth highlighting here. Firstly, late industrialisation has resulted in a relatively under-developed vocational education and training system in the Irish context, a system with few formal structures or mechanisms to ensure a stronger link between employers and education/training provision and to facilitate responsiveness to local and national labour market conditions. As a result, there are limitations on the extent to which PLC courses provide vocational skills relevant to labour market demand, especially in a rapidly changing context. A new initiative, involving the establishment of the National Skills Council and Regional Skills Fora, has the potential to provide a mechanism for ensuring a closer match between provision and demand. In conjunction with the existing labour market intelligence produced by the Skills and Labour Market Research Unit (SLMRU) in SOLAS and the Expert Group on Future Skill Needs (EGFSN), this development aims to provide a more complete picture of the nature of current and future labour market demands that would enable FE and higher education providers to plan course provision more closely aligned to labour market needs. Prioritisation of skills needs is to be overseen by the new National Skills Council. The new Regional Skills Fora aim to facilitate ongoing employer-educator dialogue to match identified needs with sustainable provision in each region.

Secondly, Ireland has seen a very significant expansion of higher education provision to the point where the majority of school leavers go on to tertiary education. This means that many learners view FE as a 'second best' option if they do not receive the grades to enter higher education directly. Somewhat paradoxically, the role of FE as a route into higher education potentially further reinforces this view of the sector as of lesser status. The relatively recent creation of SOLAS, which has overall responsibility for further education and training, has created the opportunity to bring about greater coherence within the sector as a whole. However, a large body of international research points to the difficulties in successfully introducing VET qualifications without the necessary institutional supports. Indeed, as Young (1993) suggests, 'inequality or parity of esteem between academic and vocational courses is . . . primarily a contextual question which cannot be resolved by innovations in curricula, methods of assessment or qualifications systems alone' (p. 213).

Notes

1 There are three types of secondary school in Ireland: voluntary secondary schools, vocational schools (or community colleges) and community/comprehensive schools. Voluntary secondary schools were geared towards providing an academic education and were mainly set up by Catholic religious orders. Vocational schools were introduced in the 1930s to provide an education largely geared towards preparation for manual occupations. Community/comprehensive schools were introduced from the 1960s in an effort to bridge the gap between the more academic voluntary secondary schools and trade-oriented vocational schools. There are legacy differences in governance and funding, but all school types operate within the same curriculum and assessment framework.
2 In 2017, a total budget of €830m was invested in FET through Exchequer funding and the National Training Fund (NTF) and additional expenditure from the European Social Fund (ESF).
3 The VTOS programme is an educational and training opportunities scheme for unemployed persons designed to develop employability or further opportunities leading to employment.
4 Youthreach is directed at unemployed early school leavers aged 15–20 and provides the opportunity to identify viable options within adult life and acquire certification.
5 PLC courses are mostly provided in vocational schools with some provision in voluntary secondary and community and comprehensive schools and generally lead to Major FETAC awards made by Quality and Qualifications Ireland (QQI) at NFQ Level 5 or NFQ Level 6.
6 While in Ireland, this target is seen as ambitious given the starting point, it would, of course, be seen as modest by international, and even UK, standards. For example, Scotland, with a population of just over half a million more than Ireland, currently has a target of 30,000 apprentice starts by 2020 and already has over 26,000 starts in 2017.
7 The PLC *Conditions of approval* (Department of Education and Skills, 2012) include 'In approving courses the Department has regard to ensuring appropriate provision on a geographic basis' and 'Providers must include a Labour Market Justification (LMJ) with applications for all new courses, showing: (1) How the course provision meets with Government policy; (2) What particular skill gaps or areas of skill growth, both locally and nationally, the course will address; and (3) Specific data and information on progression options, local agreements with employers, information on outcomes for previous learners'.
8 McGuinness et al. (2014) draw on international expert evidence for various countries and find that in countries such as Germany, Australia and the Netherlands, employers play a strong role in the FET provision and planning process. These higher levels of employer engagement ensure that that programmes are more fully aligned with the needs of the vocational labour market.

References

Bergin, A., Kelly, E., and McGuinness, S. (2012) *Explaining Changes in Earnings and Labour Costs during the Recession*, ESRI Economic Renewal Series 009, Dublin, ESRI.

Coolahan, J. (1981) *Irish Education: History and Structure*, Dublin, IPA.

Department of Education and Skills (2012) *PLC Conditions of Approval*, Dublin, Department of Education and Skills.

Dougherty, K. J. and Kienzl, G. S. (2006) 'It's not enough to get through the open door: Inequalities by social background in transfer from community colleges to four-year colleges', *Teachers College Record*, vol. 108, no. 3, pp. 452–487.

Gallacher, J. (2006) 'Blurring the boundaries or creating diversity? The contribution of the further education colleges to higher education in Scotland', *Journal of Further and Higher Education*, vol. 30, no. 1, pp. 43–58.

Gallacher, J. (2017) 'Higher education in the college sector: Widening access or diversion? Questions and challenges from the Scottish experience', *Journal of Education and Work*, vol. 30, no. 7, pp. 712–721.

Hannan, D. F., McCabe, B., and McCoy, S. (1998) *Trading Qualifications for Jobs: Overeducation and the Irish Youth Labour Market*, Dublin, ESRI General Research Series.

McGuinness, S., Bergin, A., Kelly, E., McCoy, S., Smyth, E., Watson, D., and Whelan, A. (2018) *Evaluation of PLC Programme Provision*, ESRI Research Series No. 61, Dublin, ESRI.

McGuinness, S., Bergin, A., Kelly, E., McCoy, S., Smyth, E., Whelan, A., and Banks, J. (2014) *Further Education and Training in Ireland: Past, Present and Future*, ESRI Research Series No. 35, Dublin, ESRI.

NESC (1993) *Education and Training Policies for Economic and Social Development*, Dublin, NESC.

O'Sullivan, D. (2005) *Cultural Politics and Irish Education since the 1950s*, Dublin, IPA.

SOLAS (2017) *FET Services Plan 2017* [Online], Dublin: SOLAS. Available at www.solas. ie/SolasPdfLibrary/FET%20Services%20Plan%202017.pdf (Accessed 2 November 2017).

Young, M. (1993) 'Bridging the academic/vocational divide: Two Nordic case studies', *European Journal of Education*, vol. 28, no. 2, pp. 209–214.

Acknowledgements

This chapter draws on two large-scale studies of further education in Ireland and so would not have been possible without the contribution of our colleagues: Seamus McGuinness, Selina McCoy, Dorothy Watson, Elish Kelly and Joanne Banks. We acknowledge the role of SOLAS in funding these studies.

Chapter 4

New frontiers in college education

Paul Little

Introduction

Tertiary education in the UK has changed considerably in recent years with a marked divergence in sub-degree and technical education across the four nations. Such change reflects the shifting attitudes of policymakers, students and employers and acknowledges that the public tertiary education sector must adapt to major economic and social challenges in the context of an increasingly complex and uncertain world. But this change to mass tertiary education brings with it inherent tensions between long-cherished beliefs about the place of universities, the privileging of the academic route and the diminished status of further education and vocational routes. Profound changes are rippling through the UK tertiary sector, and the tide of popular opinion is increasingly swinging towards value for money and employability. We are witnessing a new era in tertiary education and especially a renaissance for college education.

A new tribalism

David Goodhart (2017) makes a relevant distinction which is useful in thinking about the broader shifts that are driving change in the tertiary education sector and in the culture more broadly. He identifies two distinct modern tribes: those who have benefitted from increased economic and cultural openness – the fruits of globalisation, mass higher education and mass immigration – and those who have not. The beneficiaries he describes as 'anywheres'. They are people whose 'achieved' identities are essentially mobile; well-educated and outward-looking, they are 'comfortable and confident with new places and people'. 'Somewheres', on the other hand, are socially and geographically rooted, tend to be less well-educated and hence less affluent and feel marginalised and unsettled by the changes associated with immigration and globalisation. This divergence, Goodhart argues, helps explain the growth in populism responsible for the 2016 Brexit referendum vote in the UK and the rise of Trump in the United States.

It is worth exploring this new tribal division in more detail. The respective world views of the two tribes are not new and, from their different perspectives, understandable. What has changed is the relative influence of the two mind-sets on our culture. For a long time, the 'somewhere' perspective could be described as the British common sense; it was written into our national social contract. In the space of a few decades, however, this had changed dramatically. While the liberal, socially tolerant (though often politically somewhat intolerant) perspective of 'anywheres' has come to dominate the national conversation, 'somewheres' have felt excluded both economically and culturally. The relative powerlessness and marginalisation of British somewheres is reflected in the decline of their bedrock local technical apprenticeship provision and standards in a graduate-dominated society, the double infrastructure failure in housing (particularly in the south east of England) and transport (particularly in the north). As the baby-boomers and 1960s liberalism made their mark and higher education expanded at an unprecedented pace, the 'anywhere' view of the world dominated and in doing so displaced the 'somewheres' common-sense view of aspiration.

For somewheres, this has been a painful, alienating process. The emergence of 'mass' higher education has not only further marginalised many somewheres but has also created a separation between those somewheres who make it to university and the communities they leave. At the same time, the place of the working class has changed, with the decline in manufacturing and the near disappearance of manual labour reducing the status of workers on lower incomes. As educational success became the chief criterion both of career success and social status, those who lacked it became more and more excluded, struggling not only with the lifestyle implications of failure to attain higher education, but also the social disapprobation that came with it. As Andrew Marr writes in an article about the Queen, 'The reason aggressive meritocracy can be cruel is that it suggests that those who aren't at the top – struggling in the middle, or poor and power-less at the bottom – are supposed to understand that this isn't their misfortune, but what they, too, deserve' (Marr, 2016). Unsurprisingly, given this backdrop of growing divergence, economic change and diminishing empathy for the poor, the social contract in Britain has become much weaker.

The Brexit vote, significant in so many ways, is also deeply significant here. It challenged the anywhere view and its dominance of the political agenda, what Jeremy Cliffe has called the 'Londonisation of Britain' (Cliffe, 2015), and exposed the damage done by the widening gap between somewheres and anywheres. It acted as a reminder to the long-dominant metropolitan elite that while the expansion of higher education and the elevation of educational success into the gold standard of social esteem has been a liberation for many, for others, including around half of all school leavers, it has become a measure of their declining status; something reinforced by sharp economic difficulties faced in many areas of the country. Brexit signals a shift into a different era, one in which the any-where mindset is no longer dominant and the prevailing 'common sense' of mass immigration and mass higher education is increasingly being challenged. This troubles many, particularly on the left, but it can also be seen as an opportunity to reassert the value of locality and community in education, to re-evaluate the place of vocational and technical education and to think in different, better ways about the relationship between social mobility and education. It is the latter point I wish to explore first.

Social mobility and higher education

It is worth reminding ourselves of the dramatic changes that have taken place in this area in recent decades. As recently as 50 years ago, only 6 per cent of school leavers in England and Wales went to university, with around 90 per cent coming from private or grammar schools. Successive waves of expansion, notably in the 1960s, when a new tranche of residential universities was created, included the conversion of 35 polytechnics into new universities in 1992 and then further expanded towards a 50 per cent higher education participation target under the Blair government. The UK higher education system has not just expanded, it is also increasingly international in character; around 20 per cent of all students and 13 per cent of undergraduates come from abroad. This underlines the contrast between the international ethos of universities and the national/local focus of colleges. It can also be noted that because Scotland has a more inclusive approach to higher education, with a higher percentage being delivered in colleges compared to England or the other devolved nations, Scotland has a consistently higher participation rate. This is reflected in Scottish Higher Education Initial Participation Rate (HEIPR), which was 56 per cent in 2015–16, whereas it was 49 per cent in England.

Up to a point, this expansion has been good for social mobility. Students from all backgrounds are more likely to go to university as a result. In 2016/17, there were over 2.3 million students in UK universities, compared to a little over 600,000 university students in 1970/71 (HESA, 2012) The likelihood of those from the lowest participation areas in the country going to university increased by 30 per cent between 2004/05 and 2009/10 and by 50 per cent between 1994/95 and 2009/10 (Milburn, 2012). This is both significant and welcome. However, poorer students remain much less likely to go to university than their richer counterparts. The most advantaged 20 per cent of young people in the UK are still around seven times more likely to attend the most selective universities than the 40 per cent most disadvantaged (Milburn, 2012). An estimated 65 per cent of students in England who took A-level and equivalent qualifications in independent schools progressed to the most selective universities by age 19 by the 2014/15 academic year, compared to 23 per cent of those from state-funded schools and colleges: a gap of 42 percentage points (DfE, 2017) In 2008–09, the gap was 37 percentage points, with entry rates of 62 per cent and 26 per cent for independent and state school pupils, respectively (BIS, 2015) There is little sign of this changing. A report by independent think tank Reform found that of 29 'high-tariff' universities, only one, the London School of Economics, increased its proportion of disadvantaged students by more than one percentage point annually between 2011 and 2015. Less than a third of the universities studied made any progress at all against benchmarks (Sundorph et al., 2017). Where progress has been made, the report's authors make clear, it is mostly lower- and middle-tier universities that have done the heavy lifting.

Another trend which helps explain why social mobility has stalled in the UK is the disappearance of alternative routes to a good career or a profession. The emergence of mass higher education has coincided with the dismantling of polytechnic sub-degree qualifications in England (HNDs, HNCs) and the decline in apprenticeships and other vocational qualifications (City & Guilds, BTEC, NVQs, GNVQs, SVQs) which formerly gave young people from working class backgrounds an opportunity to enter secure, well-paid occupations with opportunities for progression. The loss of these routes has largely left only the royal road of access to the professions through higher education, which has reinforced elite domination of the professions. Social background continues to drive access to graduate options and to the top jobs. Clearly, unpicking what journalist Clare Foges describes as 'the knot of preferment and privilege that has built up over generations' is a big task (Goodhart, 2017, p. 265).

Rather than pushing more and more less advantaged students into (usually non-elite) universities and then into often low-grade, non-graduate employment, social mobility policies should increasingly target investment in technical and vocational education and promote stepping stones which can ultimately lead to professional jobs. In expanding university education for the 50 per cent, we have neglected to preserve sufficient intermediate tertiary craft qualifications to both address skill shortages and to safeguard the lower-level 'breadwinner' jobs once associated with the artisan male working class. At a very minimum, we need a more balanced approach to social mobility, one which not only makes room for the aspirations of those at the bottom of the mobility ladder with the drive and ability to move up, but also values the role and contribution of those who remain rooted in terms of place and social class.

Education and training

One casualty of the massification of higher education in a liberal, meritocratic society has been the relative loss of esteem and status for technical education and vocational training. As noted, the expansion of higher education access has coincided with the steep decline in manufacturing, as well as in the availability of non-academic routes to high-income, high-status roles. There was a sharp fall in sub-degree technical courses at Levels 4 and 5. At the same time, white-collar professional work expanded, a great deal of skilled machine work disappeared, replaced by automation, and there was a growth in low-skill, low-wage employment (Goodhart, 2017). The result was an hourglass economy, with a big squeeze on middle-income jobs and a significant expansion at the top and bottom of the labour market.

The impact of these changes has been acute at the bottom of the hourglass. The Joseph Rowntree Foundation's *UK Poverty 2017* report found that 3.7 million workers – one in eight – live in poverty in the UK. Work can no longer be considered a direct route out of poverty, and reliance on so much low-paid, low-skilled work is holding back the UK's productivity, which is very low when considered alongside other comparable countries (JRF, 2017)

The low-pay, low-productivity equilibrium exacerbated by a negligent under-investment in the national vocational skills system was further tilted away from the squeezed middle and bottom end of the market by 'over qualification' (Wolf, 2016). Over the last 20 years, numerous UK labour market studies have reported that between one-fifth and one-third of graduates are in jobs for which graduate-level skills are not required. Indeed, tracking research notes that such 'over education', often leading to underemployment, is on the increase in the UK (Purcell et al., 2012).

The dismantling of the adult education sector that has taken place since 2010 has also made it difficult for the 17 per cent of students who leave school functionally illiterate and the 22 per cent who leave school functionally innumerate to catch up. The Organisation for Economic Cooperation and Development (OECD) reports that there are an estimated nine million working-age adults in England with low literacy or numeracy skills or both, with the problem particularly acute among 16–24 year-olds. England therefore has some of the least literate and numerate young people in the developed world. Low basic skills are a problem in the workplace – more than five million of the low-skilled are in work – and at all levels of education, including higher education. England, the report notes, has more university students with weak literacy and numeracy skills than most countries. The report calls for shorter professional programmes for those with low basic skills and a reduction in student numbers in university programmes 'in favour of more suitable programmes, particularly in the Further Education (FE) sector' (Kuczera et al., 2016).

The call for greater focus and investment in further education is not surprising. For the past few decades, further education has felt the pinch of cuts orchestrated by minsters who knew little of this part of the system, being, by and large, the product of the royal route from A-levels/Highers to an elite university. In 2014, almost a quarter (24%) of all Westminster MPs went to Oxbridge, compared to less than 1 per cent of the public, while 83 per cent went to university. Almost two-thirds (59%) of David Cameron's 2014 Cabinet were graduates of Oxbridge (Social Mobility and Child Poverty Commission, 2014). Furthermore, the astonishing churn of 61 Secretaries of State responsible for skills policy in England over the last three decades – according to a 2014 City and Guilds study – suggests that this is not an area repeated governments have taken all that seriously (City and Guilds, 2014). Responsibility for the sector has also shifted between departments ten times in the machinery of government changes since the 1980s. Further education colleges have fewer legal protections than schools or universities and have a much less vocal lobby than those parts of the education system, which makes them vulnerable to cuts in times of financial constraint and also the subject of frequent reform by ministers keen to make an impression during their usually short tenure in post. The City and Guilds report found that since 1981, there had been 28 major acts of parliament related to the development, organisation and structure of vocational and further education and skills training in the UK, as well as major reviews including the Dearing, Beaumont, Cassels, Tomlinson, Leitch, Wolf and Richard reviews. This level of churn – in both policy and personnel – is clearly disruptive and has created a kind of 'collective amnesia' which sees policymaker after policymaker try to reinvent the wheel when it comes to technical and vocational education, while fostering a culture of short-termism and reaction in sector leadership (City and Guilds, 2014).

The decline in esteem for technical and vocational education mirrored the growing dominance of higher education. Tony Blair's 50 per cent target for higher education participation, however, raised more questions than it answered, not least how the demand for sub-graduate level technicians would be met and how the 50 per cent who failed to meet the higher education grade would feel about it. The decline in technical education reflected and fed into the increasing sense of powerlessness and exclusion felt by Goodhart's somewheres. The unprecedented growth in higher education also had cost implications, with Labour introducing tuition fees in 1999 to transfer part of the cost. The reforms have had very mixed outcomes. There is a clear risk that the burden of debt created by the loans system will fall disproportionately on less well-off students whose parents cannot afford to pay the fees up front.

While universities have been largely protected from cuts to the public purse, college funding in the UK has fallen sharply. A study by the Institute for Fiscal Studies reported that FE and sixth form colleges in England have not seen an increase in per student funding in 30 years. By comparison, school funding is set to be 70 per cent higher in 2020 than it was in 1990. While in 1990 FE spending per student was 45 per cent higher than secondary school spending per student, it will be 10 per cent lower in 2019/20 (Belfield, Crawford, & Sibieta, 2017) In Scotland, there was an 18 per cent real-terms drop in Scottish government funding to colleges between 2010/11 and 2014/15. At the same time, a requirement to prioritise full-time courses led to a sharp decline in the numbers of part-time learners, 48 per cent between 2007/08 and 2014/15; overall, student numbers decreased by 41 per cent over the period. The number of under-25s in the system, however, had increased by 14 per cent over the past eight years, the report said, with full-time numbers increasing year on year between 2009/10 and 2013/14 (Audit Scotland, 2016a). The Scottish higher education sector, on the other hand, had seen an increase in overall income of 38 per cent (to £3.5 billion) over the decade leading up to 2014/15, according to Audit Scotland, most of that coming from public sources. Total Scottish Funding Council funding allocated to universities in 2014/15 was £1.2 billion (Audit Scotland, 2016b), compared to Scottish Government funding for colleges of £548 million. (Audit Scotland, 2016a)

Despite substantial public investment in higher education, partly at the expense of further and technical education and the college sector, higher education students are less and less satisfied with the quality of the education they receive. The Higher Education Policy Institute's 2017 Student Academic Experience Survey reported that there are now almost as many students in the UK who feel they have received poor value for money (34%) as students who feel they have had good value (35%). A continuation of current trends would produce a negative view for the first time in 2018. This is already the case in England, where 32 per cent perceive good value, compared to 37 per cent who perceive poor value (Neves and Hillman, 2017)

And while some universities offer high level technical courses with links to industry and a strong vocational focus, it is far from clear, as David Goodhart notes, that this is enough to 'reboot the middle level of technical/vocational training'. Goodhart quotes Alison Wolf, who explains that 'universities are self-contained and separate from the workplace. They cannot . . . possibly keep up with all the changes which take place in a fast-developing industry', while university teachers 'however vocational their speciality, are making their careers as academics and researchers, not as practitioners of whatever profession, trade or calling they teach' (Goodhart, p. 164). Although the UK government has to some extent recognised the problem and attempted to redress it by increasingly the number of apprenticeships, there have been quality issues with many (BBC News, Education Editor, 2016), too few are at a higher level and its apprenticeship levy on large employers, while a good idea in principle given British employers' reluctance to invest in training, has prompted a 59 per cent fall in the number of new apprenticeships (*The Guardian*, 2017). Colleges are best placed with their direct links to industry and the workplace to play a pivotal role in delivering the full family of apprenticeship qualifications, including graduate-level apprenticeships, as they are known in Scotland, or degree apprenticeships, as they are referred to in England.

A new era in tertiary education

The mass expansion of higher education and the comparative neglect of technical and vocational education represent fundamentally consistent policy failure, particularly for those young people who have no interest in pursuing an academic route, or no aptitude for it. The dominance of one part of the system at the expense of another is reflected not only in terms of the respective funding settlements for higher and further education but also in terms of the relative esteem in which each sector is held. For far too long, further and technical education has been given a low priority by politicians and journalists alike. This has begun to change over the past decade both north and south of the border. The election of a Conservative-led coalition government in 2010 led to a greater emphasis on the expansion of vocational rather than higher education. In a statement to Parliament in 2010, Vince Cable, the new Secretary of State for Business Innovation and Skills, highlighted that:

The reality is that our best FE Colleges and advanced apprenticeships are delivering vocational education every bit as valuable for their students and the wider economy as programmes provided by Universities. There could be a law of diminishing returns in pushing more and more students through University.

(Cable, 2010)

Cable refined his vision for the College and Skills sector, launching his 'Dual Mandate' consultation paper in 2015 calling for employers and FE providers to look into how the vocational education system could meet future skills challenges. Cable described his aspiration 'for the country to have a world-class standard of vocational education that can meet the future staff needs of industry, which are rapidly evolving' (Cable, 2015). Further education featured more prominently in key policy documents, just as more recently it featured in the UK government's industrial strategy (DBEIS, 2017), with a wider acknowledgement that the needs of the economy cannot by met simply by the continuing expansion of the higher education sector. Shorter tertiary qualifications have 'virtually disappeared' in England, Alison Wolf writes, while a third of graduates 'now do jobs which are clearly "non-graduate" in their content and demands'. At the same time, we continue to produce too few workers with high level technical and cognitive skills of the sort the OECD believes essential to seizing the benefits of participation in 'global value chains' which represent the 'new phase of globalisation'. (Wolf, 2017). These concerns are made more acute, of course, by the huge drag poor productivity places on the UK economy and the realisation that Brexit will increase our reliance on home grown talent to address emerging skills gaps in industries such as construction, engineering, health and the digital sector.

While the rhetoric of politicians is becoming more favourable, institutions themselves have generally been slower to adapt, in part because, for much of the college sector, day-to-day concerns of reacting to the latest political wheeze or adapting to the latest funding cut trump any thought of longer-term strategy. However, 'We are entering a "new normal" era of globalised geopolitical, financial and societal volatility, uncertainty, complexity and ambiguity . . . with the consequence that over this next 50 years, skilling, upskilling and reskilling with the latest technology will be more vital than ever' (BE&IS and DIT, 2017). The challenges we are facing demand a tertiary education sector that is agile, adaptable and resilient, not bound to traditional practice but willing and ready to change. We need a coherent system that is nevertheless diverse enough to deliver the higher-and mid-level skills that regional, metropolitan and national economies need. This will require the availability of many more tertiary choices, with a variety of providers able to offer different types and modes of provision. A part of this new normal must be a reassertion of the role of technical and professional education as a critical community resource, a role largely eclipsed in the rush to grow mass higher education and our universities as global brands.

Scottish colleges however offer a model for inclusive growth in higher education and the kind of change the FE and Skills sectors as a whole require. Over the past decade, the Scottish Government has targeted investment of over 650m in its colleges estate, through its tertiary funding agency, the Scottish Funding Council (SFC), to create 15 new college campuses, upgrade nine campuses and establish five new specialist facilities. Indeed, the Scottish Government encourages its college sector to deliver more than further education and apprenticeships. It relies on it to widen access to higher education both directly and indirectly, to develop Scotland's young workforce, to ensure inclusive skills growth and to promote innovation, especially in SMEs.

In order to increase the proportion of the population with higher education qualifications right across Scotland, the Government has actively encouraged the expansion of college-based higher education, placing no limits on such growth. Colleges provide 28 per cent of all higher education-level studies in Scotland, as compared with 6 per cent in England and 1 per cent in Wales. College-based higher education in Scotland is more cost-effective than university-based provision. Moreover, places at Scottish universities continue to be capped centrally, unlike in England where this cap was lifted in 2016. In addition, Scotland has a smaller number of post-92 universities than south of the border. The Scottish tertiary sector is characterised by greater alignment, collaboration and articulation. This is in contrast to the English sector, where Further Education Colleges more often compete than collaborate with universities. According to SFC data, some 47 per cent of Scottish students taking Higher National qualifications at college progress to degree level study at university, but less than a quarter receive full credit, necessitating the majority of college students to take five or six years of study to obtain an Honours degree. (SFC, 2016).

Scotland has, over the last five years, witnessed the emergence of regional colleges, created as part of the Scottish Government's reform agenda to rationalise public sector provision and share services. This process saw the creation of three multi-college regions and a reduction in the number of overall colleges from 43 in 2010 to 25, during a period in which funding was heavily cut and the curriculum refocused on under-25s. The mergers, though not without challenges, delivered colleges which were, in the judgement of the Scottish Funding Council, 'more resilient and sustainable for the future', better suited to the delivery of skills and engagement with employers and universities and more focused on 'putting the learner at the centre' (SFC, 2016).

Indeed, the Scottish Government's most recent evaluative report on its college sector entitled 'Delivery for All' (2018) concludes that: 'Scotland's Colleges have implemented the most profound set of public sector reforms in Scottish tertiary education for more than a generation' whilst simultaneously improving the life chances of the most disadvantaged and also generating a skilled workforce to ensure continued economic growth. It also recognises that the quality of learning at colleges has never been higher, with 95 per cent of college learners progressing on to a positive destination and over 97 per cent of all college learning leading to a recognised qualification. This report also indicates that there is a more than 90 per cent satisfaction rate reported by college students (Scottish Government, 2018).

This step change in performance was achieved whilst still keeping equality of opportunity at the very heart of its dual role to deliver for the people and economy of Scotland. The report highlights the considerable success of the sector in supporting those furthest from the workplace including deprived communities, learners with additional support needs and those suffering from a range of disabilities, older learners, women, care-experienced students and learners from black and ethnic minorities. The report also cites the Commission on Widening Access's findings that colleges play a distinctive role in Scotland's most deprived communities, providing 'a crucial alternative route into higher education and can play a powerful role in expanding the limited applicant pool resulting from the school attainment group' (Scottish Government, 2018, p. 3). Over the past decade, colleges have grown female participation rates by 19 per cent and older participation by 18 per cent.

The significant economic contribution to the long-term value to the Scottish economy from college graduates is detailed in a similarly recent report from Strathclyde University's Fraser of Allander Institute (2017). It notes that Scotland's colleges are significant economic institutions in their own right, playing a 'crucial role' in developing Scotland's growth potential through enhancing human capital, developing a more productive workforce and generally delivering long-term sustainable national and regional inclusive growth. The Fraser of Allander Report recognises that colleges are supportive learning environments for the development of life skills which boost employability prospects. The importance of these wider benefits of learning have been recognised in the earlier work of Schuller et al. (2004). They transcend 'traditional' economic factors to have positive impacts on mental health, well-being and mental illness, especially from participation in adult learning (Chevalier and Feinstein, 2004). Such parental education also plays an important role in their child's educational outcomes and social mobility (Office for National Statistics, 2002). A college education has also wider social benefits: moderating anti-social behaviour, maturing attitudes, supporting greater social cohesion and very pertinently for Scotland, delivering increased political and voting awareness (Colleges Scotland, 2017).[1]

In addition to building inclusive workplaces and enabling individual learners to flourish, the Fraser of Allander Institute report notes that the college sector is a key source of work-based upskilling and process innovation especially for small to medium-sized companies, also improving their management practices, efficiency and overall productivity. Such interventions are particularly valued in Scotland's more remote and rural enterprises. A more productive economy is able to produce more and better quality, goods and services. This in turn leads to greater investment in public services, better living standards and greater national prosperity. The report also evidences that Scotland has actually caught up in recent years with the rest of the UK in terms of productivity (Fraser of Allander Institute, 2017).

Scotland's college sector has contributed to greater economic certainty in Scotland. In more recent years, the Scottish economy has had to respond to a diverse set of economic challenges including: the 2008 financial crisis, significant fiscal consolidation, downturn in the oil and gas industry and the uncertain outlook post-Brexit. A focus on developing Scotland's young workforce led by the college sector and continuous in-work retraining have helped address the emerging skills gaps, with 81 per cent of Scottish employers who recruit college leavers finding them well prepared for work. This has also contributed to a significant decline in Scotland's unemployment rate, down from a high of almost 9 per cent in 2010 to below 4 per cent in 2017 (Fraser of Allander Institute, 2017).

The college sector in Scotland has proved itself to be an important multiplier. Annually, it contributes almost £15BN to the Scottish economy, 8.8 per cent of the total economic output of the nation. The taxpayer sees an average annual rate of return of 15.6 per cent on their public investment in this sector, whilst the individual college learner will yield a 14.8 per cent annual return or £6.30 for every £1 they personally invest in their technical and professional education or, indeed, a £55k lifetime college graduate premium (Fraser of Allander Institute, 2017).

Scotland's renaissance in college education gained a game-changer impetus with the establishment, in Glasgow, of the UK's first 'Super College', a powerhouse of higher level vocational qualifications to 40,000 students in the city (CoGC, 2010). The City of Glasgow College was founded in 2010 as a result of a pioneering multi-college merger of three specialist Scottish colleges: Central College (of Commerce) Glasgow, Glasgow Metropolitan College (itself a previous merger of Glasgow College of Building & Printing and Glasgow College of Food Technology) and Glasgow College of Nautical Studies. The new Super College, responsible for one in ten of all college students in Scotland, originally occupied 11 legacy city sites and secured an unprecedented £200 million in private-sector financing together with 25 years of funding commitment from the Scottish Government to create what is probably Europe's largest technical college campus. Its ambitious aim is to 'guarantee employability and prosperity for its diverse student cohort' (Little, 2016, p. 49)

One of the things that makes the College different is the relative security it has in planning for the future; its diversity of non-governmental income and financial stability enable the sort of long-term strategic planning that has often eludes sector leaders, buffeted by the relentless winds of reform, particularly south of the border. Another is the sheer quantum of the 464 higher education courses it offers: 73 per cent of funded full-time provision is at higher education level. Enrolling learners from less-advantaged backgrounds on to higher education courses is a vital part of the College's contribution to the widening access agenda in Scotland, an important Government priority which has not been satisfactorily addressed by the more global-facing Scottish university sector. The College accounts for the majority share of the 23 per cent of students studying higher education in a college setting who are from Scotland's most deprived communities. Such is the transformational nature of this new hybrid institution that the College is now the third most popular destination for school leavers in Scotland going into higher education, ahead of Edinburgh University, while almost a quarter of its students (24 per cent) come from the most deprived 10 per cent of postcodes in Scotland (Little, 2016, p. 50).

'Learning 4.0' at City of Glasgow College is characterised by a pedagogic approach that is increasingly personalised and blended to ensure that individual students 'flourish'. This approach also means listening much more carefully to learners and also working even more closely with employers to ensure the right inputs into the curriculum and the most tailored work experiences are organised. The College takes seriously the very latest research from the OECD, which highlights that social and emotional skills, such as communication and readiness to learn, are just as important in the modern workplace as high-level technical skills and strong cognitive skills in literacy, numeracy and problem-solving (OECD, 2017). Strong partnerships underpin the City of Glasgow College Industry Academy model, ensuring that students are job-ready with excellent transversal skills which equip them well for their careers within the labour market. The success of this personalised learning approach can be seen in the consistently improving performance of College students, year on year (see Figure 4.1). Across full-time further education, full-time higher education and part-time further and higher education, the College has demonstrated a clear upward trend

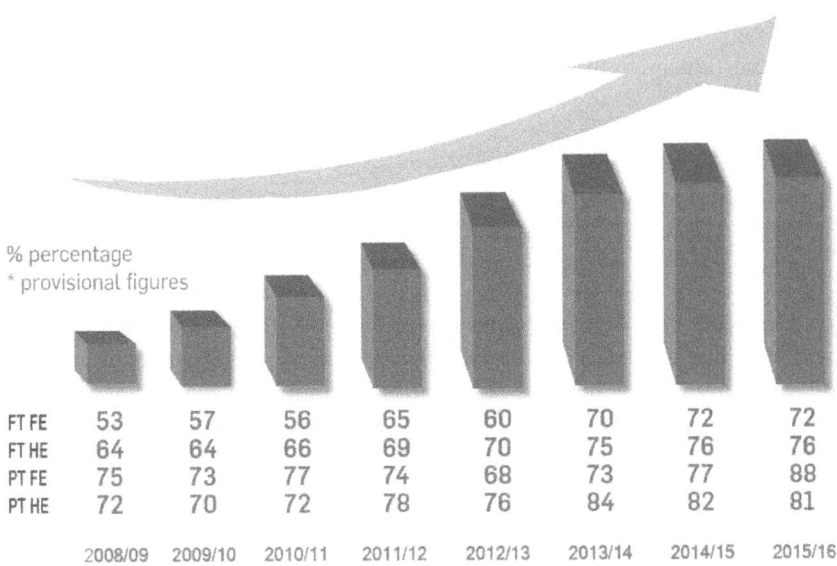

	2008/09	2009/10	2010/11	2011/12	2012/13	2013/14	2014/15	2015/16
FT FE	53	57	56	65	60	70	72	72
FT HE	64	64	66	69	70	75	76	76
PT FE	75	73	77	74	68	73	77	88
PT HE	72	70	72	78	76	84	82	81

% percentage
* provisional figures

Figure 4.1 Growth in student success rates at City of Glasgow College

in student performance since its merger, all the more remarkable given that 34.7 per cent of the college's students are from the most deprived areas in Scotland.

Despite the pivotal role played by Scotland's colleges, they seldom get the credit they deserve in public discourse. One considerable asset of the 'Super College' model is its capacity to command the attention of policymakers, employers and the media. The lower priority accorded the sector has left it subject to excessive and intrusive reform and comparative funding neglect. For far too long, colleges have lacked the time and security they need to plan in a meaningful, long-term way about where they can make most impact and how it can be sustained. The challenges of social mobility, widening access and addressing skills shortages cannot be tackled by universities alone. It is more vital than ever that colleges are allowed to play an equal part in a more diverse tertiary ecosystem to offer a real alternative with genuine employment prospects to learners who are either not interested in pursuing an academic route or unsuited to it, but who want to pursue higher skill acquisition at a different pace or for a shorter period. The VACU challenges we now face as a society demand this. Business as usual is no longer an option. The clamour for rebalancing the inexorable expansion of higher (academic) education at the expense of higher (or even mid-level) vocational education is growing ever louder in policymaking and media circles. Many more leading academics and influential journalists are challenging the current conventional wisdom. Chang (2011) likens the higher education system of the OECD club of rich countries to a:

> theatre in which some people decided to stand to get a better view, prompting others behind them to stand. Once enough people stand everyone has to stand, which means that no-one is getting a better view, while everyone has become uncomfortable.
>
> (Chang, 2011)

In debunking the myth of the 'Knowledge economy', Professor Chang exposes the 'zero-sum game of sorting' and 'degree inflation'. In calling for our 'over-enthusiasm' to be 'tamed', he cites the Swiss paradox of a nation at the very top of the international productivity league, yet with less than half of the university education of its main competitors. Meanwhile, *The Economist* concludes that repeated governments have overestimated the economic returns of higher education, noting that degrees are increasingly about signalling rather than becoming (*The Economist*, 2018). It points out that the ubiquity of the degree means that many workers go to university out of 'obligation' rather than choice, and, indeed, many are not suited to this less practical approach to learning.

As Iosue and Mussanu write: 'We pay too little attention to the cracks in the foundation of our education system and too much financial attention polishing the dome of our rich and solidly footed campus steeples' (Iosue and Mussano, 2014). This is a luxury we simply can no longer afford.

Note

1 In the Scottish Independence Referendum, the Electoral Commission noted a remarkably high turnout (84.6%) of the eligible, and recently enfranchised 16+ electorate. The turnout of the 16–17 youth vote was significantly higher (75%) than that of their 18–24 year old university counterparts (54%).

References

Audit Scotland (2016a) *Scotland's Colleges 2016*, Audit Scotland.

Audit Scotland (2016b) *Audit of Higher Education in Scottish Universities*, Audit Scotland.

BBC News, Education Editor (2016, November 11) 'Education', *BBC News* [Online]. Available at www.bbc.co.uk/news/education-37939366 (Accessed 10 March 2018).

Belfield, C., Crawford, C, and Sibieta, L. (2017) *Long-Run Comparisons of Spending per Pupil across Different Stages of Education*. London, Institure for Fiscal Studies.

Cable, V. (2010, July 15) 'A new era for universities', *2010 to 2015 Conservative and Liberal Democrat Coalition Government*. Available at www.gov.uk/government/speeches/a-new-era-for-universities (Accessed March 2018).

Cable, V. (2015, March) *A Dual Mandate for Adult Vocational Education*, UK Government, Department for Business, Innovation and Skills, London, Crown.

Chang, H. J. (2011) *23 Things They Don't Tell You about Capitalism*, London, Penguin.

Chevalier, A. and Feinstein, L. (2004) Healthy Returns on Education. In *The LoWER Annual Conference* 2004, 23–24 April 2004, London, UK.

City and Guilds (2014) *Sense and Instability: Three Decades of Skills and Employment Policy*, London, City and Guilds.

Cliffe, J. (2015, May 14) *Britain's Cosmopolitan Future: How the Country Is Changing and Why Its Politicians Must Respond*, *Policy Network* [Online]. Available at www.policy-network.net/publications/4905/Britains-Cosmopolitan-Future (Accessed 11 March 2018).

CoGC (2010) *About Us, City of Glasgow College* [Online]. Available at www.cityofglasgowcollege.ac.uk/about-us (Accessed 11 March 2018).

Colleges Scotland (2017) *Keyfacts 2017*, College's Scotland.

Department for Business, I. a. (2015) *Widening Participation in Higher Education*, UK Government, Department for Business, Innovation and Skills, London, Crown.

Department for Business, Energy & Industrial Strategy (2017) *UK Industrial Strategy: A Leading Destination to Invest and Grow*, UK Government, Department for Business, Energy & Industrial Strategy and Department for Industrial Trade, London, Crown.

Department for Education (2017) *Widening Participation in Higher Education, England, 2014/15 Age Cohort, SFR 39/2017*, Department for Education, London, Crown.

The Economist February (2018) 'Why governments have overestimated the economic returns of higher education', *The Economist* [Online]. Available at www.economist.com/the-economist-explains/2018/02/27/why-governments-have-overestimated-the-economic-returns-of-higher-education (Accessed at 20 May 2018).

Fraser of Allander Institute (2017) *The Value of College Graduates to the Scottish Economy*, Fraser of Allander Institute, University of Strathclyde.

Friedman, S., Laurison, D., and MacMillan, L. (2014) *Social Mobility, the Class Pay Gap and Intergenerational Worklessness: New Insights from the Labour Force Survey*, Social Mobility and Child Poverty Commission, London, Social Mobility and Child Poverty Commission.

Goodhart, D. (2017) *The Road to Somewhere: The Populist Revolt and the Future of Politics*, London, Hurst.

The Guardian (2017, November 23) 'Calls for change to apprenticeships after numbers fall by 59%', *The Guardian* [Online]. Available at www.theguardian.com/education/2017/nov/23/rethink-apprenticeship-scheme-employers-and-unions-urge (Accessed 12 March 2108).

HESA (2012) *Student Record 1970/71 to 2011/12*, Higher Education Statistics Agency.

Iosue, R., & Mussanu, F. (2014) *College tuition: Four decades of financial deception*. Indianapolis, Blue River Press.

Joseph Rowntree Foundation (2017) *UK Poverty*, York, Joseph Rowantree Foundation (JRF).

Kuczera, M., Field, S., and Windisch, H. C. (2016) *Building Skills for All: A Review of England*, Paris, OECD.

Little, P. (2016) *Possibility Thinking: Reimaging the Future of Further Education and Skills*, FETL (Further Education Trust for Leadership), London, RSA (Royal Society for the encouragement of Arts).

Marr, A. (2016, April 17) 'The Queen at 90: How has she remained so popular for so long?', *The Times* [Online]. Available at www.thetimes.co.uk/article/the-queen-at-90-ggls8tf5m (Accessed 12 March 2018).

Milburn, A. (2012) *University Challenge: How Higher Education Can Advance Social Mobility*, London, Crown.

Neves, J. and Hillman, N. (2017) *2017 Student Academic Experience Survey*, HEPI Higher Education Policy Institute.

OECD (2017) *Education at a Glance*, Organisation for Economic Co-operation and Development [Online]. Available at www.oecd.org/education/education-at-a-glance-19991487.htm (Accessed March 2018).

Office for National Statistics (2002) *National Educational Longitudinal Survey*, Office for National Statistics.

Purcell, K., Elias, P., Atfield, G., Behle, H., Ellison, R., Luchinskaya, D., Snape, J., Conaghan, L., and Tzanakou, C. (2012) *Futuretrack Stage 4: Transitions into Employment, Further Study and Other Outcomes*, Higher Education Careers Service Unit and Warwick Institute for Employment Research.

Schuller, T., Preston, J., Hammond, C., Brasset-Grundy, A., and Bynner, J. (2004) *The Benefits of Learning: The Impact of Education on Health, Family Life and Social Capital*, Abingdon, UK: Routledge.

Scottish Government (2018) *Scotland's Colleges: Delivering for All*, Scottish Government, Crown.

SFC (2016) *Impact and Success of the Programme of College Mergers in Scotland*, Scottish Funding Council.

Sundorph, E., Vailev, D., and Coiffait, L. (2017) *Joining the Elite: How Top Universities Can Enhance Social Mobility*, Reform.

Wolf, A. (2016) *Remaking Tertiary Education: Can We Create a System That Is Fair and Fit for Purpose*, London, Education Policy Institute.

Wolf, A. (2017, July) 'Degrees of failure: Why it's time to reconsider how we run our universities', *Prospect Magazine*. [Online]. www.prospectmagazine.co.uk/magazine/degrees-of-failure-do-universities-actually-do-any-good (Accessed 20 May 2018)

Part II

Skills, colleges and vocational education and training

Chapter 5

FE colleges in England and the skills policy agenda

Ewart Keep

Introduction

This chapter explores the actual and potential role of further education (FE) colleges in England within the national skills policy agenda. As English FE provision shares a common labour market and economic base with the rest of UK, some relatively fleeting comparisons with policy and practice in other UK nations will be made.

A backdrop of uncertainty

Skills policy in England is being driven by a dawning realisation that we are facing major changes within the economy and labour market. The as yet unknown impact of the UK's exit from the European Unit (Brexit) has combined with weak productivity growth trends to spark debate about the future shape and trajectory of the economy. Overlaying this is a growing international debate about the potential impact of technological change and the effects that robotisation, artificial intelligence and automation might have upon both the quality and quantity of work that is available and the skills that will be needed in future (see, for instance, Frey and Osborne, 2013; OECD, 2016; REC, 2017; TUC, 2017; Manyika et al., 2017; Future of Work Commission, 2017). The problem is that hard facts (as opposed to speculative forecasts) are as yet in short supply, and the scale and nature of the changes that will ensue remain highly uncertain and contested (see Malton, 2017). Therefore, the appropriate nature of the response from education remains unresolved.

At the same time, it is increasingly recognised that all is not well with the state of the employment relationship and job quality in the UK. After three and a half decades in which the mainstream political consensus has been to laud the UK's 'flexible' labour market policies and regulatory models, the downside of this in the shape of low pay, job insecurity and exploitation of vulnerable workers has started to become more apparent and to provoke unease. In Scotland, this issue has been confronted head on via a government sponsored Fair Work Convention, which has led to a Scottish Labour Market Strategy focused on the notion of 'fair work' and with an aim to improve employment relations and job quality (Scottish Government, 2016a, 2016b; Keep, 2017a).

In England, although there has been considerable government rhetoric about helping 'struggling to get by' workers and their families, concrete action has yet to emerge, but public debate about employment has undergone a major change as growing concerns about the quality of many jobs has become increasingly apparent (D'Arcy and Hurrell, 2014; D'Arcy, 2017; Taylor et al., 2017; Future of Work Commission, 2017; Findlay et al., 2017; SMC, 2017a, 2017b). Partly as a result of the geographical pattern that underlay the Brexit referendum voting, these general concerns have been heightened in relation to those areas of the country that are seen as becoming left behind in terms of economic growth trends and productivity levels and wage levels (DfE, 2017a; SMC, 2017b; Keep, 2015, 2016a).

In overall terms, therefore, skills policy in England is being fashioned and delivered within an environment which is febrile and where anxiety about future economic and social trends has largely replaced earlier, more optimistic discourses about a knowledge-driven economy and greater prosperity for all. Deep-seated structural problems relating to economic inequality, power and social class are more readily apparent and more politically salient than has been the case for a long time. The problem resides in knowing what to do about them and in resolving which elements of these challenges skills policy can tackle on its own and which can only be addressed in concert with other facets of policy.

Uncertainty about the role and responsibilities of employers

A recurring theme throughout what follows is the importance of choices made by employers and their interactions with the education and training system, both generally and with FE (Keep, 2012; Green and Hogarth, 2016). A central concern for the last three decades or more has been an unwillingness and/or inability on the part of government to resolve what exactly are the rights, roles and responsibilities (the 3R's) of employers within the education and training system (Gleeson and Keep, 2004; Keep, 2012).

Employer choice shapes competitive strategy and product market strategy, product/service quality/specification, people management systems and strategies, and production technologies, work organisation and job design (Keep et al., 2006). These decisions in turn structure the level of demand for skills, as well as how effectively skill gets utilised within the productive process. They will also exert a major influence over how well learning to earning transitions operate; the relative size of initial vocational education and training (VET) being delivered via workplace learning (apprenticeships) rather than classroom based teaching; and the levels of adult workplace learning and which employees will receive this. As a result, the performance and outcomes of education and training is to a significant degree dependent, not upon its own efficacy, but upon structural forces within the economy and the employment relationship.

The key point is that without an adequate volume of demand from employers, the economic and employment benefits of high quality college education will not be realised (Keep et al., 2006; Keep, 2016b). Unfortunately, employers' demand for skills is often lower (in terms of overall volume and qualification levels required) than official policy presumes (Keep et al., 2006; Keep, 2015). Thus the OECD's (2013) PIAAC adult skills survey demonstrated that the UK had the second lowest (after Spain) demand from employers for workers educated beyond compulsory schooling out of the 22 nations covered in the first wave of PIAAC (OECD, 2013). The survey also indicated we have the second highest levels (after Japan) of workers over-qualified for their jobs (30%) – for further details, see Keep (2016b). Employers' levels of investment in skills and their provision of training to their workforce have also been in decline (see below).

As this chapter will argue, resolving what the 3R's relating to employers should be, and strengthening interchange and cooperation between colleges and employers, is of critical importance to the success of current policies – a point that has in recent times increasingly been acknowledged by the government (Greening, 2017; DfE, 2017a). The broader issue of boosting the underlying levels of demand for skills from employers and of enabling and assisting them to deploy workforce skills to maximum productive effect remains, in England at least, to be addressed (Keep, 2016b).

Skills policy

Skills policy can be conceived of as covering a spectrum of analytical and policy stances (Keep, 2017b). At one end is a narrow model that concentrates on supplying greater volumes of human capital via an expanded education and training system. At the other end is a much broader approach that encompasses not just the supply of skills, but also efforts to stimulate underlying levels of demand for skill within the economy and to ensure that skills once created are effectively utilised within the productive process (Keep, 2016b). In essence, England conforms to the first model, whereas Scotland is closer to the second (for an overview of the contrasting national approaches, see Keep, 2017a). This fundamental choice has profound implications for the potential roles of colleges, some of which will be touched upon below.

Economic policy and the industrial strategy

Despite talk about creating a world–class technical education system, colleges get a walk-on part in the government's industrial strategy (DBEIS, 2017), much of the skills elements of which is in fact a rather traditional science and innovation strategy. The central focus is thus upon scientific research, research and development, and knowledge transfer driven innovation. FE is there to deliver the science, technology, engineering and maths (STEM) skills at intermediate and sub-degree level that employers want, and to address the latest manifestation of a supposed 'technician crisis'.

Social mobility and the inclusion agenda

FE has always been seen as a second chance provider that helps deliver social inclusion, and it has been allotted major responsibilities in delivering on the UK government's social mobility agenda (DfE, 2017a). As will be discussed below, this is a problematic role, not least as social mobility policy is struggling to deliver the scale of results that is required (SMC, 2017a). Progress in lifting people out of poverty, allowing them to progress into better quality and higher paid work and ensuring that their children can achieve better outcomes than their parents have all proved far harder to achieve than was initially anticipated within government (SMC, 2017b).

As Alan Milburn, the then-head of the Government's Social Mobility Commission (SMC) observed in his foreword to the Commission's report on the progress made between 1997 and 2017, 'there is currently no prospect of the Government achieving its ambition of Britain becoming a high-skilled high paying economy' (SMC, 2017b, p. 4). The subsequent resignation of Milburn and his fellow commissioners in protest at their perception of the UK government's lack of commitment to action indicates that social mobility policy is not going according to plan.

Skills policy overview

From an overall perspective, a complex and fragmented college 'sector', covering about 240 institutions (for details, see Hupkau and Ventura, 2017) sometimes working alongside, sometimes working in competition with independent training providers (ITPs), is addressing a multi-faceted policy agenda that is still driven by a very traditional skills supply model that assumes that demand for skills is relatively high, and that if government can get colleges (and others) to deliver what is 'needed', employers and the working of market forces will do the rest in terms of ensuring that a more highly skilled workforce delivers enhanced productivity, more competitive firms and greater social equity (DfE, 2017a; Greening, 2017). For example, there is a belief that boosting the supply of skills can stimulate productivity within particular localities and help transform local economies towards a higher skills equilibrium, thereby lifting demand for skill from employers and improving opportunities for social mobility (DfE, 2017a). This conforms to a very traditional skills supply-push model that has been an important strand in English policy since at least 2002 (Keep, 2006; Keep and Mayhew, 2010).

Yet another 'skills revolution'...

In order to deliver the goals outlined above, FE finds itself facing yet another 'perfect storm' of reform. For example, the last Secretary of State for Education described the current reform of vocational qualifications as 'the greatest shake-up in further education in 70 years' (Greening, 2017, p. 3). These reforms cannot be reviewed in detail, but references to more comprehensive treatments of the reforms are offered where available. In overall terms, government rhetoric stresses the need for FE to deliver on a range of extremely ambitious economic and social goals and on yet another attempt at catalysing a 'skills revolution' (Greening, 2017; DfE, 2017a, p. 24), while failing to acknowledge that these policy goals have remained unachievable for the last 35 years or more (Keep, 2006; Keep and Mayhew, 2010). Moreover, many of the initiatives are as yet evolving, and arriving at any judgement as to their likely success is problematic.

The key elements of the reforms include:

Further moves towards marketisation of FE are ongoing in order to help promote efficiency and effectiveness. Policy in England has opted for wide-scale marketisation of education and training provision across schools, colleges and universities, in the belief that the market and informed choices therein (by parents, students and employers) are the best and most rational resource allocation mechanism, and that by placing spending power in the hands of students (via loans for post-19 FE and HE) and by funding following the student at lower ages, education and training providers will be forced to respond to and reflect demand (Keep, 2016a; Frontier Economics, 2016). However, overlaying this enthusiasm for markets, there is a strand of official thinking that continues to favour traditional models of skills forecasting and planning and which also hankers after greater cooperation and a systems-based approach for some forms of provision (DfE, 2017a). How the tensions between these forces will be resolved is as yet profoundly unclear.

FE provision has been rationalised through a series of Area Based Reviews (ABRs) which have led to proposals for college mergers and new patterns of cooperation.

The Adult Education Budget is about to be devolved from central government to localities, represented by Local Enterprise Partnerships (LEPs) and Combined Authorities (Keep, 2015, 2016a). As noted above, the government's industrial strategy (DBEIS, 2017) and those elements of its social mobility strategy that relate to education (DfE, 2017a) both have a strong local component and aim to see education and skills supply transforming productivity, promoting occupational and sector rebalancing between localities and powering higher levels of economic growth and job opportunities in areas that currently lag behind.

A complex set of apprenticeship reforms are ongoing (see Lanning, 2016). In the context of this chapter, there are two issues. First, can colleges retain or increase their role in apprenticeship provision (see Westwood, 2016)? Second, will moves towards a massive expansion of 'degree apprenticeships' (aided by the impact of the apprenticeship levy and the willingness of university business schools and other providers to help firms convert their traditional, pre-existing graduate training schemes into graduate and MBA 'apprenticeships') mean that there is a danger that another vocational brand and associated stream of activity is about to be partially graduatised and allocated to universities?

Yet again, vocational qualifications are undergoing a major transformation, with the development of T levels to act as the technical mirror image of academic A levels (see DBIS/DfE, 2016; DfE, 2017a). The T levels will reflect career pathways and occupational families via 15 pathways, and will incorporate a significant mandatory element of work placement (45 days). As T levels will only exist at Level 3, the majority of 16–18-year-old students in most colleges will not be on the T levels (see below), but will be on what is called the 'transition year', the purposes, contents and certification arrangements for which remain to be resolved.

A set of new Institutes of Technology (IoTs) are to be established in partnerships between colleges, local universities and employers (DfE, 2017b). Each IoT will specialise in a particular occupational or sectoral area, and will pioneer new provision at sub-degree level.

In the last couple of years, there has been a growing if rather belated acknowledgement that the focus has shifted too much towards initial learning and has underplayed the importance of adult and lifelong learning. Work by the Institute for Public Policy Research for the J P Morgan Chase Foundation on adult skills (Dromey and McNeil, 2017), coupled with a Government Office for Science Foresight (GOSF) project on the changing nature of work and the need for adult learning, has served to put this issue back on the agenda (see Campbell, 2016; Green et al., 2016; Green and Hogarth, 2016; GOSF, 2017), where there is an acceptance that new policies on adult training may be required. The first, albeit small-scale, fruits of this realisation are already emerging in the shape of pilot schemes for a National Retraining Scheme, which will be fully operational by 2022 (for further details, see DfE, 2017a).

FE's current performance in relation to policy goals

Despite current policy rhetoric focusing upon technical education, a 'technician crisis' and a remodelling of vocational courses to support a high status technical route, the reality is that FE provision for 16–18-year-olds is driven by foundation learning (i.e. sub-formal educational qualification level) and qualifications at Levels 1 and 2 (where Level 1 has no international qualifications equivalent, and Level 2 represents lower secondary achievement or its vocational equivalent), rather than at Level 3 (which is equivalent to upper secondary education) or above.

Thus, in 2016/17, the enrolments at ages 16–18 at different levels were as follows:

> Entry/Foundation Level – 119,450; Level 1–198,830; Level 2–427,780; Level 3–620,650

For adult (aged 19+) students, the enrolment figures are even more stark (see Table 5.1):

Table 5.1 Enrolments in FE in England

Level	2016/17
Total learners	**1,080,400**
Below Level 2 (excluding English and maths)	377,200
English and maths*	358,400
Level 2	465,800
Level 3	158,700
Level 4+	16,100
No Level Assigned	34,100

Source: Adult (19+) Education and Training Participation by Level (2010/11 to 2016/17) in Further Education and Skills Statistical First Release: November 2017. Accessed February 2018

Qualifications reforms, IoTs and a recently announced government review of sub-degree level provision (Levels 4 and 5) speak to a desire to shift the balance of provision upward, but this will be challenging. Current patterns reflect the reality of FE's critical role in catering for those students who performed relatively poorly in their lower secondary phase and who schools do not want to retain in the upper secondary phase; its importance as a 'second chance' provider for adults that can deliver social inclusion gaols; and the fact that demand for craft and technician skills is limited (Keep and James, 2010) and is often being met through higher rather than further education (Wolf, 2016, see below). Also, as previously noted, a great many jobs do not require much by way of qualifications (Lloyd et al., 2008; Keep et al., 2006).

FE in decline?

Overlaying this is the fact that English FE has experienced an overall decline in learner volumes, from about six million leaners in 2005 to just four million in 2014 (for details, see Hupkau and Ventura, 2017). Much of this fall has been in adult provision, a development occasioned by the New Labour government's decision to shift adult funding from shorter courses to longer qualification-bearing provision, coupled with the more recent move to student loans funding for adults at Level 3 and above (Hupkau and Ventura, 2017).

Between 2013/14 and 2014/15 adult FE leaners (i.e. those aged over 19) fell by 11 per cent. One major factor in this has been the government's decision to fund Level 3 and above courses for post-19's via the student loans system (shared with higher education). As Burke (2017) outlines, this has had a major negative impact on provision, with student numbers at Levels 3, 4 and above falling from 273,400 in 2012/13 to 195,200 in 2013/14 and 169,400 by 2015/16. The latest figures for 2017/18 indicate another drop of 17 per cent compared to the same time last year. This reflects a wider backdrop of falling participation in learning by 25–64-year-olds across the UK. It declined from 20 to 14 per cent of the adult population between 2010 and 2016. This was the largest fall in Europe in that period and contrasts with significant increases in France (from 5 to 19 per cent in the same period) (Tait, 2017).

Employer retreat

This picture also needs to be seen in the context of a labour market where employers' own training efforts are in decline. The incidence of training across the whole workforce peaked in about 2000 and by 2010 was back to levels last seen in 1993 (Mason and Bishop, 2010), and there has been a much sharper reduction in the average number of hours of training per worker, with the level having fallen by between 40 and 50 per cent between 1997 and 2012 (Green et al., 2013). Since 2005, employer funding for training has declined. It is important to note that all these indicators started to decline before the recession struck in 2008. For further discussion of employer retreat and its causes and consequences, see Keep (2015).

Issues and questions for future policy development

Given the foregoing, what are the big issues and questions that policy and practice need to address in order to help ensure that FE can play its part in delivering economic and social goals?

Stability and evolution

One of the most important lessons that English policymakers have repeatedly failed to grasp is that change is not cost free (Keep, 2006; Norris and Adam, 2017). Indeed, the opposite is clearly the case – change is very expensive, risky and disruptive. New institutions take time to set up and get running, and it takes longer still for them to establish the trust and respect that is often required for them to deliver on their remit (Atkinson et al., 2017). New programmes and qualifications require significant lead times to be designed and delivered, and for qualifications it can take decades for them to seep into the consciousness and understanding of employers. For example, in England, we have created and then abolished new vocational qualifications so rapidly that the vast bulk of employers were unaware that the reform had been instigated, still less that it had failed! Whether policymakers can now give the current reforms time to be delivered and to bed in before further change ensues is an open question, but without greater stability long-term progress may be hard to achieve.

Resources

The FE sector in England has sustained significant cuts in its funding since 2010. As Belfield et al. (2017) record, across 16–18 provision FE has been the biggest loser. Thus, 'in 1990–91 spending per student in further education was nearly 50 per cent higher than spending on pupils in secondary schools, but in 2015–16 it was 10 per cent lower' (2017, p. 7). The head of the government's official educational inspectorate (Ofsted) has noted that the FE 'sector will continue to struggle' without an increase in the base level of funding for 16–18-year-olds (Burke, 2018). Moreover, as noted above, spending on adult skills has been much reduced, and, excluding apprenticeships, the entire devolved Adult Education Budget now represents no more than 2.3 per cent of the annual spending on education and training in England (Keep, 2016a).

The impact of these cuts has become more and more noticeable, and in its policy paper on the role of education in promoting social mobility, the DfE admitted:

> Historically we have not done enough to invest in further education, which is the sector responsible for delivering training from basic skills to post-graduate degrees, including the bulk of technical education. The hard work and dedication of teachers and college leaders has not been matched by successive governments who have overlooked further education . . . We want genuine partnership with the further education sector: a self-confident sector with autonomy to use its own professionalism and expertise, alongside the proper investment and capacity building from government to raise quality and ensure that best practice is identified and shared.
>
> (DfE, 2017a, p. 26)

However, the sums of money announced to rectify this decline in funding have, to date, been exceedingly small, and most of this has been allocated to establishing new sub-degree technical provision through the creation of the IoTs and to supporting the development and delivery of the new T levels.

The space for vocational learning and the role and prestige of colleges

The traditional skills policy agenda for FE has been very wide-ranging and encompassed many different roles, student groups and social and economic aims, and this continues to pertain (Bailey and Unwin, 2014). The role of colleges within governments' skills strategies is, to some extent at least, that of a 'gap filler', dealing with those skill needs and student groups that schools and universities are less willing or less adept at catering for, and this means that colleges have a complex 'mission' to pursue and a broad-ranging set of stakeholders with which to engage. As a result there are important questions, largely unresolved, about what the distinctive mission of FE colleges should be in relation to vocational provision. The scale, nature and status of the 'vocational space' and colleges' role within it remain a set of contested issues.

To put it briefly, this has two aspects. First, what is the nature and status within society and the labour market of learning that is labelled as 'vocational' (Brockmann et al., 2011), particularly those elements of which that are delivered outside universities? This has been heightened by the relative decline in the importance (in numerical terms) of the craft and technician skills that have traditionally been associated with college provision (Bailey and Unwin, 2014).

Second, in England, high-status vocational provision has been increasingly been allocated to or appropriated by universities, leaving colleges with a less glamourous and implicitly lower status role to fulfil. As Wolf (2016) points out, the expansion of English higher education has to a considerable extent been built on an acceptance that the most appropriate way to prepare those going into technical and associate professional occupations has been a three-year full honours degree rather than shorter, sub-degree level courses offered by FE. In many other countries, including to some extent Scotland, the strand of vocational preparation aimed at those entering such occupations would be the core (or at least a very major element) of what vocational colleges existed to do within the context of a model of tertiary education (Wolf, 2016).

The question is, therefore, whether T levels, IoTs, ongoing reforms to apprenticeship and a larger role for colleges within this strand of provision can together deliver the government's aim to 'establish a technical education system that rivals the best in the world to stand alongside our world-class higher education system' (DBEIS, 2017, p. 8) or whether the gravitational 'pull' of mass HE and the potential expansion of degree level and above apprenticeships mean that FE is left with a largely social inclusion role, to which higher status technical education continues to play second fiddle.

Colleges and their relationship with employers

In a speech to business leaders on the government's vocational reform programme, the previous Secretary of State for Education made a pledge that, 'we are putting you, the employers, at the heart of the reform. To be frank, everything that I've set out today . . . lives or dies on the strength of your involvement and commitment to work in partnership' (Greening, 2017, p. 4). The DfE's subsequent social mobility plan also stresses the centrality of employer engagement in and commitment to delivering the various elements of its vocational reform programme.

Two recent action research projects, both funded by the J P Morgan Chase Foundation underline the scale of the difficulties attendant upon these ambitions, particularly when small and medium-sized enterprises (SMEs) are involved. The first provided business support and subsidised human resource (HR) management consultancy services to SMEs in three locations (Stoke-on-Trent, Hackney and Glasgow). Its aim was to improve the overall quality of people management policies and practices in the firms in order to allow them to recruit and train young people more effectively and to utilise their employees' skills to greater productive effect (Atkinson et al., 2017, p. 6). In the event, the baseline people management capabilities of the SMEs engaged with turned out to be much lower than had initially been anticipated, and the project expended the majority of its resources simply dealing with relatively basic transactional issues and enabling the firms to become legally compliant in respect to employment regulations. The project's evaluators concluded that 'many SMEs felt that they were not ready for transformational work. Managers had a purely transactional and compliance-based view of HR and were simply not prepared in outlook or leadership to take on significant change' (Atkinson et al., 2017, p. 26) and that to bring about the desired changes to the majority of SMEs would require a much longer and sustained period of engagement and considerable resources. Their recommendation was that policymakers should invest in a stable, strengthened local business support infrastructure that can underpin the evolution of local skill ecosystems (Atkinson et al., 2017, p. 55).

This brings us neatly to the second of the J P Morgan Chase projects, which is ongoing at the time of writing. This is the East London Vocational Education and Training: Innovation Through Partnership (ELVET) programme, managed by the UCL Institute of Education (IoE) in partnership with the Association of Colleges (AoC). ELVET aims to test out new ways of colleges working with employers to improve training provision and labour market outcomes in social care, digital and creative occupations. The project has a broader context of exploring how colleges can help create local High Progression and Skills Ecosystems (HPSE) – see Hodgson et al. (2017a) for details.

ELVET's exploration of building linkages to employers that move from one-way engagement (college to employer) to a genuine two-way partnership suggests that the establishment and development of such relationships is an extremely time- and resource-intensive activity (Hodgson et al., 2017b). Looking across the developed world, it is apparent that in the majority of developed countries, strong collective employer representation and organisation that can deliver a coherent employer view and concert employers' collective actions on skills and training are preconditions for a successful education and training system. Disorganised employers will in all probability lead to a poorly functioning and ineffective education and training system (Martin and Swank, 2012; Keep, 2012; Green and Hogarth, 2016; Martin, 2017). Given English employer retreat from investing in skills and their long record of passivity and disengagement from an active role in education and training policy, achieving a lasting and broad-reaching change in their role within the education system will not be easy, and will take a considerable and concerted effort. It is also the case that international research suggests that although ecosystems approaches hold considerable promise, they are complex to construct and require considerable patience and capacity building if they are to be successful (Buchanan et al., 2017).

New, integrated models of economic and social action at the local level

There are two final, inter-linked 'wild card' elements in the possible evolution of colleges' roles in England. These are the devolution of the Adult Education

Budget and the potential this is opening up for experimentation with a local skills 'offer' that is more closely integrated within a wider focus on inclusive growth and improved job quality. At present, there exists a spectrum of different models of how skills policy should be structured at the local level. At one end are traditional skills supply models that stress matching demand and supply at local and occupational levels, and also the idea that a local supply-push effect can deliver economic revitalisation and greater social mobility (City Growth Commission, 2014; Local Government Association, 2015). In other words, it is a localised version of the policies and beliefs that have powered English national level skills policies for three and half decades. At the other end of the spectrum are new approaches that argue that both economic success and greater labour market progression are likely to be delivered only when skills policies are closely tied to interventions concerned with economic development, business support and improvement and with policies that explicitly seek to deliver inclusive growth and fair work – i.e. better quality employment (for an overview, see Green et al., 2017). It has also been argued (Rubery et al., 2017) that besides linking up skills with other policy areas, education and training itself will need to adopt a more integrated and sophisticated approach that embraces human development across the life course.

The development of these models has been supported by the Joseph Rowntree Foundation and other charities and campaign groups and in part reflects research by regional studies experts that argues that the policy challenge posed by the need to achieve spatial economic rebalancing, inclusive growth and better work are very considerable (Martin et al., 2015; Pike et al., 2016). One possible indicator that this integrated approach is gaining traction is the fact that the Greater London Authority (GLA) has produced alongside one another a draft economic strategy (Mayor of London, 2017a), a draft skills strategy (Mayor of London, 2017b) and a consultation on a Good Work Standard (Mayor of London, 2017c) that to some extent inter-relate and are intended to be mutually reinforcing. This plainly carries echoes of Scotland's Fair Work Convention and the resultant Scottish Government Labour Market Strategy (Scottish Government, 2016a, 2016b). Parallel efforts are in train in Leeds and Greater Manchester. The main stumbling block is liable to be the limited capacity that local authorities and LEPs currently possess, in terms of the expertise, resources and staffing required to design and deliver a more joined-up and holistic policy package (Keep, 2016a; Payne, 2018).

Final thoughts

English FE finds itself torn between delivering a social inclusion, second-chance agenda and trying to upgrade the status of its traditional vocational education and training offering. The dominance of the former has tended to depress its status vis-à-vis other education providers. It is short of resources and is facing another wave of radical and unpredictable reforms, particularly in terms of the

T levels and apprenticeships. From a policy perspective, it is also profoundly unclear what constitutes successful performance by FE colleges (Hadawi, 2018).

At a macro policy level, colleges find themselves tied to a very traditional skills supply strategy that no longer has large sums of public money behind it, and this in turn is tied to a fairly narrow and traditional 'industrial strategy' that has far more to say about the role of HE and science than it does about vocational education and training. This kind of approach is increasingly questioned by the OECD and has been rejected by some countries (see Keep, 2017a). For example, Scotland has integrated skills and the work of colleges into policies that try to address skills supply, demand and utilisation in the round (Keep, 2017b). It will be interesting to observe the relative success of these two models over the next few years.

References

Atkinson, C., Lupton, B., Kynigho, A., Antcliff, V., and Carter, J. (2017) *People Skills: Building Ambition and HR Capability in Small UK Firms*, London, Chartered Institute for Personnel Development.

Bailey, B. and Unwin, L. (2014) 'Continuity and change in English further education: A century of voluntarism and permissive adaptability', *British Journal of Educational Studies*, vol. 62, no. 4, pp. 449–464.

Belfield, C., Crawford, C., and Sibieta, L. (2017) *Long-Run Comparisons of Spending Per Pupil across Different Stages of Education*, London, Institute for Fiscal Studies.

Brockmann, M., Clarke, L., and Winch, C. (eds.) (2011) *Knowledge, Skills and Competence in the European Labour Market: What's in a Vocational Qualification?*, London, Routledge.

Buchanan, J., Anderson, P., and Power, G. (2017) 'Skill ecosystems', in Warhurst, C., Mayhew, K., Finegold, D., and Buchanan, J. (eds.), *The Oxford Handbook of Skills and Training*, Oxford, Oxford University Press, pp. 444–465.

Burke, J. (2017, December 1) 'Advanced learner loans less popular than ever', *FE Week*, p. 6.

Burke, J. (2018, January 12) 'DfE disappoints as it rejects a 16-to-18 funding-rate rise', *FE Week*, p. 7.

Campbell, M. (2016) 'The UK's skills mix: Current trends and future needs', in *GOSF Future Skills and Lifelong Learning Evidence Review*, London, Government Office for Science Foresight.

City Growth Commission (2014) *Human Capitals: Driving UK Metro Growth through Workforce Investment*, London, Royal Society for the Arts.

D'Arcy, C. (2017) *Low Pay Britain 2017*, London, Resolution Foundation.

D'Arcy, C. and Hurrell, A. (2014) *Escape Plan: Understanding Who Progresses from Low Pay and Who Gets Stuck*, London, Resolution Foundation.

Department for Business, Energy and Industrial Strategy (2017) *Industrial Strategy: Building a Britain Fit for the Future*, Cm 9528, London, DBEIS/HMSO.

Department for Business, Innovation and Skills/Department for Education (2016) *Post-16 Skills Plan*, Cm 9280, London, HMSO.

Department for Education (2017a) *Unlocking Talent, Fulfilling Potential: A Plan to Improve Social Mobility through Education*, Cm 9541, London, DfE.

Department for Education (2017b) *Institutes of Technology Prospectus*, London, DfE.

Dromey, J. and McNeil, C. (2017) *Skills 2030*, London, IPPR.

Findlay, P., Warhurst, C., Keep, E., and Lloyd, C. (2017) 'Opportunity knocks? The possibilities and levers for improving job quality', *Work and Occupations*, vol. 44, no. 1, pp. 3–22.

Frey, C. B. and Osborne, M. A. (2013) *The Future of Employment: How Susceptible Are Jobs to Computerisation?*, Oxford, Oxford University, Martin School.

Frontier Economics (2016) 'Understanding the further education market in England', *BIS Research Paper* No. 296, London, Department for Business, Innovation and Skills.

Future of Work Commission (2017) *Report of the Future of Work Commission*, London, Future of Work Commission.

Gleeson, D. and Keep, E. (2004) 'Voice without accountability: The changing relationship between employers, the state and education in England', *Oxford Review of Education*, vol. 30, no. 1, pp. 37–63.

Government Office for Science Foresight (2017) *Future of Skills and Lifelong Learning*, London, GOSF.

Green, A. and Hogarth, T. (2016) 'The UK skills system: How aligned are public policy and employers' views of training provision?', in *GOSF Future Skills and Lifelong Learning Evidence Review*, London, Government Office for Science Foresight.

Green, A., Hogarth, T., Barnes, S.-A., Gambin, L., Owen, D., and Sofroniou, N. (2016) 'The UK's skills system: Training, employability and gaps in provision', in *GOSF Future Skills and Lifelong Learning Evidence Review*, London, Government Office for Science Foresight.

Green, A., Kispeter, E., Sissons, P., and Froy, F. (2017) *How International Cities Lead Inclusive Growth Agendas*, York, Joseph Rowntree Foundation.

Green, F., Felstead, A., Gallie, D., Inanc, H., and Jewson, N. (2013) 'What has been happening to the training of workers in Britain?', *LLAKES Research Paper* No. 43, London, Institute of Education, LLAKES.

Greening, J. (2017, November) *Speech at DfE Skills Summit*, London, DfE.

Hadawi, A. (2018, February 9) 'Ofsted is measuring the wrong things', *FE Week*, p. 17.

Hodgson, A., Spours, K., Jeanes, J., Smith, D., Vine-Morris, M., Vihriala, R., Bollam, J., Cook, B., Clendenning, D., Harris, M., and Kazempour, T. (2017a) 'Education, skills and employment in East London: An ecosystem analysis', *ELVET Programme Research Briefing* No. 1, London, UCL Institute of Education, Centre for Post-14 Education and Work.

Hodgson, A., Spours, K., Jeanes, J., Smith, D., Vine-Morris, M., Vihriala, R., Bollam, J., Cook, B., Clendenning, D., Harris, M., and Kazempour, T. (2017b) 'Beyond employer engagement: Exploring the nature of partnership working for skills development', *ELVET Programme Research Briefing* No. 2, London, UCL Institute of Education, Centre for Post-14 Education and Work.

Hupkau, C. and Ventura, G. (2017) 'Further education in England: Learners and institutions', *CVER Briefing Note* No. 1, London, Centre for Vocational Education Research.

Keep, E. (2006) 'State control of the English VET system: Playing with the biggest trainset in the world', *Journal of Vocational Education and Training*, vol. 58, no. 1, pp. 47–64.

Keep, E. (2012) 'Education and industry: Taking two steps back and reflecting', *Journal of Education and Work*, vol. 25, no. 4, pp. 357–379.

Keep, E. (2015) 'Unlocking workplace skills: What is the role of employers?', *CIPD Policy Report*, London, Chartered Institute for Personnel and Development.

Keep, E. (2016a) *The Long-Term Implications of Devolution and Localism for FE in England*, London, Association of Colleges.

Keep, E. (2016b) 'Improving skills utilisation in the UK: Some reflections on what, who and how?', *SKOPE Research Paper* No. 123, Oxford, SKOPE.

Keep, E. (2017a) 'English exceptionalism re-visited: Divergent skill strategies across England and Scotland', *Journal of Education and Work*, vol. 30, no. 7, pp. 741–749.

Keep, E. (2017b) 'Current challenges: Policy lessons and implications', in Warhurst, C., Mayhew, K., Finegold, D., and Buchanan, J. (eds.), *The Oxford Handbook of Skills and Training*, Oxford, Oxford University Press, pp. 671–691.

Keep, E. and James, S. (2010) 'What incentives to learn at the bottom end of the labour market?', *SKOPE Research Paper* No. 94, Cardiff, Cardiff University, SKOPE.

Keep, E. and Mayhew, K. (2010) 'Moving beyond skills as a social and economic panacea?', *Work, Employment and Society*, vol. 24, no. 1, pp. 565–577.

Keep, E., Mayhew, K., and Payne, J. (2006) 'From skills revolution to productivity miracle: Not as easy as it sounds?', *Oxford Review of Economic Policy*, vol. 22, no. 4, pp. 539–559.

Lanning, T. (ed.) (2016) *Where Next for Apprenticeships?*, London, Chartered Institute for Personnel and Development.

Lloyd, C., Mason, G., and Mayhew, K. (eds.) (2008) *Low-Wage Work in the UK*, New York, Russell Sage Foundation.

Local Government Association (2015) *Realising Talent: A New Framework for Devolved Employment and Skills*, London, Local Government Association.

Malton, C. (2017) 'The future of work: What do we know?', *WONKHE Blog* [Online]. Available at http://wonkhe.com/blogs/the-future-of-work-what-do-we-know/ (Accessed 4 November 2017).

Manyika, J., Lund, S., Chui, M., Bughin, J., Woetzel, J., Batra, P., Ko, R., and Sanghvi, S. (2017) *Jobs Lost, Jobs Gained: Workforce Transitions in a Time of Automation*, New York, McKinsey Global Institute.

Martin, C. J. (2017) 'Skill builders and the evolution of national vocational training systems', in Warhurst, C., Mayhew, K., Finegold, D., and Buchanan, J. (eds.), *The Oxford Handbook of Skills and Training*, Oxford, Oxford University Press, pp. 36–53.

Martin, C. J. and Swank, D. (2012) *The Political Construction of Business Interests*, Cambridge, Cambridge University Press.

Martin, R., Pike, A., Tyler, P., and Gardiner, B. (2015) *Spatially Rebalancing the UK Economy: The Need for a New Policy Model*, Seaford, Regional Studies Association.

Mason, G. and Bishop, K. (2010) 'Adult training, skills updating and recession in the UK: The implications for competitiveness and social inclusion', *LLAKES Research Paper* No. 10, London, Institute of Education, LLAKES.

Mayor for London (2017a) *The Mayor's Economic Development Strategy for London: Draft for Consultation*, London, Greater London Authority.

Mayor for London (2017b) *Skills for Londoners: A Draft Skills and Adult Education Strategy for London*, London, Greater London Authority.

Mayor for London (2017c) *The Mayor of London's Good Work Standard: A Call for Evidence*, London, Greater London Authority.

Norris, E. and Adam, R. (2017) *All Change*, London, Institute for Government.

Organisation for Economic Cooperation and Development (2013) *OECD Skills Outlook 2013*, Paris, OECD.

Organisation for Economic Cooperation and Development (2016) 'Structural transformation in the OECD: Digitisation, deindustrialisation and the future of work', *OECD Social, Employment and Migration Working Papers* No. 193, Paris, OECD.

Payne, J. (2018) 'In the DNA or missing gene? Devolution, local skills strategies and inclusive growth in England', *SKOPE Research Paper* No. 126, Oxford, Oxford University, SKOPE.

Pike, A., MacKinnon, D., Coombes, M., Champion, T., Bradley, D., Cumbers, A., Robson, L., and Wymer, C. (2016) *Uneven Growth: Tackling City Decline*, York, Joseph Rowntree Foundation.

Recruitment and Employment Confederation (2017) *The Future of Jobs*, London, REC.

Rubery, J., Johnson, M., Lupton, R., and Roman, G. Z. (2017) *Human Development Report for Greater Manchester*, Manchester, Manchester University, European Work and Employment Research Institute.

Scottish Government (2016a) *Fair Work Framework*, Edinburgh, Scottish Government.

Scottish Government (2016b) *Scotland's Labour Market Strategy*, Edinburgh, Scottish Government.

Social Mobility Commission (2017a) *Social Mobility in Great Britain: Fifth State of the Nation Report*, London, SMC.

Social Mobility Commission (2017b) *Time for Change: An Assessment of Government Policy on Social Mobility 1997–2017*, London, SMC.

Tait, C. (2017) *New Tricks: Innovative Approaches to Lifelong Learning*, London, Fabian Society.

Taylor, M., Marsh, G., Nicol, D., and Broadhurst, P. (2017) *Good Work: The Taylor Review of Modern Working Practices*, London, HM Government.

Trades Union Congress (2017) *Shaping Our Digital Future: A TUC Discussion Paper*, London, TUC.

Westwood, A. (2016) 'Why colleges and universities should be offering more and better apprenticeships', in Lanning, T. (ed.), *Where Next for Apprenticeships?*, London, Chartered Institute for Personnel and Development, pp. 44–49.

Wolf, A. (2016) *Remaking Tertiary Education*, London, Education Policy Institute.

Chapter 6

SkillsFuture

Breaking new ground, creating new
pathways

Ng Cher Pong

Impact of VUCA and extension of working lives

Introduced by the US Army War College in the 90's, the acronym VUCA
(which stands for Volatility, Uncertainty, Complexity, Ambiguity) was initially
used to describe the geopolitical environment post-Cold War. However, in
recent years, especially after the Great Recession, VUCA has become a widely
used term for the general business environment. This is an apt descriptor set
against a backdrop where entire industries are being disrupted. The scale and
pace of the transformation are unprecedented – driven by primarily by technology and automation and, in some instances, also by innovations in business
models. Coupled with globalisation, such transformation has spread across the
world at breakneck speed. Many business leaders have rallied their companies
to innovate, with the message of 'disrupt yourself or be disrupted by your
competition'.

These widespread disruptions at the workplace have profound implications
for jobs and skills. According to the OECD Policy Brief on the Future of
Work,[1] mid-level routine jobs have been made redundant across the EU, Japan
and the US over a 12-year period, while new jobs are being created. Nowadays, job titles that were unheard of 10–15 years ago, such as data scientists,
cyber security specialists, bloggers and digital marketers, populate the online
job boards. This trend will, at the minimum, continue unabated, as technology
affects a broader segment of the workforce. VUCA therefore accelerates the
pace of skills obsolescence.

At the same time, the retirement age in most developed countries is being
raised, in tandem with improved health and increased longevity. Today, new
entrants into the workforce are likely to have careers spanning four to five
decades. As working lives are extended, individuals will need to make more
effort to remain employable throughout this period.

The combined effect of these two driving forces, that is, an ever-changing
external environment and the lengthening of working lives, is that reskilling and
upskilling becomes even more imperative for individuals in order for them to be
prepared for the new jobs that are being created.

SkillsFuture – Singapore's skills strategy

In Singapore, we launched a new national skills strategy known as SkillsFuture in 2015. To drive and coordinate the implementation of this, a new statutory board, SkillsFuture Singapore, was formed in 2016, reporting to the Ministry of Education. SkillsFuture seeks to help build the foundations for a highly skilled, productive and innovative economy for Singapore. However, it serves not only an economic objective. SkillsFuture is also about helping individuals to realise their full potential, regardless of their starting points. Through an integrated and high quality system of education and training, it is envisaged that individuals will be able to continually learn and deepen their skills throughout life, driven by their passion and interests. By reskilling and adapting, they will remain employable even as industries transform in a VUCA environment. SkillsFuture will therefore empower Singaporeans to take charge of and steer their education and training, as well as their careers. By doing this, we seek to nurture a workforce that is adaptable and nimble, responding quickly to changes in their industries and workplaces.

There are three distinct segments of stakeholders – employers (including organisations representing groupings of employers such as Trade Associations and Chambers), individuals (including unions which represent the interests of workers) as well as education and training providers. In each country, the relationship between these three stakeholders define and shape the skills ecosystem. The skills ecosystem is a complex one, comprising several dimensions: how skills are imparted, acquired and utilised; how skills are recognised and rewarded at the workplace, which affect an individual's decision on whether to deepen skills; and how society values skills and the mastery of skills.

In developing the different programmes and initiatives under SkillsFuture, we have drawn many lessons from education and training systems across the world, especially from Germany and Switzerland, and adapted them for our purpose. As details of the SkillsFuture programmes and initiatives are available at www.skillsfuture.sg, it is not the intention of this chapter to elaborate on them. Rather, this chapter will focus on how education and training systems around the world are evolving, and what we have learned from them in developing SkillsFuture.

Globally, there are four broad shifts in the education and training landscape:

a   A rebalancing between academic and vocational pathways;
b   A rebalancing between learning in school and learning at the workplace;
c   A rebalancing between front-loading the learning and spreading out learning throughout life; and
d   A rebalancing between learning technical skills and transversal skills (or more commonly known as 'soft skills').

Rebalancing between academic and vocational pathways

Academic pathways are favoured in many countries over vocational pathways and are generally viewed as the more established route to success in life. In East Asian countries, including Singapore, this is often exacerbated by a Confucian tradition that values scholastic achievements over vocational skills.

Globally, there has been a sharp increase in the proportion of individuals with tertiary education who are now entering the workforce. As shown in the chart below, the proportion in the 25–34-year-old age group has nearly doubled in the OECD countries over the last two decades (see Figure 6.1).

At the same time, unemployment rates for tertiary-educated individuals in this same age group in the OECD countries has hovered below 8 per cent (see Figure 6.2). This reflects the corresponding growth in employment opportunities for tertiary-educated graduates.

However, the unemployment rate has gradually crept upwards in many countries in recent years, which is an early warning sign of a potential mismatch between the demand and supply. This is particularly so if tertiary education does not equip these graduates with the skills required by industry. Policymakers are also increasingly worried about graduate underemployment, which is difficult to measure. So, while the overall increase in educational attainment is encouraging, it is important to have a good spread of tertiary-educated individuals across both the academic and vocational pathways, in order to avoid skills mismatch and graduate unemployment.

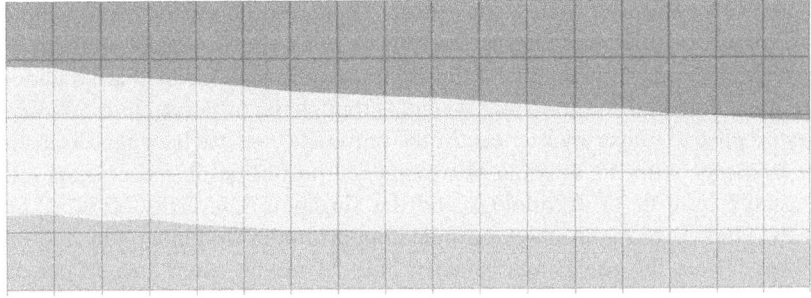

Figure 6.1 Educational attainment for 25–34-year-olds by qualification, as % share of OECD population, 1998–2015

Source: OECD Educational attainment and labour-force status, data retrieved on 1 Oct 2016

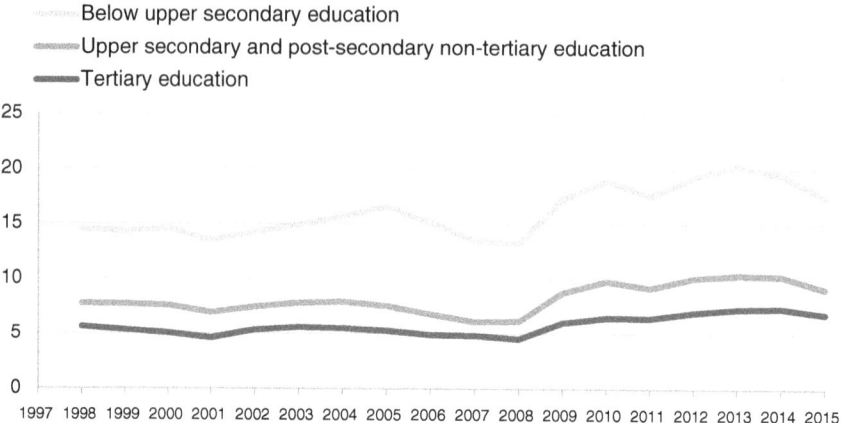

.... Below upper secondary education

▬▬▬ Upper secondary and post-secondary non-tertiary education

▬▬▬ Tertiary education

Figure 6.2 Unemployment rates for 25–34-year-olds with tertiary education, as % of corresponding group in labour force, 1998–2015

Source: OECD Educational attainment and labour-force status, data retrieved on 1 Oct 2016

Switzerland, for example, has been successful in striking a good balance between the two pathways. Two-thirds of each birth cohort progresses through the vocational pathway. They receive well-structured and rigorous training as apprentices in companies, after which many of them stay on as employees. Those who do well in their apprenticeships also have the option to progress further onto universities, particularly the universities of applied sciences. Good employment outcomes and the porosity across the education and training landscape are key to how Switzerland has made both the academic and vocational pathways attractive.

In Singapore, the polytechnics and Institute of Technical Education (ITE) cater to about two-thirds of each birth cohort. These institutions focus on technical and vocational skills and prepare students to enter the workforce immediately upon graduation. As such, they differ from the universities, which are traditionally more focussed on academic studies, although some polytechnic graduates may progress to university later on. At the university level, we have also diversified the landscape with the building of two applied universities in recent years – the Singapore Institute of Technology and the Singapore University of Social Sciences. These have significantly expanded opportunities for higher education for graduates from the polytechnics and the ITE. As a result, more than 40 per cent of the polytechnic students qualified for the more academic pathway but chose to pursue applied studies in areas such as digital animation, precision engineering, retail management and nursing instead. This is the outcome of sustained – and ongoing – efforts to build multiple pathways in the education and training system to cater to different interests and forms of learning, with connections across these diverse pathways and no dead ends (see Figure 6.3).

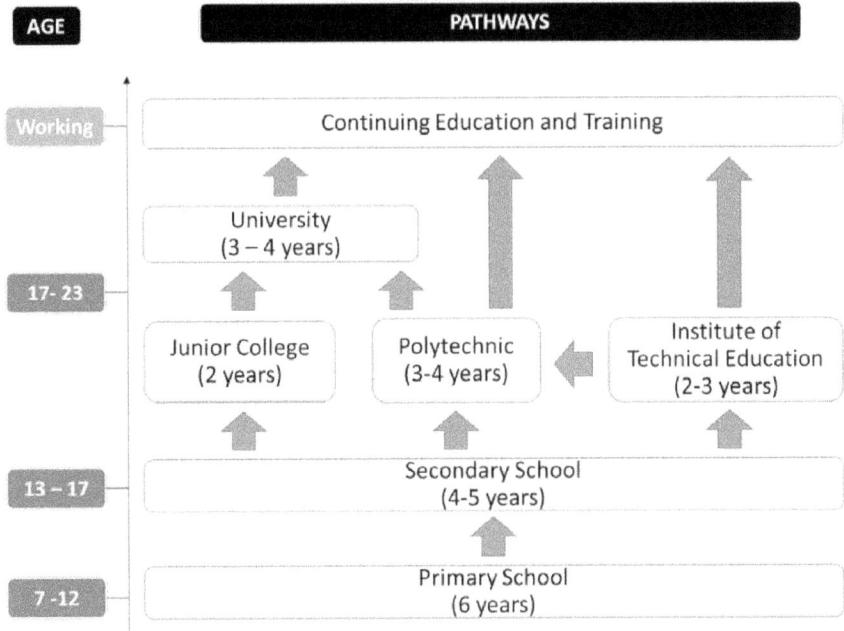

Figure 6.3 Educational pathways in Singapore

To ensure strong industry orientation across the publicly-funded tertiary institutions in Singapore, employment outcomes of graduates are measured and published by the Ministry of Education annually. A survey is conducted six months after graduation, and the average employment rate and starting salary are made available at the course level. Employment outcomes for fresh graduates have been good thus far – at least 80 per cent of them secured permanent full-time jobs each year, across the past five years.

In the skills ecosystem, supply-side interventions targeted at the education and training institutions are necessary but insufficient on their own. Equally important is that employers cannot be entirely qualifications-based in making decisions on who they hire and promote. Enterprises should be prepared to look beyond qualifications and hire individuals based on their passion and interests. Even if these individuals may not immediately have the full repertoire of skills required for a particular job, they will be able to pick them up with some training and most importantly, with the right attitude. Employers also need to make the most of the skills acquired by their employees. Demand-side interventions to engage companies and to co-share the cost and risks of such hires, especially via training subsidies, have therefore been undertaken in Singapore to extend the philosophy of 'multiple pathways, with no dead ends' from the education sector into the labour market.

Rebalancing between learning in school and learning at the workplace

Globally, there is also recognition of the importance of shifting the location where learning takes place. Education models in most countries, including in Singapore, are still very much classroom-centric and institution-centric. Our ability to codify skills and competencies, and to systematically impart them to the next generation of workers have improved by leaps and bounds over the past few decades. The use of technology in education such as through simulators and immersive media equipment has also contributed to this in recent years.

Even so, there are limitations to how much we can simulate the real workplace environment within a training institute, especially for the learning of soft skills. At the same time, the extent and pace of industry transformation have made it more difficult for education institutes to stay current. These account for the resurging interest in apprenticeships among policymakers around the world, including Singapore, which has recently introduced the SkillsFuture Earn and Learn Programme (ELP). The ELP is structured like an apprenticeship programme, although the training duration is shorter (i.e. about 12 to 18 months), and it targets fresh graduates from the polytechnics and ITE. With the reliance on workplaces to impart skills and competencies, apprenticeships enable authentic, real-life and hands-on learning. The participation of employers also substantially lowers the risk of a mismatch between what is taught and what is required by industry. In addition, workplace learning facilitates skills mastery in the longer run, as an individual is able to continually hone and deepen his or her skills.

The current distinction between learning in an educational institution and at the workplace is an artificial one. It is likely to become increasingly blurred, with the need for workers to continually reskill and upskill throughout their careers. How seamlessly we can support and coordinate the learning experiences for each learner between the two different settings will determine the quality of workplace learning.

In most countries, this is often the Achilles heel of apprenticeships and accounts for the high drop-out rates among apprentices. Most countries that have successful apprenticeship models have taken hundreds of years to build up their existing systems to support workplace learning. They have evolved a corporate culture in which companies view training as part and parcel of their business operations. In Germany, for example, companies continue to invest in the future and take on a steady stream of apprentices to build up their manpower pool for the long-term. Skilled craftsmen in these countries similarly see training of the next generation as their responsibility. Accordingly, the training of a

Meister in Germany includes, among other skills, training on pedagogy. Such tradition and culture does not exist in most other countries, so, not surprisingly, they will take some time to build a similar system to support and enable workplace learning. Patience, therefore, is a pre-requisite for policymakers.

Employers who are not accustomed to delivering structured training must first be convinced and see the value in doing so. They must be persuaded that a 'plug and play' approach towards talent is not sustainable. This is particularly true for emerging skills, such as cyber security, which are in short supply globally. In such areas, even companies that have deep pockets will not be able to acquire talent in sufficient numbers and quality to meet their demand. Shifting towards an 'invest and build' strategy towards talent therefore makes good business sense. Employers who are convinced about this will have to build up workplace training capabilities over time in order to keep their workforce resilient, adaptable and highly skilled.

Small and medium-sized enterprises, or SMEs, face much greater hurdles. For them, the lack of economies of scale to train and retrain may necessitate them to work either directly with their competitors or via industry associations to make workplace training a reality. Many SMEs also do not have adequate HR capabilities to enable workplace learning. There is therefore a small firm effect on training participation rates in most countries. However, given that SMEs employ the bulk of the workforce in almost all countries, it is crucial to reach out to and support them in training, especially in efforts to build workplace training capacity.

In Singapore, we are piloting different models to bridge the learning in schools with learning at the workplace, through a combination of strengthening industry involvement and making available government support. Not only are industry internships compulsory for most courses offered by the polytechnics and ITE, enhancements are being made to lengthen them and make them more structured to achieve the learning outcomes. We have also been introducing a range of work-learn programmes that involve close partnerships between tertiary institutions and industry. In 2015, we launched the first batch of ELPs. These programmes target fresh graduates from the polytechnics and ITE, and facilitate their transition to the workplace. Government grants are offered to lower the cost of participating in such programmes for companies. In 2017, our universities have also launched work-study degree programmes, which are structured as cooperative education and contextualised for participating companies in Singapore. Similar to what we observed in Germany and Switzerland, some progressive employers in Singapore, too, have stepped up to create industry training centres together with the government. This has been done for key industries such as cyber security and supply chain and logistics, in order to train for the broader industry and build up a talent pipeline. Ultimately, the key to such models is finding a practical model that works for all the stakeholders involved for each programme – the prospective students or trainees, the participating employers and the education institutes.

Rebalancing between front-loading the learning and spreading out learning throughout life

Concentrating learning in the first two decades of an individual's life is clearly an outdated concept in a rapidly changing world. Yet, education is still very much front-loaded. While general and tertiary education is subsidised in most countries, education budgets are seldom extended to adult education and lifelong learning. Instead, companies and workers have been expected to bear the majority of their own training and development costs. While this model has worked previously, it has increasingly come under strain. This is primarily because the overall cost required to keep skills current and workers employable has continued to escalate, as skills become obsolete at a faster rate and as the likelihood of career disruptions increases.

At the individual level, learning how to learn has become a critical foundational skill for one to stay adaptable and employable. It is not limited to learning techniques, but also extends to self-motivation – it is hard to be disciplined to continually learn, unlearn and relearn, especially for working adults who juggle the demands of their workplace, as well as their personal and family life. Individuals need to be self-directed learners who take personal responsibility to develop and deepen their skills. Given that the future economy will be technology-based, Singapore has also introduced a national SkillsFuture for Digital Workplace programme. This initiative seeks to equip Singaporeans with digital confidence and a positive mindset towards innovation, and functional skills to work in technology-rich environments.

Grooming and nurturing self-directed learners has therefore been embedded as one of the desired outcomes of education in Singapore. At the same time, we are increasing government expenditure on continuing education and training, in order to lower the cost for enterprises and individuals. Government subsidies are primarily supply-side driven, i.e. they are disbursed to approved training providers in order to lower the course fees for their programmes. Through supply-side funding, subsidies are directed to training in skills and competencies that are demanded by industry. Co-payment by employers and/or trainees is also required. Increased levels of subsidy are also made available to targeted segments of the population, such as low-wage workers and mature individuals (who are more likely to require a top-up or refresh in their skills and competencies).

To spur individuals to act, we have created a lifelong learning account for all Singaporeans aged 25 years and above in 2016. Each Singaporean receives an initial amount of S$500 in credit, which works out to about £300. Known as the SkillsFuture Credit, it can be used by individuals to pay for course fees from a pre-approved list of training programmes offered by both public and private training providers. There is no expiry date to the credit. The government has also committed to periodically topping up the account in the future. The policy objective for the SkillsFuture Credit is to empower all Singaporeans to become lifelong learners and to take ownership of their learning. Demand-side subsidy, such as the SkillsFuture Credit, is placed in the hands of consumers and is hence much less directed. However, it is very visible to the public, generates substantial interest and is more likely to lead to action. An early indication of the effect of the SkillsFuture Credit is a spike in training participation rate in Singapore, as shown in the figure below (see Figure 6.4).

Another key hurdle to lifelong learning is the availability of high quality and industry-relevant training programmes. Publicly funded education and training institutions that have traditionally focused on training young people will have to evolve their roles. They should see themselves as playing a critical role in not only pre-employment training, but also continuing professional development. This will entail offering a suite of part-time, evening and even weekend courses.

A vibrant adult education and training sector is required to enable continuous upskilling and reskilling, and to support the transformation that is happening across many industries. In Singapore, we have extended government subsidies to both public and private training providers. All our publicly funded universities have committed to setting up new units that are dedicated to lifelong learning, and see themselves playing a major role in SkillsFuture. Beyond offering the traditional part-time degree and postgraduate programmes, these centres deliver short modular and certificate courses targeted at working professionals. The range of training programmes available is expected to increase significantly, especially in areas of industry demand, such as robotics, advanced manufacturing, data analytics and artificial intelligence.

At the same time, all training providers, whether public or private, will need to have trainers which are plugged into the latest industry developments and

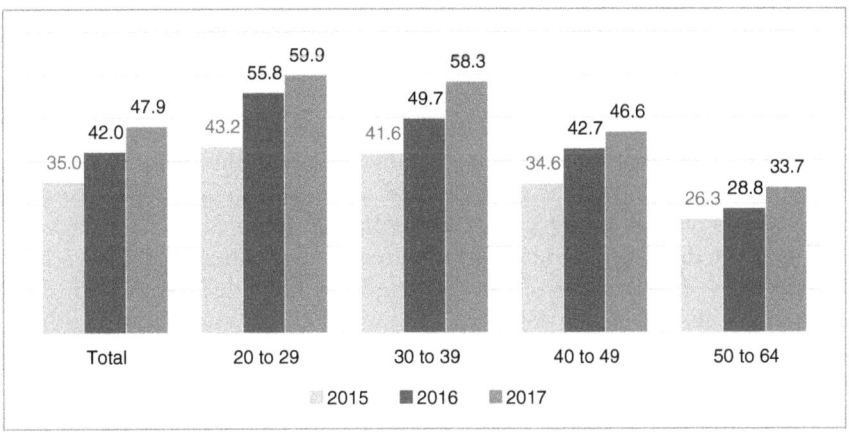

Figure 6.4 Training participation rate (%) of Singapore resident labour force aged 15–64 years old

Source: Singapore Ministry of Manpower, Labour Force in Singapore 2016 and 2017, data retrieved on 19 Mar 2018

skills requirements by industry players. Part of this will involve employing a pool of professional adult educators who are drawn from industry and who are able to help working adults upgrade their skills and stay relevant to the industries they work in. The challenge will be to create a culture of mentorship within industry, while also ensuring that practitioners are well-equipped with the pedagogical and instructional skills to pass on to less experienced trainees.

Such growth should however not come at the expense of quality. This is why some form of government regulation is required to accredit training organisations and the courses offered, as well as for adult educators. Apart from its regulatory role, SkillsFuture Singapore also operates the Institute for Adult Learning as the centralised training institute for adult educators in Singapore. This helps us to maintain standards. At the same time, the institute's dual role in research also enables us to drive evidence-based innovations in adult education.

Rebalancing between learning technical skills and learning transversal skills

The tension between these two driving forces manifests itself most evidently in curriculum design for pre-employment training to prepare individuals for good jobs and to ensure that they have a strong foundation from which to continually adapt and reskill.

On the one hand, the depth of technical skills and competencies required by employers is increasing. An engineering student, for example, will increasingly need to know about the Internet of Things technology – how to use an inter-connected network of electronics that are embedded in devices, sensors and software to collect data and improve system performance. It is not limited to knowledge about hardware, nor only about software. It has therefore become much more complex to be adequately prepared for the future jobs that have emerged.

On the other hand, transversal or soft skills are also becoming ever more important, with employers looking for individuals with the ability to communicate effectively, to work in cross-cultural teams, and to collaborate. Each of these skills is difficult to impart in a traditional classroom.

This is the dilemma faced by most education and training institutions – how to effectively deliver a curriculum that nurtures individuals with both deep technical skills, and strong soft skills. There are no easy solutions. The most obvious and logical approach would be to introduce some form of workplace training in order to enable the learning of soft skills. However, in most instances, the existing curriculum is already very packed, and carving out additional time for workplace training is not straightforward. In these instances, there is scope for employers, especially those lacking internal capabilities, to work more closely with training institutions to develop customised training programmes for the workplace. This will enable their staff to obtain the necessary technical and soft skills and be more effective at work.

Yet, if we see learning as not being limited to the curriculum in a training institute, and as not being restricted to what an individual needs to know upon graduation, the canvas becomes very much expanded. By placing more emphasis on the foundational soft skills required to start work – including the competency of learning how to learn, an education institute can reorient aspects of its curriculum and student experience to lay the foundation for lifelong learning among its graduates.

Similarly, continuing education and training for working adults will also need to adopt a holistic approach by deepening both technical and soft skills. In Singapore, we are developing skills frameworks that provide information on job roles, career pathways, and the skills needed to progress in each key sector. Within these frameworks, we have identified both the occupational or technical and the generic or cross-cutting skills needed for each job role. This signals to individuals that working towards a promotion or a new job may not simply be about getting better at what they do, but also about picking up new skills such as management and leadership. It also signals to employers that these areas must be addressed when developing their workforce and to training providers to cater to such needs.

Conclusion

We are entering a period of massive disruption and innovation caused by technology and globalisation, and the world of education is not spared. Recalibration in some combination across all four areas is necessary, and technology has the potential to be harnessed purposefully as a key enabler for the rebalancing, provided individuals are confident and comfortable enough to do so. With the right mindset towards technology, working adults can take advantage of it to facilitate learning at their own pace and convenience, throughout their entire life, be it to keep abreast of the latest industry developments or to pick up other new, relevant skills.

Within a high skills, high-productivity industry ecosystem, enterprises will compete on the basis of innovation and skills. Accordingly, they will value skills development and take a long-term view. They will be prepared to invest and build a strong talent pipeline with deep skills. Many companies will build up workplace training capabilities, and encourage their employees to continually upskill and reskill themselves. Some companies may also pool their resources to develop industry training centres, which will be particularly beneficial to SMEs. Governments can also play a part by providing incentives and subsidies to encourage this positive behaviour by companies. Driven by strong demand, a vibrant education and training landscape will emerge, involving high quality training providers from both the public and private sectors. Collectively, they will offer a wide array of industry-relevant learning opportunities across different levels and skills. Most of these training programmes will be short and modularised, with technology used widely and purposefully to enhance and scaffold the learning. For individuals, opportunities to learn, unlearn and relearn throughout their lives abound – whether via formal training programmes or at workplaces. Such a supportive environment will enable working adults to be adaptable and stay relevant. Learning will become a way of life and even upon retirement, individuals will continue to be passionate about learning, stay mentally active, and remain socially engaged in their golden years. All these will be hallmarks of a successful national skills strategy.

Note

1 OECD (2016). "Automation and Independent Work in a Digital Economy", Policy Brief on The Future of Work, OECD Publishing, Paris [Online]. Avaiable at www.oecd.org/els/emp/Policy%20brief%20-%20Automation%20and%20Independent%20Work%20in%20a%20Digital%20Economy.pdf (Accessed 18 March 2018).

Chapter 7

The art of balance
How Chinese vocational education integrates with industry

Ni Tang and Dayong Yuan

Introduction

China has the world's largest vocational education system, with 10,893 secondary vocational education schools and 1,359 higher vocational colleges; altogether, there were around 30 million students in vocational education by 2016. Vocational education is considered as the booster of economic and social development, so the issue of school and enterprise cooperation and integration must be seen as an important task.

In the Chinese context, vocational education is a key means of employment promotion and industry upgrading. Employment and industry are the aims of the integration of industry and vocational education and the cooperation between school and enterprises. China's economy has entered a period of rapid growth in gear shifting and upgrading. It is necessary to speed up the transition from 'made in China' from 'qualified made in China' to 'quality made in China' and 'excellent made in China' by promoting China's economy to a the high-end of the global industrial value chain and nurturing a large number of highly skilled workers with professional skills and craftsmanship.

School/college-enterprise cooperation is a multi-stakeholder work which is regulated by many departments including the Ministries of Education, Labour, Finance etc. The Ministry of Education promotes and implements student internships, teacher 'go-to' business practices, a skilled worker's studio and other forms of cooperation. In addition to the specific system of cooperation between vocational schools/colleges and enterprises, it is necessary to concentrate more on seeking breakthroughs in setting up and perfecting vocational education mechanisms in industries, innovating vocational education in the form of collectivised education and modern apprenticeships and establishing new forms of school/college and enterprise cooperation.

There are kinds of school/college-enterprise cooperation which are very popular in China, such as the establishment of industry vocational guidance committees, various forms of industry participation in vocational education and the Ministry of Education's organisations to set up dialogue and forum activities for local government, industry and enterprises. We will now explain the forms and models of the integration and how they work in practice.

The main modes of Chinese vocational education-industry integration

Cooperation between vocational schools/colleges and enterprises

School/college-enterprise cooperation is an important feature of vocational education, which is indispensable in the running of vocational education. Closer links between businesses and learning institutions will pave the way for greater progress in the quality of training. In China, the development of vocational school/college-enterprise cooperation has gone through some major stages. The industrialisation in the 20th century encouraged the development of vocational schools in China and led to the birth of the earliest school-enterprise cooperation mechanism. In the 1950s, when the People's Republic of China was just founded, the education system could not meet the needs of economic and social development. Under this context, the then President Liu Shaoqi advocated and implemented the Part-Work-Part-Study education alongside full-time in-school education. Following the introduction of 'Open and Reform' policy in 1980s, the 'school-enterprise cooperation' idea received more and more attention. In 2005, the State Council stated clearly in '*Decision on Vigorously Developing Vocational Education*' the importance of 'the model of integrating working and learning and school/college-enterprise cooperation' (State Council, 2005). In 2010, the Chinese government issued '*The National Guideline for Mid-and Long-term Education Reform and Development (2010–2020)*' (The Office of National Mid-and Long-Term Education Reform and Development Plan Working Group, 2010). This stated the need to include 'integrating working and learning' and 'school–enterprise cooperation' in the list of the main reform trials within the national VET system (Zhao, 2011). In 2017, the General Office of the State Council issued the latest move to promote integration – '*Several Opinions on Deepening the Integration of Education and Industry*', which stated that enterprises will be encouraged to participate in the operation of vocational education and higher education solely or jointly and establish more intern vacancies for students to strengthen cooperation with educational institutes (The General Office of the State Council, 2017).

Following government policies, some vocational schools and colleges are working intensively with enterprises and some businesses are investing in vocational schools and colleges to build skills pools. School/college-enterprise cooperation can be summarised in some main patterns according to varied combination of time, space and organisational factors. (1) Students work in the positions of official employees for internships (ding gang shi xi). This kind of internship usually means the '2 +1' model, which means a three-year vocational training programme, students spending the first two years in school and the third year in an enterprise internship (which is normally employment-related). This is the most common form of cooperation in China. (2) Work-study rotation (gong xue jiao ti): schools and companies jointly develop training programmes under which the students rotate work in businesses and study in schools (for a certain period of time or in each semester). (3) 'Training orders' (ding dan pei yang): according to their own needs, enterprises may specify in advance the number of graduates they will need, which is often accompanied by joint curriculum development and teaching and learning organisation and generally requires the businesses to pay for part of the training – for example, the 'Haier class' or 'Siemens class' is a common form of such a model. (4) Teaching factories (jiao xue gong chang): schools set up their own enterprises, or the other way around: enterprises move their workshops into the schools (Zhao, 2011).

After decades of efforts, different patterns of cooperation between schools/colleges and enterprises have emerged. A study demonstrates that, in terms of the differences in the level of school/college-enterprise cooperation, the eastern and central regions are generally better than the western regions, and the higher vocational colleges are better than the secondary vocational schools; medical and health care, construction, electronic information and manufacturing are better than public administration, art design, media, finance, commerce, tourism, agriculture, forestry, animal husbandry and fishery. The average duration of school/college-enterprise cooperation is relatively short, with 9.7 per cent programmes being less than one year, 22.3 per cent being one to two years, 50.5 per cent being two to five years and only 16 per cent of programmes being more than five years (Wu and Ouyang, 2017).

Modern apprenticeship pilot project

The introduction of Germany's dual-system vocational education model started in the early 1980s in China. At that time, with the help and guidance of the education sector and direct help from Germany, the dual system was piloted in individual schools. These cooperation projects basically copied the dual-system model in Germany. However, due to the limited enthusiasm for participation among enterprises in China and the 'transplant' nature of the projects, these dual-system pilot projects had limited effectiveness. Copying the dual system was difficult to achieve full success, and so the Chinese vocational education system began to consider how to reform the dual system and adapt it to the actual conditions in China.

In response to the industrial upgrading and the shortage of skilled workers in China, in recent years, the Chinese government attaches great importance to the development of vocational education. The rise of modern apprenticeships in Western countries has aroused great interest in education policymakers in China since the 2010s. In order to deepen the integration of vocational education and industry and to further improve the mechanism for school-enterprise cooperation and encourage innovation in technical and skills training, the Ministry of Education issued the 'Opinions of Ministry of Education on Piloting Modern Apprenticeships' in 2014. Opinions pointed out that it is necessary to actively promote the integration of school enrolment and enterprise recruitment, deepen reform in training mode with work-study integration, strengthen the numbers of faculty members with a combination of full-time teaching staff and part-time teachers from enterprises and form a teaching management and operation mechanism that is compatible with the modern apprenticeship system (MOE, 2014). In 2015, the Ministry of Education promulgated the '*Notice on Carrying out the Work of Modern Apprenticeship Pilot Project*'(MOE, 2015a) announcing the implementation plan of the modern apprenticeship pilot project and then selected 165 qualified cities, industrial organisations, enterprises, secondary vocational schools and higher vocational colleges to carry out modern apprenticeship pilot projects. In 2017, the Ministry of Education organised the annual inspection for the first batch of pilot units and selected 203 qualified cities, industrial organisations, enterprises, secondary vocational schools and higher vocational colleges as the second batch of modern apprenticeship pilot units (MOE, 2017). In total, there were 368 units selected to carry out modern apprenticeship pilot project (some units left the pilot project afterwards). Among the first and the second batch of modern apprenticeship pilot units, there were 19 qualified cities, 17 industrial organisations, 13 enterprises, 65 secondary vocational schools and 254 higher vocational colleges. Higher vocational colleges have an important role in carrying out modern apprenticeship pilot projects, accounting for 69 per cent of all units (Figure 7.1). In 2018, the Ministry of Education will select about 140 new modern apprenticeship pilot units.

It can be observed from the above that the Ministry of Education in China has developed the modern apprenticeship pilot project in accordance with the

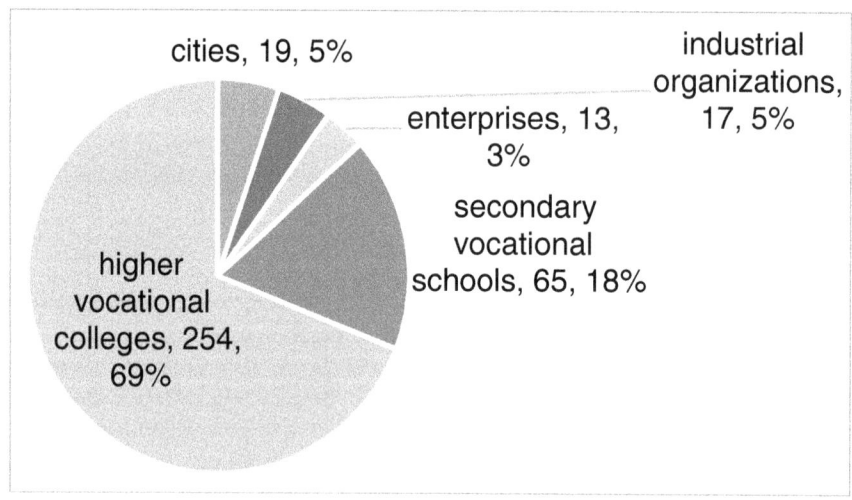

Figure 7.1 The proportions of different pilot units of the modern apprenticeship pilot project by 2017

(Source: author's own compilation base on MOE, 2015a, 2017)

four types: local governments; industrial organisations; enterprises; secondary vocational schools and higher vocational colleges. The reason why it was divided into four categories was that different subjects who wish to participate in the modern apprenticeship system could exert their respective advantages and play unique roles in gaining experience and breakthroughs in different fields. To promote the combination of the vocational education system and the country's labour and employment system requires multiple institutional guarantees and practical norms.

Different types of pilot works have different tasks and goals. This has strict requirements in the pilot project mid-term monitoring. All pilot units must firmly grasp the core elements of their work and work together to improve the framework of modern apprenticeships with Chinese characteristics. The local government-led pilot work focus on trying to make breakthroughs in policy assurance and system design. The industrial organisation led pilot work focus on exploring ways to strengthen the constraints in form of industry body regulations on substantive participation of enterprises in vocational education and the development of industrial (professional) apprenticeship standards to meet the requirements of the high level enterprises. The enterprise-led pilot work focuses on combining its own cadre team and staff team building in work implementation, internal guarantee and management and explores effective ways to deepen the participation in vocational education. Vocational schools and colleges led pilot work focus on formulation of management practices, close cooperation between schools and enterprises and guarantee of effective teaching in accordance with the actual conditions of school-enterprise training.

In addition to the modern apprenticeship pilot project conducted by the Ministry of Education, the Ministry of Human Resources and Social Security also issued a *Notice on Launching New Apprenticeship in Enterprises* in July 2015, carrying out pilot works in large and medium-sized enterprises in selected provinces and cities (MOHRSS, 2017). In September 2015, the National Development and Reform Commission also issued the '*Pilot Programme for Dual-subject Cultivation Reform of Technical and Skilled Talents for Industrial Transformation in Old Industrial Bases*' and carried out a pilot project in three northeastern provinces, including Inner Mongolia (NDRC, 2017). These are both essentially modern apprenticeships pilot projects. In fact, many regions and schools have autonomously conducted various forms of modern apprenticeship practice exploration before these pilot projects, and this trend has been rapidly developing in recent years. Modern apprenticeship has become a hot word in the field of policy and practice in vocational education and an important form of vocational education–industry integration in China.

Grouped school-running in vocational education

Vocational education group is a combination of a number of independent legal entities of vocational schools and colleges, related enterprises and institutions, etc. It is a school-running complex taking leading enterprises or high level institutions as the core and linking each member with other institutions or organisations. The exploration of grouped school-running in vocational education in China started in the 1990s and is a hot issue in the current vocational education reform. In line with practices within industry, it introduced the group management mode of enterprises into vocational education and further expanded its connotation. It aims at relying on industries and joint ventures to strengthen the links between schools, schools and enterprises to achieve resource sharing.

In order to promote the healthy development of grouped school-running in vocational education, in June 2015, the Chinese Ministry of Education issued the 'Opinions of the Ministry of Education on Further Promoting Grouped School-running in Vocational Education' (MOE, 2015b). The implementation of grouped school-running in vocational education in China is not only an organisational form and an effective way to deepen the integration of vocational education and industry and cooperation between schools and enterprises, but also an important form for implementing the system of running vocational education through government coordination, industrial guidance and enterprise participation. Nowadays, grouped school-running in vocational education is an important highlight of the reform and development of vocational education in China and is gradually becoming a business card of vocational education with Chinese characteristics going out to the world.

After more than two decades of development, under the guidance of government policies at all levels, the number of vocational education groups in China has witnessed a rapid growth. As of the end of 2016, there were 1,406 vocational education groups nationwide, representing an increase of 15.15 per cent from 2015 and 34.16 per cent from 2014. In terms of group type, there were 1,095 industrial vocational education groups and 311 regional vocational education groups, accounting for 77.88 per cent and 22.12 per cent of the total group size, respectively. Compared with 2014, the number of industrial vocational education groups and regional vocational education groups increased by 293 and 65, respectively, with increases of 36.53 per cent and 26.42 per cent (The Chinese Society of Vocational and Technical Education, 2017a). The total amount and growth rate of industrial vocational education groups are significantly higher than that of regional vocational education groups, which fully reflects the unique characteristics of 'industrial' of grouped school-running in vocational education. From the view of the member unit, the total number of member units of vocational education groups reached 35,945 in 2016. The proportions of the types of organisations involved were as follows: secondary vocational schools 12.77 per cent; higher vocational colleges 3.44 per cent; universities 1.48 per cent; government departments 4.72 per cent; industrial associations 4.85 per cent; enterprises 67.80 per cent; research institutes 1.86 per cent; and other units 3.07 per cent. Enterprises are important subject of grouped school-running in vocational education. Among them, there were 147 national top 500 enterprises that participated in grouped school-running, with a participation rate of 29.4 per cent. Besides, there were 4,591 secondary vocational schools and 1,236 higher vocational colleges that participated in grouped school-running in vocational education, respectively accounting for 47.58 per cent of the total number of secondary vocational schools and 90.95 per cent of the total number of higher vocational colleges in this country (The Chinese Society of Vocational and Technical Education, 2017b).

With the substantial increase of the number of vocational education groups, the coverage of grouped school-running has been continuously expanded, laying a good foundation for comprehensively promoting the integration of vocational education and industry. At present, the grouped school-running in vocational education has covered all provinces except Tibet Autonomous Region in China. The number of vocational education groups in most provinces (autonomous regions and municipalities directly under the Central Government) increased in varying degrees. In 2016, the numbers of vocational education groups in the eastern, central and western regions were 725, 331 and 350, respectively, of which the number of vocational education groups in eastern region accounted for 51.56 per cent. Compared with 2014, the growth rates of the vocational education groups in the eastern, central and western regions were 20.63 per cent, 47.11 per cent and '57.66 per cent, respectively. The growth rate in the western region was higher than those in the eastern and central regions. In terms of industry coverage, vocational education groups have covered the vast majority of the three industries groupings, with 98 or 8.95 per cent in the primary sector, 530 or 48.40 per cent in the second sector and 467 or 42.65 per cent in the tertiary sector.[1] The proportion of vocational education groups serving three sectors is close to the proportion of the three sectors in the total Chinese economy. According to the specific industries in which vocational education groups are distributed, the comprehensive agricultural vocational education groups, the electronic information vocational education groups and the financial and commercial vocational education groups occupy the largest share of their respective primary, secondary and tertiary sectors (The Chinese Society of Vocational and Technical Education, 2017c).

Grouped school-running in vocational education has made a great contribution to the integration of vocational education and industry in China. It promoted the optimisation of vocational education resources and achieved resource sharing in terms of programmes, curricula, teachers and practical training bases development. The implementation of grouped school-running in vocational education in China improved the overall quality of talent cultivation. In 2016, the number of students trained by vocational education groups reached 1.22 million. Vocational education groups have highlighted the dominant position of enterprises in the cultivation of technical and skilled talents and realised the joint training of talents by the 'dual subjects' of school and enterprise. Vocational education groups have also become the important carriers of the task of implementing modern apprenticeship pilot projects in this country.

The basic experience for Chinese vocational education-industry integration

Adherence to the vocational education–industry integration is an important measure for deepening the reform of the vocational education system and the only way to encourage innovation in various types of vocational education at all levels. After decades of development, China has further improved the integration of industry and vocational education and the national system of cooperation between schools and enterprises and improved industry's participation in the vocational education system. It has led the reform of the vocational education system in all regions and vocational schools with special policies, special measures and special inputs and has formed some basic experiences.

Policy support and departmental linkage

Vocational education–industry integration is a kind of cross-border integration and cooperation. Since the 1990s, according to the economic and social development needs, China has promulgated a series of policies and measures based on the *'Labour Law', 'Education Law', 'Vocational Education Law', 'Higher Education Law'* and the *'Employment Promotion Law'* and other laws and regulations to improve the integration of vocational education and industry. At the same time, different ministries and commissions have actively implemented the strategic plan of developing vocational education in the country. The promulgation of the policy documents on the evaluation of highly skilled personnel, the quality of personnel training for vocational education, the development of colleges and universities, the construction of campus culture, teaching reform, vocational training and the construction of demonstration schools have all emphasised the integration of vocational education and industry and the cooperation between schools and enterprises. During this period, China also promulgated a number of policies that specifically targeted the cooperation between schools and enterprises in vocational education and adopted a series of special measures to lead the integration of vocational education and industry. Various operational mechanisms were established and perfected, and the integration of vocational education and industry has achieved a series of outcomes.

Mechanism for industry's participation

In order to deepen the integration of vocational education and industry, China sought breakthroughs in establishing and perfecting the mechanism for industry's participation in vocational education.

First, there was the establishment of industry guidance platforms. In recent years, the Ministry of Education entrusted relevant industry authorities or industry organisations to take the lead and continue to set up a steering committee for vocational education in the industry. The Ministry of Education encouraged cooperation in industries such as machinery, non-ferrous metals, supply and marketing, water conservancy and other industries to formulate special policies and classifications to promote the joint implementation of education and teaching reform by schools and enterprises. Throughout the country, vocational education and teaching committees have also been set up to carry out various forms of industry participation in vocational education. For example, the educational administrative department proactively joined the relevant departments of industry to establish the joint council and the board of directors to improve the work charter, management system and work procedures and standardise and improve the governance structure of vocational education groups. The Ministry of Education also organised the establishment of a steering committee for experts on modern apprenticeships in the country to conduct activities such as consultation, guidance, training, assessment, inspection and promotion of exchanges for the modern apprenticeship pilot projects. Second, the Ministry of Education and industry and trade organisations stepped up efforts to hold dialogues between vocational education and industry. Educational institutions, localities, industries and enterprises jointly agreed on the integration of vocational education and industry and the cooperation between schools and enterprises. Various forms of activities have also been held all over the country. Third, holding exchanges of experiences and academic forums on the theme of integration of vocational education and industry, including regional, national and international symposia and academic forums, has resulted in the establishment of platforms for education, industry, academia and government to jointly promote the integration of vocational education and industry and successfully promoted the theoretical research level and practical level of school-enterprise cooperation.

Increase of special funds investment

In recent years, the central government has continued to invest special funds in the form of project construction and pilot projects to support vocational education in piloting modern apprenticeships and piloting vocational education groups and supporting vocational schools and colleges to deepen the integration of vocational education and industry and enhance the capacity of serving industry development in vocational schools and colleges. In 2010–2013, the central government invested RMB 1,666.7 million in implementing the project of building vocational training bases and supporting 910 vocational training bases in 715 vocational colleges to guide these vocational schools and colleges to actively explore the new model of government-school-enterprise cooperation based on the construction of productive training bases on campus.

In 2016, the National Development and Reform Commission, the Ministry of Education and the Ministry of Human Resources and Social Security jointly launched and implemented the project of integration of vocational education and industry. During the 'Thirteenth Five-Year Plan' period, it plans to invest RMB 5 billion to support about 100 vocational colleges to deepen the integration of vocational education and industry, accelerate the construction of a modern vocational education system and comprehensively enhance the ability of vocational education to serve the economic and social development. Some parts of the country have also started the implementation of the project of vocational education-industry integration. For example, during the 'Thirteenth Five-Year Plan' period, Jiangsu Province focused on building 100 deep-integration training platforms (bases) for vocational education-industry integration in higher vocational education. In 2016, it started the construction of the first batch of 30 training platform (base) projects with a provincial financial input of RMB 69.75 million.

Creation of social and cultural environment

Among the various elements of social ecology that affect the integration of vocational education and industry and the development of school-industry cooperation, the elements of cultural ecology are the key ones that embody the society's will, psychology and value orientation in promoting the integration of vocational education and industry. To mobilise the enthusiasm of industry and enterprises and the public to participate in vocational education, the Ministry of Education has taken a series of measures to promote the integration of vocational education and industry and the spread and diffusion of the school-enterprise cooperation system. It has also encouraged shared ways of thinking about vocational education in industry and vocational schools and colleges and the establishment of a cooperative atmosphere.

First, China attaches great importance to publicising vocational education and its cooperation with enterprises. Through various media, it vigorously publicises the national vocational education policies, the cooperation between schools and enterprises and the deeds of outstanding talents. By adding the category of vocational education awards and organising publicity and exhibitions of various types of vocational education and school-enterprise cooperation, the cultural influence of vocational education and the integration of education and industry has been increased. Second, in 2015, China established the national 'Week of Vocational Education Activities'. During this week, vocational schools/colleges and enterprises are open to the public. Model workers, masters, entrepreneurs, technical experts and outstanding graduates are invited to go to schools, and dialogues between industry and vocational schools/colleges and other activities are held. Third, in 2008, China established the National Vocational Schools/ College Skill Competition System for vocational schools and colleges, aiming at promoting the integration of vocational education and industry, the cooperation between schools and enterprises and the combination of talents training and industrial development.

Conclusion

Since the 21st century, the integration of vocational education and industry in China has achieved remarkable results in terms of systems, models and service. Vocational education with basic characteristic of school/college-enterprise cooperation has been deeply embedded in economic transformation and industry upgrading and has played an increasingly important role in various fields. However, the integration of vocational education and industry in China also encountered many difficulties. First, although the government recognises the importance of establishing a system and mechanism for the integration of vocational education and industry, the laws in the economic field basically do not involve a central focus integration of vocational education and industry, reflecting the lack of related legal and policy support systems for vocational school/college-enterprise cooperation. Second, the authority of industry guidance for vocational education is not clear, and policies to support and encourage industry organisations to participate in vocational education are still not sound. Third, vocational education in China is in the initial stage of the development of the market mechanism. The opportunities and conditions for enterprises to express wishes are not yet mature, and their internal driving force for participation in vocational education is not enough.

In the future, in order to further deepen the integration of vocational education and industry, Chinese government at all levels should gradually promote vocational school/college-enterprise cooperation through innovations in laws and regulations in various fields such as economy, education and labour, and take measures to breakdown barriers between administrative departments and strengthen coordination and cooperation. Meanwhile, the government should innovate the top-level design of the vocational education system as soon as possible, provide a good environment for the development of vocational education and coordinate the management of the governments, schools/colleges, enterprises, industries and make the rights, duties and responsibilities of all parties clear and definite in the integration of vocational education and industry. China should also explore and establish a long-term mechanism for the promotion of integration of vocational education and industry, improve the basic system for cultivating high quality technical talents and respect the decisive role of market in the integration of vocational education and industry. Attention should be paid to avoiding government-led vocational education, which can lead to the situation of divorces from social needs in vocational education.

Note

1 The primary industry refers to agriculture, forestry, animal husbandry and fishery (excluding agriculture, forestry, animal husbandry and fishery services).

Secondary industry refers to the mining industry (excluding mining auxiliary activities), manufacturing (excluding metal products, machinery and equipment repair industry), electricity, heat, gas and water production and supply and construction.

The tertiary industry as a service industry refers to other industries except primary industry and secondary industry. Tertiary industries include: wholesale and retail trade, transportation, storage and postal services, accommodation and catering, information transmission, software and information technology services, finance, real estate, leasing and business services, scientific research and technical services. They also include industry, water conservancy, environment and public facilities management, residential services, repair and other services, education, health and social work, culture, sports and entertainment, public administration, social security and social organisations, international organisations and agriculture and forestry, as well as animal husbandry and fishery services in grazing and fisheries, mining auxiliary activities in the mining industry, metal products, machinery and equipment repair in the manufacturing industry.

References

The Chinese Society of Vocational and Technical Education (2017a) *Report on the Development of Grouped School-Running in Vocational Education in China*, Beijing, Language & Culture Press, pp. 3–5.

The Chinese Society of Vocational and Technical Education (2017b) *Report on the Development of Grouped School-Running in Vocational Education in China*, Beijing, Language & Culture Press, pp. 19–21.

The Chinese Society of Vocational and Technical Education (2017c) *Report on the Development of Grouped School-Running in Vocational Education in China*, Beijing, Language & Culture Press, pp. 10–14.

The General Office of the State Council (2017) *Several Opinions on Deepening the Integration of Education and Industry* [Online]. Available at www.gov.cn/zhengce/content/2017-12/19/content_5248564.htm (Accessed 30 December 2017).

MOE (Ministry of Education of the People's Republic of China) (2014) *Opinions of Ministry of Education on Piloting Modern Apprenticeships* [Online]. Available at http://old.moe.gov.cn//publicfiles/business/htmlfiles/moe/s7055/201409/174583.html (Accessed 18 December 2017).

MOE (Ministry of Education of the People's Republic of China) (2015a) *Notice on Carrying Out the Work of Modern Apprenticeship Pilot Project* [Online]. Available at http://old.moe.gov.cn//publicfiles/business/htmlfiles/moe/A07_sjhj/201501/182996.html (Accessed 18 December 2017).

MOE (Ministry of Education of the People's Republic of China) (2015b) *Opinions of the Ministry of Education on Further Promoting Grouped School-Running in Vocational Education* [Online]. Available at www.moe.edu.cn/srcsite/A07/s3059/201507/t20150714_193833.html (Accessed 20 December 2017).

MOE (Ministry of Education of the People's Republic of China) (2017) *Notice of the General Office of Ministry of Education on Announcement of Selection of the Second Batch of Modern Apprenticeship Pilot Units and the Annual Inspection Results of the First Batch of Modern Apprenticeship Pilot Units* [Online]. Available at www.moe.gov.cn/srcsite/A07/moe_737/s3876_cxfz/201709/t20170911_314178.html (Accessed 18 December 2017).

MOHRSS (Ministry of Human Resources and Social Security) (2017) *Notice on Launching New Apprenticeship in Enterprises* [Online]. Available at http://kjs.mof.gov.cn/mofhome/mof/zhengwuxinxi/zhengcefabu/201508/t20150805_1405492.htm (Accessed 20 December 2017).

NDRC (National Development and Reform Commission) (2017) *Pilot Program for Dual-Subject Cultivation Reform of Technical and Skilled Talents for Industrial Transformation in Old Industrial*

Bases [Online]. Available at www.ndrc.gov.cn/zcfb/zcfbtz/201511/t20151118_758880. html (Accessed 20 December 2017).

The Office of National Mid-and Long-Term Education Reform and Development Plan Working Group (2010) *The National Guideline for Mid-and Long-Term Education Reform and Development (2010–2020)* [Online]. Available at http://old.moe.gov.cn/publicfiles/business/htmlfiles/moe/info_list/201407/xxgk_171904.html (Accessed 17 December 2017).

State Council (2005) *Decision on Vigorously Developing Vocational Education* [Online]. Available at www.moe.edu.cn/jyb_xxgk/moe_1777/moe_1778/tnull_27730.html (Accessed 17 December 2017).

Wu, J. and Ouyang, H. (2017) 'Study on long-term mechanism of cooperation between vocational schools and enterprises under the effective intervention of the government', *Vocational Education Forum*, vol. 10, pp. 18–28.

Zhao, Z. (2011) *Presentation on the 4th International INAP Conference* [Online]. Available at www.inap.uni-bremen.de/dl/pres11/keynotes/Keynote2-Zhiqun%20Zhao-School-enterprise%20Cooperation%20in%20China%20s%20Vocational%20Education%20 and%20Training.pdf (Accessed 17 December 2017).

Part III

Colleges and vocational qualifications

Chapter 8

Apprenticeships and social mobility

Real choices for young people

Conor Ryan[1]

Introduction

There has been a growing political interest in apprenticeships as a vehicle for improving skills across the UK for the past decade. Apprenticeships are increasingly seen as a way to improve employability skills for young people, an alternative to traditional university routes and a way of upskilling the adult workforce. An apprenticeship differs from other forms of education – including that traditionally delivered by colleges – in the combination it offers of work-based competency training and theoretical knowledge in a skilled occupation. Crucially, the learner is employer-based rather than college-based. Key skills such as English and maths are usually part of an apprenticeship, as are 'personal learning and thinking skills' and employee rights and responsibilities. An government definition of English apprenticeships in 2013 also defined them as requiring 'substantial and sustained training, lasting a minimum of 12 months and including off-the-job training' leading to 'full competency in an occupation, demonstrated by the achievement of an Apprenticeship standard that is defined by employers' (DBIS, 2013a, p. 9). Since 1994, there has been a revival in apprenticeships in the UK, notably in England, but with that revival, there has also been a widening – and a blurring – of the definition of an apprenticeship and what it means to the apprentice. Colleges have a particular role in strengthening the educational content of apprenticeships.

This chapter examines how the apprenticeship system should develop if it is to provide real choices for young people, while also meeting the skills needs of employers and the wider economy. We will see how getting this right could have significant economic benefits, not least for individuals, but doing so will require some important policy changes, where colleges can have a crucial role in helping to strengthen the quality of apprenticeships. In one sense, the government has created the right levers. Since April 2017, larger employers have been required to contribute 0.5 per cent of their wage bill to an apprenticeship levy, unless they can demonstrate they are providing sufficient apprenticeships themselves. But quality could suffer if the emphasis is too much on quantity. When the Conservative government was re-elected in 2017, they committed to providing three million apprenticeships by 2020 in England. Apprenticeships are a devolved matter in the UK, enabling the Scottish, Welsh and Northern Ireland governments to take their own approaches to the issue, though all have been committed to increasing apprenticeship numbers. The Conservative manifesto also promised to 'drive up the quality of apprenticeships to ensure they deliver the skills employers need' (Conservative Party, 2017, pp. 54–55). In Scotland, the Scottish National Party government has said it will use its share of the levy funding to support the delivery of 30,000 modern apprenticeship starts each year by 2020, as well as being for other workforce skills development programmes (Scottish Government, 2017). In Wales, the Apprenticeships Skills Policy Plan commits the government to 100,000 all-age apprenticeships by 2022, with more targeted at 16–19-year-olds and more at level 4^2 and above, with a promise to continue to monitor the effectiveness and relevance of Foundation (level 2) apprenticeships (Welsh Government, 2017). In some ways, Northern Ireland has the most clearly defined model in the UK: in future, it will only offer apprenticeships from level 3 upwards and require them to last at least two years. Progression is part of the design. However, currently it has more level 2 than level 3 starts (Department for the Economy, 2014).

Were all this political enthusiasm matched by policy clarity, apprenticeships could become as important a driver of social mobility as growing working class participation in higher education. In the UK, social mobility is defined by the government as referring 'to the ability of individuals from disadvantaged backgrounds to move up in the world, akin to the notion of equality of opportunity' (Department for Business and Skills, 2011, p. 6). Theorists of social mobility note that there are two forms of social mobility: absolute, where your progress is not at the expense of others; and relative, where you may be displacing someone probably from a better off background who may otherwise have gained that opportunity. With a substantial expansion of apprenticeships, there should be opportunities for such absolute mobility (Machin, 2017). But there are real tensions that are preventing such ambitions, particularly in England. This chapter compares the experience of England and Scotland – too often, governments are more inclined to look overseas for good practice rather than within their own country – and we see important lessons for both nations in how the apprenticeships policy should develop.

The first tension relates to the target audience for apprenticeships. The rhetoric is often directed at young people, yet the reality is that two-fifths of all apprenticeships in England are taken by those aged over 25 (House of Commons Library, 2016). The second relates to quality. The majority of apprenticeships for young people are at level 2 rather than level 3, and some 40 per cent of young people who complete a level 2 apprenticeship do not progress to a level 3. While small employers in particular seem to value the level 2 apprenticeship (CIPD, 2016), young people would normally be better served progressing to a higher level automatically. The third issue is around length and content. Lorna Unwin and Alison Fuller argue persuasively that a key problem with today's apprenticeships is their legacy from the Youth Training Scheme, which means that they are primarily competence based, particularly at level 2. This has led to a lot of 'conversions' where existing employees are relabelled as apprentices to gain state funding for the employer. Unwin and Fuller argue that 'while acquisition of qualifications is clearly important for individuals, this should not be the sole purpose of an apprenticeship, and particularly not when the qualifications gained have such variable currency in the labour market' (Fuller and Unwin, 2011, p. 33). They argue that even though there is a requirement that apprenticeships include a knowledge component, the content represents a 'thin curriculum' compared to the requirements of other European countries (Fuller and Unwin, 2011). Certainly, the extent to which students receive off site education in colleges during the working day and learn a broad range of skills within a company is variable and impeded by length, compared with a typical German apprenticeship. Take Webasto, an auto-components company near Munich, an example cited by the Sutton Trust in one of its apprenticeship reports (Sutton Trust, 2013, p. 12):

> Isabell Schreck, 22, is an apprentice as industrial administrator in Munich, working for the auto parts company Webasto . . . While on her three-year programme, Isabell has spent blocks of time at a local vocational school. She has worked for up to six months in each of a half-dozen different areas of the company. The job of industrial administrator involves sales, customer management and use of information technology. Isabell's apprenticeship has seen her work as an IT assistant, a sales administrator, in the logistics team, in the assistant managing director's office, in marketing, purchasing and corporate communications. In each role, she has been expected to work for one to six months. During her apprenticeship, she has also spent days or weeks at a time learning theoretical aspects of her role at the vocational college. At the end of her three years, she must sit an externally marked exam in accounting, business studies and social studies, alongside an intermediate exam she passed after 15 months' training. The Chamber of Commerce ensures quality control in her apprenticeship, and like a growing number of apprentices, Isabell has the option of going on to study at university for a degree supported by the company while still working at Webasto.

What is standard practice for the equivalent of a level 3 apprenticeship in Germany would signify the best of such apprenticeships in England. A combination of a strong college-based curriculum with a varied and engaging workplace experience is what an apprenticeship should be – something that benefits the employee as much as the employer. Without clearer knowledge content, apprenticeships may not provide the range of transferable skills increasingly required in a world which is constantly changing, with greater automation and technological advance.

At level 3 and above, there is evidence that apprentices can earn as much over a lifetime as those on A levels, those with higher apprenticeships and those on many English degree courses (after factoring increased years of earnings and the absence of student debt). But if this is to be a genuine option for young people, those options need to be universally of a high standard, with clear expectations of what should be included in an apprenticeship for it to have the title.

Young or old: who are the apprentices?

In 2015/16, there were over 500,000 apprenticeship starts in England (DfE, 2017a), and in the first nine months of 2016/17, there had been 440,000 starts (DfE, 2017b), broadly the same as in 2013/14 after the definition of apprenticeships was tightened (DfE, 2017a). As Figure 8.1 shows, there has been some shift towards advanced and higher apprenticeships, with 40 per cent at level 3 in 2016/17 compared with 33 per cent in 2013/14 (although the percentage was higher in 2012/13). There has also been a significant growth at level 4 and above, with those now representing 7 per cent of all apprenticeships, compared to 1 per cent in 2011/12. However, more than half of all apprenticeships are at level 2.

However, as Table 8.1 shows, nearly half of all apprenticeship starts are by people aged 25 or over, with 28 per cent aged 19–24 and only a quarter aged under 19 (DfE, 2017c). The change in age started in the mid-2000s but only really accelerated after 2008 and particularly after the election of the coalition government and its the abolition of Train to Gain, an adult skills programme

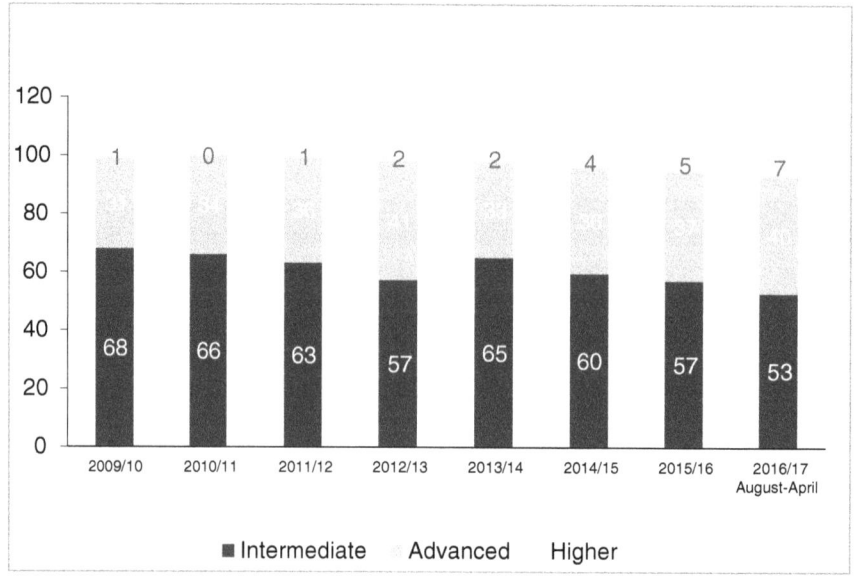

Figure 8.1 Apprenticeship starts by type by academic year

Source: Department for Education data (DfE, 2017d).

Table 8.1 Apprenticeship achievements (starts) in England by year and age

Age \ Year	2009/10	2012/13	2013/14	2014/15	2015/16
Under 19	73,000	61,000	65,000	71,080	73,620
	(117,000)	(115,000)	(120,000)	(126,000)	(131,000)
19–24	64,000	79,000	87,000	91,310	90,140
	(114,000)	(165,000)	(159,000)	(160,000)	(154,000)
25+	34,000	113,000	104,000	98,520	108,040
	(49, 0000)	(230,000)	(162,000)	(214,000)	(224,000)
Total	172,000	253,000	256,000	260,910	271,800
	(280,000)	(510,000)	(440,000)	(500,000)	(509,000)

Source: Department for Education data (DfE, 2017d).

introduced by the Labour government. Apprenticeships are still not the option they should be for young people.

Nearly 272,000 people complete apprenticeships in England each year. That total has been broadly unchanged in recent years – it was 258,000 in 2011/12 – despite the increased policy emphasis. However, this does represent a substantial increase from the 42,000 completions in 2001/2 or the 112,000 in 2007/8 (although some of the difference may reflect statistical changes). The big drive on expanding apprenticeships was started by Peter Mandelson as Business Secretary in 2009. His *Skills for Growth* report promised 35,000 more government-funded apprenticeships and UCAS equivalent tariffs to apprentices to qualify for university places (Curtis, 2009). At that stage, virtually all apprenticeships were for young people, although funding for adult apprenticeships for the over-25's was introduced in 2003 for older workers, to expand and meet their skills needs (NAO, 2012). The coalition was equally keen after 2010, but the definition of what constituted an apprenticeship loosened somewhat. This was exemplified in 2012 when it was reported that Morrisons supermarket chain employed 52,000 apprentices – a tenth of all those in England – most of whom were existing employees aged over 25, and many of which lasted six months or less (BBC News, 2012). In a way, the rapidly growing apprenticeship programme had inherited many of the problems attached to the Train to Gain programme championed by Gordon Brown as Chancellor in the Labour years, which the coalition had scrapped; it was accrediting existing skills as much as developing new ones and creating huge deadweight costs. The outcry following the Morrisons revelations led to a review by Doug Richard and a tightening of the apprenticeship criteria. In 2013, the government announced that apprenticeships would need to be at least 12 months 'to ensure quality' and would be developed by employer's groups, initially called Trailblazers. English and maths would have to form part of each programme and assessment would be tightened up (DBIS, 2013b). These reforms were followed by the creation of the

Institute of Apprenticeships in 2016 with a responsibility for quality, standards and assuring assessments (DfE, 2017e). The Institute will have an important role ensuring that a new apprenticeship levy operational from April 2017, delivers more new apprenticeships. The levy, which is paid by large employers with an annual pay bill in excess of £3 million amounts to 0.5 per cent of an employer's pay bill and is forecast to raise £3 billion a year by 2020. Those employers who pay can use the levy to invest in apprenticeships and will have their contributions topped up by the government by 10 per cent. Other employers will still contribute to the cost of apprenticeships, but will do so directly with the provider, and the government will pay a portion of the cost.

These structural changes could help improve the quality and number of apprenticeships. But there is a tension between the two objectives. The government is committed to delivering three million new apprenticeship starts between 2015 and 2020, an objective reaffirmed in the 2017 Conservative manifesto (Conservative Party, 2017, p. 53). The target would represent an increase of 25 per cent on the number in the previous parliament. Despite a promise to improve standards of training and assessment at the same time, the danger is that the numerical target places quantity ahead of quality. Even after the 2013 announcement on tougher standards, Ofsted, the inspectorate for the sector in England, has reported that too many apprentices in the food production, retail and care sector 'were simply completing their apprenticeship by having low level skills, such as making coffee, serving sandwiches or cleaning floors'. Ofsted also found cases where workers did not know they were apprentices and reported that one in three of 45 providers they visited did not provide sufficient high quality training that stretched the apprentices and improved their capabilities (Ofsted, 2015), cited in (Lanning, 2016). Such training is unlikely to provide much economic benefit, nor will it contribute to social mobility through the advancement of the apprentices.

The returns on apprenticeships

The potential economic returns on apprenticeships are significant both for the UK as well as for individuals. The Centre for Economics and Business Research found that apprenticeships contributed as much as £34 billion to the UK economy, with the economy benefitting by £21 for every £1 invested from the public purse (CEBR, 2014). However, not all apprenticeships are equal, and this is reflected in the returns to those who do them. For example, one study found that the wage returns to level 2 apprenticeships in retail, and to level 2 and 3 apprenticeships in health and social care, are non-existent (Broughton, 2015). However, there is also evidence that at the right level apprenticeships can bring returns as high as A levels and university degrees. Analysis by the Boston Consulting Group for the Sutton Trust has shown that higher apprenticeships at level 5 result in greater lifetime earnings than undergraduate degrees from non-Russell Group[3] universities. Across a lifetime, someone with a higher (level 5) apprenticeship averages earnings of around £1.44m, while someone with a degree from a non-Russell Group university earns just under £1.38m on average (when student debt repayments are considered). As Figure 8.2 shows, the returns for Russell Group university degrees are higher – at £1.6m and those from Oxbridge higher still at £1.79m. Of course, there are specific reasons why lifetime earnings differ between apprenticeships and degrees – apprentices earn for the three years that undergraduates are studying and they do not incur student debt, which is now estimated at over £57,000 for disadvantaged students and £50,800 on average (Belfield et al., 2017). As Figure 8.3 shows, the annual income of a graduate is over £1000 higher for a non-Russell Group degree, £5,000 higher for a Russell Group degree and £11,600 higher for Oxbridge. But the differences with a significant number of degrees remain small, highlighting the potential of higher apprenticeships to offer real choice, free of debt. The differentials may be lower in Scotland where the absence of tuition fees means graduate debt is lower. Interestingly, the earning potential of an advanced apprenticeship at level 3 is also slightly better than that of someone whose highest qualification is at A-level (Kirby, 2015).

These potential returns are not matched by sufficient opportunities for young people to access such opportunities. There are only 39,000 new higher apprenticeships each year and only a quarter are taken by the under-25s. This means

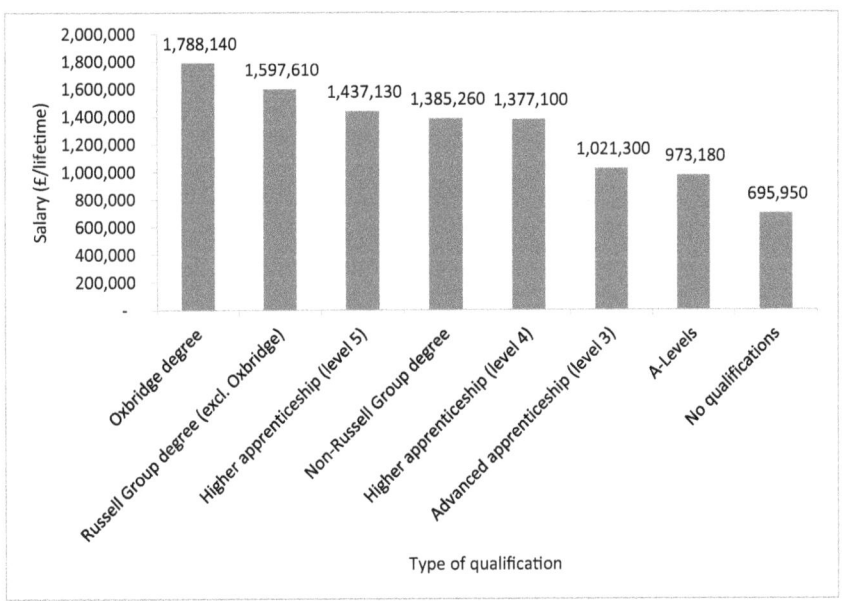

Figure 8.2 Average lifetime earnings by type of qualification, overall

Source: Kirby (2015)

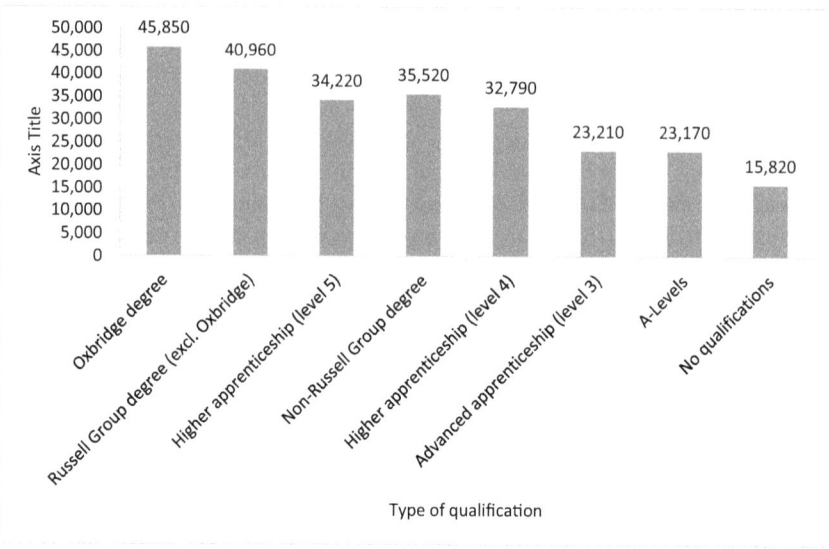

Figure 8.3 Average lifetime annual income by type of qualification
Source: Kirby (2015)

that around 9,400 young people are on higher apprenticeships in England (DfE, 2017f), compared with 320,000 UK-based new undergraduates each year in England (UCAS, 2017). The higher apprenticeship figures do not include some company school leaver schemes, such as those in accountancy and other financial service firms, but they are a good illustration of the challenges translating the theory of choice into practice. There are clear opportunities for colleges to deliver more higher apprenticeships, though it is likely that it will take significant adoption by Russell Group universities for them to become a widely-accepted alternative to traditional degree courses.

Structural issues

The delivery of apprenticeships is dependent on buy-in by employers. Successive governments in England have sought to engage employers in different ways. The Labour government created sector skills councils linked to different economic sectors. These still play a major role in setting standards and awarding apprenticeships. There are 16 sector skills councils (SSCs) and five sector skills bodies that work with over 550,000 employers to define skills needs and standards in their industry. Their representative body says that the SSCs work with over 7,500 training providers and 500,000 apprentices in England, Scotland and Wales to provide them with their final apprenticeship certificate. They also provide quality assurance of the Apprenticeship process with and on behalf of The Education and Skills Funding Agency, the National Apprenticeship Service and employers (FISSS, n.d.). In some parts of England, colleges initiated apprenticeships because employers were either thin on the ground or reluctant to come forward, but this approach potentially reduces the distinctive benefit of apprenticeships (as work-based) as much as the limited educational offer in the weaker apprenticeships currently on offer.

The coalition government created a parallel structure to the SSCs of employer 'trailblazers' to design new apprenticeship standards for occupations within their sectors, as part of its plan to implement the Richard Review. The new entities were intended to ensure higher standards for apprenticeships, particularly after the Morrisons embarrassment. New emphasis was placed on English and maths within specifications and on synoptic assessment when apprenticeships were coming to an end. Trailblazers were defined in a way not all that different from the original goal of sector skills councils, but it was apparently hoped that the focus on apprenticeships and the more dynamic name would help improve standards and increase the numbers of employers offering apprenticeships (DBIS, 2013a).

Since April 2017, a new government body, the Institute for Apprenticeships, has had responsibility for apprenticeship standards in England. An employer-led organisation, it considers and approves expressions of interest, apprenticeship standards and assessment plans submitted by employer groups (DfE, 2017e). All of this has been given greater impetus by the introduction of the apprenticeship levy. The combination of these changes has the potential to drive up standards, but only if the new regulator and the employer-led organisations take a fundamental look at the structure of apprenticeships in England. This means a stronger focus on apprenticeships as a high quality route for young people to gain the skills and competencies they need for a career. In other words, a real focus on level 3 and above apprenticeships for the under-25s – rather than a catch all that includes low level programmes akin to the old discredited Youth Training Scheme – accreditation of existing employee skills as happened under Train to Gain and a rebadging of existing adult training programmes by firms in order to escape the levy.

Changing public attitudes

It has long been a criticism of British attitudes that they value academic over vocational education. This has impacted colleges as much as apprenticeships. Critics charge snobbery and contrast the British public's views with those in countries that have strong vocational systems, notably Germany, Austria and Switzerland. Although public opinion in those countries is not quite as neutral between the academic and vocational as some imagine, employers undoubtedly respect those with apprenticeships as much as graduates.

> German firms don't view dual training as something for struggling students or at-risk youth. 'This has nothing to do with corporate social responsibility',

an HR manager at Deutsche Bank told the group I was with, organized by an offshoot of the Goethe Institute. 'I do this because I need talent'. So too at Bosch. 'Building world-class diesel parts is hard', the executive in charge of the program explained. 'We're very careful about who we hire. We're looking for quality'.

(Jacoby, 2014)

Research by the Boston Consulting Group for the Sutton Trust has suggested reasons why such respect is greater in these countries. It found Switzerland had seven times more high quality apprenticeships per head of population than the UK. There were 43 Swiss apprentices at level 3 for every 1,000 staff, 40 in Germany and 33 in Austria. Even Australia had 39. By contrast, there were six per 1,000 in the UK, and BCG estimated a need for 150–300,000 more such apprenticeship starts at level 3 and above each year in the UK (Sutton Trust, 2013). In contrast with such continental exemplars, too many English apprenticeships were at a lower level and were more likely to be targeted at adults.

Knowing all this may help explain the caution of many teachers and parents about apprenticeships, although a growing promotion of apprenticeships as a viable alternative to university in the broadsheet press may slowly be starting to change attitudes. Polling for the Sutton Trust in 2014 suggested that public attitudes could change with sufficiently high quality apprenticeships. 34 per cent of adults in England aged 16–75 said a degree-level apprenticeship would be better for somebody's future career prospects than a university degree, compared to 21 per cent who thought a traditional degree would be better. However, 56 per cent of parents say they are likely to encourage their children to consider a university degree, while only 40 per cent would encourage them to consider an apprenticeship.

The public clearly has higher expectations for apprenticeships than current government standards. Just under two-thirds (63%) of adults in England believed that most apprenticeships should be set at A-level standard (level 3) or higher, whereas nearly two-thirds of apprenticeships started by young people in 2012/13 were only at GCSE standard (Level 2).

And young people are potentially keen. More than half (55%) of young people aged 11–16 say they would be interested in an apprenticeship rather than going to university if it was available in a job they wanted to do, but only 31 per cent say that their teachers have ever discussed the idea of apprenticeships with them at school. This may be explained not just as ignorance by teachers but a sense that existing apprenticeships are not good enough. Only 26 per cent of teachers thought (to a great or some extent) there were enough apprenticeships available at an A-level standard or higher, and 65 per cent said they would rarely or never advise a student to take an apprenticeship if they had the grades for university (Sutton Trust, 2014).

The Scottish context

There has been much discussion recently about differential rates of university access between England and Scotland. Some of which was prompted by a University of Edinburgh report, Access in Scotland, for the Sutton Trust which showed that in 2013–14, the gap in university access between those from advantaged and disadvantaged neighbourhoods was higher in Scotland than in England. While 55 per cent of Scots entered higher education by the age of 30 – higher than the 49 per cent rate in England – 21 per cent of Scots went via further education college compared to just 6 per cent in England. Indeed, the authors calculated that 90 per cent of the growth in higher education participation in Scotland since 2006 had been due to entry to college rather than university (Weedon et al., 2016). This substantial level of college entry prompts the question as to whether some Scots would be better doing a higher apprenticeship rather than going through college, perhaps hoping for articulation to university afterwards.

As with England, Scotland still has only a relatively small proportion of apprenticeships at higher level – 4 per cent in 2015/16 – but it has also a much larger proportion at level 3. Indeed, the balance of Scottish apprenticeships overall feels closer to what should be happening in England, as Figure 8.4 shows. Of modern apprentices in training at the end of the first quarter of 2017/18, only 17 per cent were aged over 25. Nearly half of all apprentices were young people aged 16–19 working towards level 3 with a higher proportion of level 3s and more per head of population. A further 17 per cent were young people under 25 studying to the same level. Only at levels 4 and 5 were the under-25's outnumbered, suggesting a similar challenge in Scotland offering higher apprenticeships as a genuine alternative to university (SDS, 2017).

What needs to change

The differences in approach between what is happening in Scotland – and the experience of countries like Germany and Switzerland – points to what needs to happen to improve apprenticeships in England. The public's and teachers' attitudes may be sceptical about the quality of apprenticeships, but their prejudice is not entirely unwarranted. The extension of adult apprenticeships, particularly as they replaced many Train to Gain programmes, devalued the apprenticeship brand, and while the government has since put in place stronger quality controls, there is still more to do if they are to fulfil their potential.

For a start, policymakers need to be clearer about what apprenticeships are and who they are for. The broadening of apprenticeships into adult skills in 2004 was a minor change at the time but has now overwhelmed the programme in England in a way that has not so far happened in Scotland. It would make sense to focus apprenticeships on young people, with an upper age limit of 25 at least for advanced and intermediate apprenticeships, and to find alternative

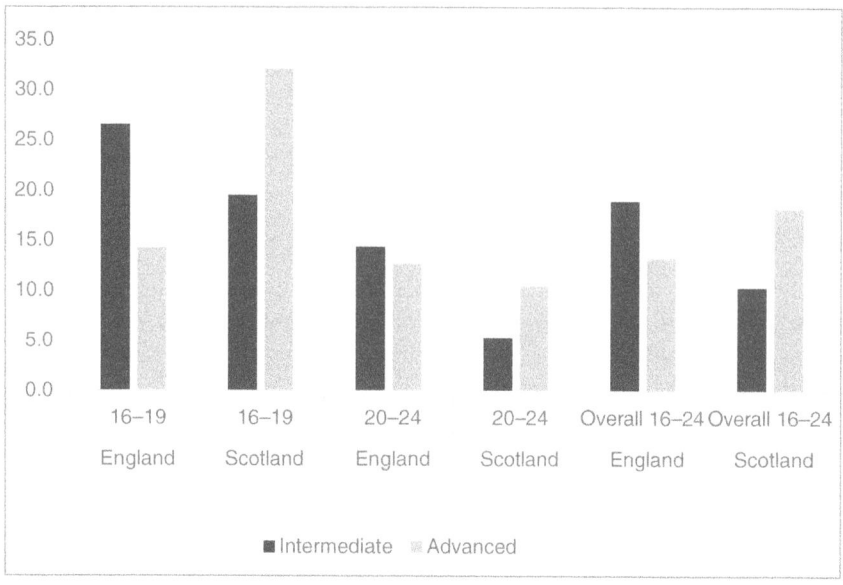

Figure 8.4 Intermediate and advanced apprenticeship starts in England and Scotland (per 1,000 population in age bracket per nation)

Source: Sutton Trust, internal document, drawing on

England: www.ons.gov.uk/peoplepopulationandcommunity/populationandmigration/population estimates/datasets/populationestimatesanalysistool

England starts by age: www.gov.uk/government/statistical-data-sets/fe-data-library-apprenticeships

Scotland: www.nrscotland.gov.uk/statistics-and-data/statistics/stats-at-a-glance/registrar-generals-annual-review/2016/chapter-1-population

for Scotland's age breakdowns by level, see page 40: www.skillsdevelopmentscotland.co.uk/media/13282/modern-apprenticeship-statistics-quarter-4-2016-17.pdf

routes for skills training and accreditation for older workers. While it makes political and business sense for employers to be driving the standards of apprenticeships, the rapidly changing work environment with the growth of automation means that it is crucial that the range of knowledge, key and life skills that apprentices learn should be both transferable and at a sufficiently high level to be of value in different sectors. This would improve employability and not just fill today's skills gaps.

The second issue is one of quality and expectations. England is unusual in having so many apprenticeships at level 2 – as opposed to Scotland, where the ratio of level 3: level 2 is reversed. The Conservative manifesto re-committed the government to its three million target by 2020, and this is having perverse effects that potentially damage young people's opportunities. A young person who gets both a level 2 and a level 3 accreditation is counted twice, as is someone with two level 2s. This is not in that person's interest. It would be far better to do as happens in Germany, where someone starts on a route that typically takes three years to get to a level 3 standard in the end. If the statisticians need to accredit at both level 2 and 3, that shouldn't mean the apprentice stopping and starting their courses. Linked to quality is the content and length of courses. Apprenticeships should be about developing new skills not accrediting existing ones, except to determine a starting point for new skills. There should also be clear expectations in the balance between knowledge and practice, with college day release the norm. Level 3 apprenticeships, lasting a minimum of two years, should be as much an option as A levels – the pre-university school exams in England, Scotland and Wales or T levels – a planned new technical qualification for English teenagers – for 16- and 17-year-olds, and there should be far more such opportunities. Colleges can play a leading role in this quality debate.

Finally, the growth of higher and degree level apprenticeships in recent years has been a positive development. But there are still too few such opportunities for young people. Most higher apprentices – in both England and Scotland – are aged over 25. Yet higher apprenticeships offer an opportunity to earn while learning, and to graduate debt-free, which should be a real choice for young people across the UK. Universities, colleges, employers and governments should work together to expand these opportunities and to offer them as a real choice for young people.

Conclusion

The revival of apprenticeships has been a positive development in the UK. But there is a danger that they miss their potential by their lack of focus and rigour. Government should refocus on young people and set higher expectations so that level 3 becomes the minimum standard for most apprenticeships. Scottish policymakers should avoid the mistakes made in England, and all UK governments should develop strong offers for young people in advanced and higher apprenticeships. Colleges have a particular role in ensuring the strong core content that is essential to the future career prospects of apprenticeships. In time, apprenticeships could offer a realistic debt-free alternative to the traditional undergraduate degree.

Notes

1 The author is grateful for additional research by Dr Rebecca Montacute, Sutton Trust Research Fellow.
2 In the UK, vocational qualifications are awarded on a scale of 1–8 with level 1 being entry level and level 8 equivalent to a PhD. Level 2 is equivalent to an intermediate school qualification, level 3 to A levels or Scottish Highers (pre-university exams), levels 4 and 5 are undergraduate level equivalents while level 6 equates to a bachelor's degree. There is a useful guide to the levels at the City and Guilds website here: www.cityandguilds.com/ qualifications-and-apprenticeships/qualifications-explained/qualification-comparisons

3 The Russell Group universities are 24 of the most selective in Britain. They have higher entry standards than most other universities.

References

BBC News (2012, April 2) 'One in 10 apprentices in England works at Morrisons', *BBC News* [Online]. Available at www.bbc.co.uk/news/uk-17564255 (Accessed 1 August 2017).

Belfield, C., Britton, J., Dearden, L., and van der Erve, L. (2017) *Higher Education Funding in England: Past, Present and Options for the Future*, London, Institute for Fiscal Studies.

Broughton, N. (2015) *The Value of Apprenticeships: Wages*, London, Social Market Foundation.

Centre for Economics and Business Research (2014) *Economic Impact of Apprenticeships: A CEBR Report for the Skills Funding Agency*, London, Centre for Economics and Business Research.

CIPD (2016) *Employer Views on the Apprenticeship Levy*, London, Chartered Institute for Personnel and Development.

Conservative Party (2017) *Forward Together: The Conservative Manifesto*, London, The Conservative Party.

Curtis, P. (2009, November 11) 'Mandelson announces 35,000 new apprenticeships', *The Guardian*.

Department for Business Innovation and Skills (2011) *Social Mobility: A Literature Review*, London, Department for Business and Skills.

Department for Business Innovation and Skills (2013a) *The future of apprenticeships in England: Implementation Plan*, London, BIS.

Department for Business, Innovation and Skills (2013b) *The Future of Apprenticeships in England: Next Steps from the Richard Review*, London, BIS.

Department for the Economy (2014) *Securing Our Success: The Northern Ireland Strategy on Apprenticeships*, Belfast, Department for the Economy.

Department for Education (2017a) *Apprenticeships Geography Data Tool: Starts 2011/12 to 2016/17 Reported to Date* [Online]. Available at www.gov.uk/government/statistical-data-sets/fe-data-library-apprenticeships#apprenticeship-starts-and-achievements (Accessed 26 October 2017).

Department for Education (2017b) *Apprenticeships by Quarter: Starts and Achievements 2002/03 to 2016/17 Reported to Date* [Online]. Available at www.gov.uk/government/statistical-data-sets/fe-data-library-apprenticeships (Accessed 26 October 2017).

Department for Education (2017c) *Apprenticeships Geography Data Tool: Achievements 2011/12 to 2015/16* [Online]. Available at www.gov.uk/government/statistical-data-sets/fe-data-library-apprenticeships (Accessed 7 August 2017).

Department of Education (2017d) *Apprenticeships Level, Framework and Sector Subject Data Tool: Starts 2011/12 to 2015/16* [Online]. Available at www.gov.uk/government/statistical-data-sets/fe-data-library-apprenticeships (Accessed 7 August 2017).

Department for Education (2017e) *Institute for Apprenticeships: About Us* [Online]. Available at www.gov.uk/government/organisations/institute-for-apprenticeships/about (Accessed 1 August 2017).

Department for Education (2017f) *Apprenticeship Programme Starts by Level and Age (2002/03 to 2016/17 Reported to Date)* [Online]. Available at www.gov.uk/government/statistical-data-sets/fe-data-library-apprenticeships#other-apprenticeship-statistics (Accessed 1 August 2017).

Federation for Industry Sector Skills and Standards (n.d.) *About Us: The Federation* [Online]. Available at http://fisss.org/about-us/ (Accessed 2 August 2017).

Fuller, A. and Unwin, L. (2011) 'The content of apprenticeships', in Dolphin, T. and Lanning, T. (eds.), *Rethinking Apprenticeships*, London, IPPR.

House of Commons Library (2016) *Apprenticeships Statistics for England*, London, House of Commons Library.

Jacoby, T. (2014, October 16) 'Why Germany is so much better at training its workers', *The Atlantic*.

Kirby, P. (2015) *Levels of Success: The Potential of UK Apprenticeships*, London, Sutton Trust.

Lanning, T. (2016) *Where Next for Apprenticeships?*, London, Chartered Institute for Personnel and Development.

Machin, S. (2017) 'Social mobility over time', *The Sutton Trust Social Mobility 2017 Summit*, London, 12 July, Sutton Trust [Online]. Available at www.suttontrust.com/wp-content/uploads/2017/08/Steve-Machins-slides.pdf (Accessed 13 March 2018).

National Audit Office (2012) *Adult Apprenticeships*, London, NAO.

Scottish Government (2017) *UK Government Apprenticeship Levy* [Online]. Available at www.gov.scot/Topics/Education/skills-strategy/apprenticeship-levy (Accessed 1 August 2017).

Skills Development Scotland (2017) *Modern Apprenticeship Statistics Up to the End of Quarter 1, 2017/18*, Glasgow, Skills Development Scotland.

Sutton Trust (2013) *Real Apprenticeships: Creating a Revolution in English Skills*, London, Sutton Trust.

Sutton Trust (2014) *Higher Ambitions*, London, Sutton Trust.

UCAS (2017) *Applicants and Acceptances by Groups of Applicants 2016*, Cheltenham, UCAS.

Weedon, E., Kadar-Satat, G., Hunter Blackburn, L., and Riddell, S. (2016) *Access in Scotland*, London, Sutton Trust.

Welsh Government (2017) *Apprenticeships Skills Policy Plan* [Online]. Available at http://gov.wales/topics/educationandskills/skillsandtraining/apprenticeships/apprenticeships-skills-policy-plan/?lang=en (Accessed 7 August 2017).

Chapter 9

Is there a higher level skills gap that colleges can fill?

Fiona Reeve and Jim Gallacher

Introduction

This chapter will examine the role of colleges as providers of vocational qualifications at higher education level in England and Scotland. It will consider the different contexts for colleges in the two nations and the nature of the contributions that colleges make at this level. The degree to which a centrally managed approach in Scotland has resulted in different outcomes from the more market driven approach in England will be considered. The extent to which colleges in both nations retain a role which is distinctly *vocational* is raised in the light of learners' increasing use of these qualifications for transition to universities. Looking forward, we reflect on future demand for higher level vocational qualifications delivered by colleges in societies where the workforce is increasingly skewed towards either degrees or lower qualifications. The UK government's own prognosis emerges from within the recent Industrial Strategy (DBEIS, 2017), where key elements have the potential to impact on colleges' higher level provision. While the strategy promises a fundamental review of higher level vocational qualifications which are taught in English colleges, the system in Scotland is a devolved matter and not under review. In Scotland, attempts are made to shape both supply and demand for vocational education and to influence employers' use of skills. In both nations, apprenticeship, including at the higher levels, is reconfirmed as a key vehicle for workforce development. The expansion of the apprenticeship system to the higher levels is already underway creating opportunities, as well as challenges, for colleges. In particular, to what extent will colleges be able to take a key role in supporting higher level apprenticeships and, through this, reassert their vocational purpose? We will draw on our earlier comparative work on vocational sub-degree qualifications to identify some of the enduring issues that colleges may face in establishing this role. Here, the renewed emphasis on apprenticeships is viewed as the latest in a series of testing contexts within which colleges seek to establish a vocational role at this higher level.

What do colleges offer at this level?

Most higher education (HE) level learning in English Further Education (FE) takes place in the 186 General FE colleges (AoC, 2017). In total 151,360 students were studying at HE level within English colleges in 2015/16, making up 9.5 per cent of HE learners in England (RCU, 2017). Interestingly HEFCE reports regional variations with three times as many students undertaking HE in FE in the North East, North West and Yorkshire and the Humber than in the London, South East and East of England regions (HEFCE, 2017). In Scotland, there has been a move away from the term *further education* to acknowledge the importance of higher level learning within the sector, which is now known as Scotland's Colleges (Gallacher, 2017). In 2015/16, there were 46,970 students studying at this level in the colleges (SFC, 2016), representing 22 per cent of all students at the undergraduate level in colleges and universities, a much more substantial proportion than we have seen in England. Again, there are variations across the sector, and regional differences have become important. While the overall percentage of college students studying at this level in Scotland is 22 per cent, within City of Glasgow College, it is 41 per cent and a further four colleges exceed 25 per cent; in contrast, at Borders College, they make up only 8 per cent of learners (SFC, 2016).

Historically, the focus for colleges at this level has been on providing part-time study for those in work through well-established Higher National Certificates (HNCs) or Higher National Diplomas (HNDs).[1] However, there has been a notable growth in full-time students as the part-time student market has declined, resulting in a shift in emphasis for many colleges towards younger, full-time students. We have also seen the development of new qualifications for emerging areas of work, including the service sector, at the technician level and for mainly public sector 'para-professional' occupations. Within Scotland, new developments have been taken forward though a national process of 'modernisation' of the existing HNCs and HNDs managed by the Scottish Qualification Authority (SQA, 2007). There has also been an interest within the SQA in developing new qualifications which are equivalent to an unclassified bachelor's degree, although this has not led to any firm proposals at a national policy level (Ingram and Gallacher, 2010). In England, policy diverged resulting in a new qualification, the Foundation Degree (FD),[2] becoming established which largely replaced the existing HND provision (DfEE, 2000; QAA, 2004). FDs are validated by universities and taught largely in partner colleges (the initial growth of FDs in universities was reversed due, in part, to alternative opportunities for degree expansion).

In summary, we can see that Scotland's colleges are making a significant contribution to HE level learning, which is proportionately more than double that made by colleges in England. It has also increasingly become full-time provision, rather than part-time for people in work. In Scotland, the HND dominates full-time provision, whereas it has been eclipsed by the FD in England. However, these programmes do not only serve as higher vocational qualifications they also have an important function in providing full-time routes through to university degrees (Gallacher et al., 2012). This applies not only to FDs, where progression was part of the design, but also to the Scottish HNDs, where there has been increasing emphasis on articulation agreements which facilitate transition to universities.

What kinds of roles do colleges play in offering higher level vocational education?

The role of colleges in contributing to the development of a highly-trained workforce has been recognised in the two nations. In Scotland, this has been re-emphasised in the recent letter of guidance to the Scottish Funding Council, which states that 'colleges are at the centre of our efforts to build the workforce Scotland's employers and economy needs' (Scottish Government, 2017a). In a recent address to the Association of Colleges in England, the Apprenticeship and Skills Minister, Anne Milton, indicated her belief that 'further education is central to the challenge of delivering a prosperous future for this country after Brexit. Ensuring that we have an adaptable workforce with the skills and opportunities to thrive. Supporting the growth of innovative, productive business' (Milton, 2017). Her address highlighted the local nature of economies and positions colleges as partners in local efforts to address the needs of employers and locally important sectors.

At the same time, in both nations, the importance of colleges in widening access to learning, including higher level vocational learning, is increasingly emphasised. The success of colleges in providing opportunities in areas of least HE participation, so-called cold spots, has been documented in England (RCU, 2017). In Scotland, it has been recognised that they have in recent years made the major contribution in providing opportunities for those from the most disadvantaged areas to enter HE (Hunter Blackburn et al., 2016). Here again, the local role of colleges is emphasised. However, there is little recognition that the skills and widening access agendas may not be coterminous, and there may be tensions for colleges in seeking to meet multiple needs. Moreover, colleges have had to operate with lower funding levels than other sectors, and funding has been squeezed during the period of austerity. For example, Audit Scotland reported a decrease in funding to Scotland's Colleges of 18 per cent over the period 2010/11 to 2014/15, which a more recent increase has yet to restore (Audit Scotland, 2016). Similarly, funding levels for further education in England have fallen further behind schools and universities. As a recent report on reform in FE notes 'there is a sense amongst many providers that currently they have to deliver much more for significantly less funding' (DfE, 2017, p. 137). The dangers of such an approach are evident in the increasing numbers of English colleges receiving 'exceptional financial support' from the government (FE Week, 2018).

A further problem for colleges is that, while delivering the skills employers need and widening access are important missions, ultimately, colleges are funded to provide qualifications and must follow the funding streams that are available. The context of frequently changing funding arrangements, arising from various waves of government policy 'reform', has proved extremely challenging for colleges in England (DfE, 2017). Yet more change is on the horizon; a review of higher level technical education in England has been announced as part of the UK's latest industrial strategy (DBEIS, 2017). The review will respond to the recommendations of the earlier Lord Sainsbury's review. It is required to consider progression routes for those qualifying from the newly announced T levels, which are located just below HE level and will be taught in schools and colleges, and from work-based routes, including apprenticeship. The focus will be on enabling progression to skilled occupations within 15 technical areas. The review has the potential to change what English colleges offer and will bring these programmes under the regulatory oversight of a new central body the Institute for Apprenticeship and Technical Education. As Parry (2017) suggests, these changes will be far-reaching, in part because eligibility for government-backed loans will be linked to qualifications meeting national standards; standards which are ultimately approved by the new employer-led Institute.

In contrast, Scotland's colleges are emerging from a process of reorganisation which has sought to end duplication in the sector and meet the needs of learners and employers within regions. All colleges now serve a region or are part of a multi-college region. In this respect, they are required by the Scottish Funding Council (which funds all colleges) to produce a Regional Outcome Agreement (ROA) which specifies the ways in which they will meet the social and economic needs of the region. Funding is then allocated on the basis of the ROA. We will return to the importance of this regional dimension later in the chapter. Alongside college regionalisation relevant policy initiatives have the potential to bring some stability to the sector. The 'Scottish Government 15–24 learner Journey Review' (Scottish Government, 2017b) develops the theme of the 'journey' from school, via education and training, into employment. The various component projects require cooperation between relevant institutions and organisations. The Scottish Funding Council (SFC) and Skills Development Scotland (SDS) are also appointing in 2018 a Director of Skills Alignment to enhance cooperation between these two agencies in skills planning. Similarly, the Scottish Government's 'Developing the Young Workforce: Scotland's Youth Employment Strategy' (Scottish Government, 2014) outlines a seven-year strategy involving greater partnership working between schools, college and employers. It includes the development of new Foundation Apprenticeships, offered by both schools and colleges to young learners, and new Graduate Apprenticeships to sit on either side of the intermediate Modern Apprenticeships. In these policies, we see greater emphasis on coordination between education and training providers and a recognition of the need for longer-term development.

Do we need more higher level vocational education and what form should this take?

As we have seen, colleges in England and Scotland make a significant contribution to increasing the volume of HE level study, widening access and addressing 'cold spots' which are not well served by universities. While the government review of higher technical learning is just beginning, there is already a considerable body of research regarding the UK's skills profile and whether we have already an oversupply at a higher education level. In their review of graduate jobs in Europe, Green and Henseke note positively that in the UK, high-skill employment is the fastest-growing segment of the economy (Green and Henseke, 2017). At the same time, UK higher education has expanded in recent decades, and taking attainment of tertiary education as the measure, they locate the UK at the upper end of participation. To assess whether supply is already outstripping demand, they consider available measures of graduate 'underemployment' such as the continuation of an earnings premium (relative to secondary education) and skills utilisation survey data. While they conclude that between 2006–12 'the prevalence of graduate jobs was more or less keeping up' with graduate supply (Green and Henseke, 2017, p. 15), they also suggest that there is a stable picture of underemployment which effects approximately 30 per cent of UK graduates per year and this implies a cause for concern. Green and Henseke also point to a number of dangers for the future: evidence from the US of stagnation of demand for high-skilled jobs and a growing danger of automation at this level; the persistence of graduate underemployment at an individual level; that uncertainty following Brexit could supress graduate job growth in the UK; and evidence from East Asia that rising numbers of graduates has led to increasing inequality amongst that group. The fear is that those who progress through less prestigious routes, such as local colleges, will be least well placed to ride out these dangers. Such concerns indicate perhaps a need for colleges to provide not more of the same, but a contribution which adds value by addressing particular locations, levels or sectors.

In her recent report, Alison Wolf examines similar questions and argues that an open-ended commitment to funding honours degrees in England, through a system of government-backed loans, has led to overexpansion at the highest level and a shrinking in importance of sub-degree qualifications and in the role of colleges (Wolf, 2016). Wolf cites earlier work by McIntosh (2013) to suggest the decline in intermediate jobs, including in administrative and skilled trade occupations, is overstated and 'large numbers of intermediate jobs remain' (McIntosh, 2013, p. 5). Wolf draws from this, and from European research on the wage returns from intermediate qualifications, to argue for the 're-creation' of a national system of sub-degree tertiary awards, like the HNCs and HNDs, which can be offered in further education colleges as well as universities. An important element of her argument is a change to the funding regime in England, to provide an entitlement to individuals which is not tied to a degree and which would reduce the 'economic inefficiencies' (Wolf, 2016, p. 8) in the system. Curiously, Wolf draws on European models but has relatively little to say about the Scottish experience, where the national system of HNC and HND qualifications has been supported by the Scottish government, and they remain an important part of the work of colleges. Here, as we have argued above, despite their vocational purposes, questions are being raised about the role they play in practice, as in many subject areas they have gained importance as transitional qualifications for full-time students progressing to an honours degree. Furthermore, HNs are disproportionally accessed by candidates from the most deprived areas, whereas those from the least deprived areas are three times more likely to enter university than opt for these college qualifications (Hunter Blackburn et al., 2016). Such patterns could be viewed as a continuation of the effects of an 'education logic' identified by Iannelli and Raffe (2007) when studying school transitions. In Scotland, they found academic qualification routes appear to lead to higher occupational status for males, in comparison to vocational routes, whilst being neutral for females. Thus, despite the health of the HN route in Scotland questions over parity of esteem remain. It is not at all clear how reviving HNC/D qualifications in England would avoid these issues.

While Green and Henseke consider European trends in employment and the increasing range of graduate jobs, Wolf is concerned about deficiencies in the study of STEM (Science Technology Engineering and Maths). This is where she suggests colleges should be contributing; indeed, the dominance of business studies amongst existing sub-degree vocational provision is viewed as evidence of a failing system. A similar focus on the need for STEM knowledge and skills is evident in the UK Government's Industrial strategy, where unmet need from employers is noted as a concern (DBEIS, 2017). However, the role of colleges in providing STEM related higher level learning is challenging, given the limited funding outlined above. A recent report indicates that the costs to English colleges of offering engineering are significant when compared to management qualifications, and the recruitment of suitable staff is a considerable barrier (Aldaba, 2017).

Nevertheless, given the uncertainty about trends in higher level jobs, at a national and European-wide level, and the strength of the universities in this 'market', the nature of the contribution that colleges can make to meeting higher vocational learning needs is uncertain. Should they offer a broad range of sub-degree qualifications across the economy; should they follow learner demand in providing vocational routes through to degree programmes and focus on strengthening transition, or should they identify areas of specialism in occupations which meet local, regional, or even national employer need? Strategic decisions will, of course, be influenced by policy initiatives and which funding streams become available. A significant policy drive in recent years has been the reform of apprenticeships, which is now reaching the higher levels. Arguably, this provides a new, and tangible, opportunity for colleges to support part-time learners and meet the needs of employers. It also provides an example of the difficult issues that arise for colleges in finding a role at this level.

Higher, degree and graduate apprenticeships

In recent years, UK governments have placed renewed emphasis on apprenticeship as a key route to developing vocational skills amongst new and existing employees. Ambitious targets have been confirmed for three million apprenticeship starts in England by 2020 (DBEIS, 2017), although concern has been expressed elsewhere in this volume (Ryan, 2018) that a danger of this target is that volume is prioritised over quality, and that to meet it, the proportion of lower level apprenticeships will remain high. In Scotland, the target is to provide 30,000 starts every year (Scottish Government, 2015). Although limited in number, developments in apprenticeships at the higher levels are now underway. In common with all apprenticeships, learners are primarily employees. Their programme must include at least 20 per cent 'off-the-job' training, and while lower apprenticeships have been encouraged to avoid embedding specific qualifications, at the highest levels, this is an important feature. In England, two categories have been delineated: degree apprenticeships, which include a full undergraduate or (rarely) a master's degree, and higher apprenticeships, which include learning at the higher education level below a degree. In Scotland, the single-term graduate apprenticeships refer to all those at the Higher National Diploma level or above. Since April 2017, a UK apprenticeship levy on large employers (above £3 million annual payroll) has operated to co-fund learners, with the government making a significant contribution. In England, all of this levy funding must be used on apprenticeships, whereas in Scotland, a proportion has been reserved to provide a Workforce Development Fund, which can be used for wider skills training. The promotion of apprenticeship at the higher levels and a new funding mechanism provide opportunities to both colleges and universities. We will now examine how the experience of previous reforms raises questions for the extent to which colleges will be able to take advantage of this opportunity or be overtaken by other providers.

What can we learn from the introduction of FDs in England and the modernisation of HNs in Scotland?

The reorganisation of apprenticeship and extension of the programme to higher levels could be viewed as just the latest wave of change to impact on colleges, particularly in England, where it extends an already long roll call of 'reform' (DfE, 2017). Arguably, there are parallels with the earlier period of change which led in England to the introduction of a new HE level award, the FD, which was aimed both at employees studying part-time and full-time students, where the content was designed to develop the necessary skills and knowledge for work and the process included work-based learning as an element. As we have seen in Scotland, a different approach to meeting skills needs was taken, with attempts made to modernise HNs to adapt to new types of employment. In a comparative study[3] of these two developments, we identified both the significant divergences in policy between the two nations and the commonalities that emerged in practice (Gallacher et al., 2009). Some of the features of this comparison have resonance for the latest apprenticeship reform, with implications for the roles for colleges within it.

Divergence in English and Scottish policy provides opportunities for home international comparison

In HN modernisation, we noted a strong role for national policy implemented through the Scottish Qualifications Authority (SQA), not only in establishing the principles guiding the process, but in coordinating the groups which worked on each national qualification. Colleges were confirmed as the main providers of these renewed qualifications, and their role was strengthened. In England, in contrast, much greater faith was placed in the ability of the market to direct development, in the form of employer engagement in partnerships with providers, universities and colleges, to develop FDs. With FDs being approved by validating universities, this, in many, cases led to a weaker role for colleges. Evidence from the study pointed to the advantages and disadvantages both approaches yielded. In England, greater responsiveness to local employment opportunities was a feature of FD development, and some bespoke programmes were created. In Scotland, by contrast, colleges found it more difficult to adapt national programmes to local needs. A concern reported by colleges and universities in England, however, was the limited nature of employer demand in practice, or its unsustainability beyond the initial years (Gallacher et al., 2009).

The approaches to implementing the higher levels of apprenticeship have already diverged in the two nations, and in ways that echo this earlier initiative. In Scotland, the government agency SDS has the role of identifying sectors for the initial graduate apprenticeship programmes, based on their assessment of current demand and growth areas. Advice and guidance are provided by a Scottish Apprenticeship Advisory Board (SAAB) subcommittee, which does have significant employer representation (SAAB, n.d.). Ultimately, SDS has taken a strong role by commissioning the first rounds of graduate apprenticeships with providers. In England, the reform has located the development of new Apprenticeship Standards in self-selecting 'trailblazer' groups of employers, who draw on national guidance (IfA, 2017). For a degree apprenticeship, the group must work with at least two universities, but the implication is that trailblazers will be heavily employer-led. The approval of a new higher apprenticeship or degree apprenticeship lies within the remit of the central body the Institute for Apprenticeship, which is also 'employer-led'. While HEFCE has provided a competitive round of funding for providers to offer new higher level apprenticeships, these programmes must conform to the new Standards developed by the trailblazers. These arrangements have clear echoes of a strong state in Scotland and a more market-led approach in England. It is interesting to note that on this occasion, the strong state approach in Scotland has not resulted in a convincing role for colleges in graduate apprenticeships. In commissioning the pilot programmes, government has sent a clear signal that universities are the locus of development, with only one college being included among initial providers, and only one graduate apprenticeship specifying an HND rather than a degree award. In England, the market approach has resulted in some colleges joining with universities to bid for HEFCE support to establish degree apprenticeships, but they are very rarely the lead partner.

The difficulty of putting employers in the driver's seat

The stated intention of the apprenticeship reform in England is to put employers in the driver's seat, since 'nobody knows the skills employers need better than the employers themselves' (HMG, 2015, p. 2). This, it is argued, will deliver the skills, knowledge and behaviours required of the workforce of the future. Since learners will be employees and paid by a combination of their employer and the state, understanding employer demand is crucial. Existing studies (Dromey and McNeil, 2017; Keep, 2015) identify problems with relying on employers to identify demand, suggesting this is weakly articulated. Evidence from our comparative study suggests that despite an important role for employers in developing individual FDs and initial rapid growth during the period of government support, this didn't prevent significant 'churn' in provision, with FDs being developed but running for a limited period as cohorts dried up (Gallacher et al., 2009). Following the withdrawal of additional support for these programmes, the FD has since dwindled in importance, particularly in universities, although as we have seen it is still a feature of provision in colleges. This FD experience suggests a strong employer role in development is not necessarily a guarantee of sustained demand. In this respect, the approach taken to apprenticeship development in England, of putting faith in trailblazer employer groups, may not be more robust in divining demand than the more top-down approach taken in Scotland. The reliance on an employer-driven approach in England also raises issues of the uneven pace of development of the standards across sectors and levels, making it difficult for colleges and other providers to plan effectively for higher apprenticeships. In this respect, the clearer roll-out of graduate apprenticeships in Scotland may have advantages for providers.

Concerns have also been raised about the patterns of use of emerging qualifications. Despite the policy focus on developing the workforce in STEM-related occupations, with the intention of attracting new recruits to those areas, early indications suggest many employers are using their apprenticeship levy funds to put existing employees through management apprenticeships, particularly at the higher levels, including the MBA (FE Week, 2017a). These initial figures have led to lively discussion of whether to trust employers to spend the levy as they see fit or seek to intervene to ensure younger apprentices are recruited (FE Week,

2017b). More concerning still has been the drop in total apprenticeship starts in England since the levy was introduced in April 2017, where there have been drops of 59 per cent and 26 per cent in the first and second quarters, in comparison to the equivalent quarters in 2016/17 (DfE, 2018). The drop in numbers applied to the lower and mid-levels rather than the new degree apprenticeships, as these were so new to the system. Debate centred on whether this overall drop was the expected effect of the introduction of an unfamiliar system, as the Department for Education insisted, or evidence that some employers were willing to treat the levy as a tax rather than participate. A recent survey from the Chartered Institute of Personnel and Development found 19 per cent of levy paying organisations were planning to write off the charge, with a further 22 per cent undecided whether to use it; the numbers treating it as a tax rose to 35 per cent amongst the smaller levy paying organisations (CIPD, 2018). Elsewhere, it has been reported that slow take-up has been due to increases in resources required to support apprentices (BBC, 2017). Smaller employers, who do not pay the levy, are a now required to pay a 10 per cent contribution towards fees and absorb the costs of releasing learners for off the job study. The limited initial take-up, particularly amongst smaller employers, is a concern for colleges, which may be better placed to serve these smaller organisations than universities. Figures in Scotland for the first two quarters post-levy indicate a very slight drop in numbers for apprenticeships overall, at less than 4 per cent (SDS, 2017). Once again, since graduate apprentices are at a very early stage, it is difficult to gauge demand at this level. It is possible that once again, some stability in the Scottish system has benefited employer recognition, as Scotland has not required that the levy is spent on a reformed set of apprenticeships but enabled access to existing frameworks.

So there is concern that in these early days of the levy, employers are not coming forward in sufficient numbers to support apprentices. The significant difficulties of engaging employers in the support of learning and assessment were identified in our comparative study (Reeve et al., 2007). In the FD development, employer engagement was positioned as central, and attempting to secure employer participation became a significant area of work for college staff. No such requirement was built into the modernisation of HNs in Scotland, and programme leaders had the flexibility to involve employers as they felt appropriate. We noted that both FDs and HNs were more successful in working with employers and incorporating work-based or work-related learning, where this emerged from a tradition of joint working in the sector: for example, in engineering (Gallacher et al., 2009). It is likely that these new developments in higher level apprenticeships will also prosper in selected sectors rather than across all occupations, despite the ambition for the reform to address needs of the wider economy. Where colleges have established relationships with employers in particular sectors, they are more likely to be able to develop a higher level apprenticeship as a viable programme. Colleges may need to be realistic about where to put efforts and seek to operate in limited occupational areas.

The lure of the degree

In designating the very highest levels as 'degree' apprenticeships and 'graduate' apprenticeships, a very clear signal is being sent that these new programmes are to be viewed as equivalent in level and prestige to traditional degrees. Indeed, a key part of the marketing pitch to learners is the opportunity to obtain a degree without the high debt now associated with the traditional route. This is consistent with the stated aim of establishing a vocational education system which is equal in prestige to the academic line, and perhaps a recognition that in the UK, degrees dominate at tertiary level. As we have seen in both nations, universities have a leading role in the piloting of these developments, though larger colleges are present as partners. Arguably, it is the higher apprenticeships in England and those graduate apprenticeships which are linked to HNDs in Scotland that provide the realistic opportunity for colleges to support apprenticeship. At this early stage, it remains unclear how significant demand for these levels will be within the apprenticeship system. The employer-led system in England has to date resulted in more Standards emerging at the two levels within the higher apprenticeship than at the new degree apprenticeship level, taking those approved and in development into account (IfA, 2018). In contrast, in Scotland, only one of the initial 11 commissioned pilots has been a HND linked Graduate Apprenticeship (SDS, 2018). While this provides some indication of interest amongst these stakeholders, it is, of course, learners who must be committed to studying the programme. What can colleges learn from previous student engagement at this level?

Despite the attempt to draw on the cachet of the degree in naming FDs, the new programmes experienced difficulty in establishing a distinct identity. For many learners, they became an initial step on the route towards a degree rather than the endpoint. Progression rates from full-time programmes on to honours degrees were high and still significant for part-time learners (Gallacher et al., 2012). This was perhaps not surprising, given each FD was required to identify progression opportunities to a degree within its design. However, our comparative study identified that progression was also significant from the Scottish HNs into degree programmes, albeit with fewer opportunities for full credit within the receiving programme (Gallacher, 2017). The experience of FDs and HNs indicates that while there is demand from learners at this level, it is much lower than for degrees, and in many cases is treated as a route to a degree, calling into question the extent to which the vocational purpose is driving recruitment. It appears that the FD and HN route is particularly useful for those that lack the qualifications for direct entry to a degree or prefer a local provider. In this respect, it can be seen as an aspect of the social inclusion role which has become important for many colleges. The importance of progression in practice creates tensions for colleges, as programme content and process are subject to influence from the receiving universities, in what has been described as a process of academic drift. At present, there are ambiguous signals about the desirability of progression within the apprenticeships system. In England, standards are required to relate to a 'stand-alone' occupation that has its own clear purpose and demand (IfA, 2017, p. 9). Yet in some occupations, including one of the most the popular, Management, the desirability of establishing a ladder of apprenticeships up to masters level is noted (Wilton, 2017). In Scotland, progression is encouraged from a lower level apprenticeship into a graduate apprenticeship but not yet explicitly addressed within the graduate apprenticeship itself. While there is a space for colleges, in both countries, to become a core provider of apprenticeships at this sub-degree level, it will require careful consideration, and activity at this level may remain subsidiary to that at the degree apprenticeship level, where universities will dominate.

The expansion of apprenticeship to the higher levels does represent an opportunity for colleges, but as we have seen above, the lesson of previous initiatives is that there are likely to be significant challenges for colleges in establishing their role. These include addressing the attraction of a full degree for both learners and employers, and the advantage that this conveys on universities, and the need to identify sustained employer demand for individual apprenticeship programmes. Here the selection of development activity, based on local understandings and evidence, will be important. How this develops within the very different national contexts should provide an opportunity for comparative research.

Conclusion

Earlier in this chapter, we identified three questions which arise for colleges as they consider their vocational purpose at this level. These questions are: should they offer a broad range of sub-degree qualifications across the economy; should they follow learner demand in providing vocational routes through to degree programmes and focus on strengthening transition; or should they identify areas of specialism in occupations which meet local, regional or even national employer need? We recognise that colleges may decide to respond to these questions in different ways, depending on local circumstances. However, in the light of the discussion presented in this chapter, we suggest that for many colleges, there may be a value in focusing on the third of these options if they wish to establish a significant role in the provision of higher level vocational education. This is particularly so where colleges face local competition from other providers, including vocationally orientated universities. In considering how colleges might respond to this third strand, we note the importance of employer demand, which will be variable by sector, expressed at different levels and influenced by the local context.

Colleges may be wise to accept that there are some occupational areas for which the natural partner has become the universities, either through policy moves, as has been the case in nursing, or through the attraction of the undergraduate and postgraduate degree, as we have seen in finance or management.

Colleges are unlikely to find a role in these areas. A more positive opportunity may be found in those sectors where there is demand for qualifications that lie just below the degree, where there is a clear rational for these as 'terminal qualifications' linked to particular roles. At present, higher education is less interested in this market, so leaving a potential role for colleges. The identification of these elusive higher technical occupations that do not need, or even desire, a degree is being taken forward differently in the two nations. Employers are increasingly put 'in the driver's seat' in England, while in Scotland, they have an advisory role. Yet what emerges from this work are qualification structures and opportunities to offer services, where colleges can respond but not strongly shape developments at a national level. This points to the importance of working instead at the local or regional level to determine, and seek evidence for, growth areas. As we have seen in Scotland, Regional Outcome Agreements are now required which identify how colleges will meet the needs of the region, including meeting employers' needs. In England, Further Education Area Reviews have been more focused on the need to reduce complexity and the number of colleges in the system, but many did document employer demand, gained in part from the evidence of Local Enterprise Partnerships. Such government-initiated processes arguably generate just the initial layer of analysis, though they may lead to other working groups that will take forward dialogue between colleges and employers. Hodgson and Spours argue that a more a more comprehensive form of engagement could be established between the two, through incentives and regulation, with colleges taking a leading role within 'High Progression and Skills Ecosystems' (2017). However, as Keep notes in his chapter (2018), the resources required for such developments may be significant. In the meantime, colleges will need to draw on their existing relationships with local employers and seek to expand these to establish evidence of real and sustained employer demand. Wheelahan and Moodie (2017) have noted the weakness of links with employers in Anglophone countries when compared with Germany and other northern European countries, and, while strengthening these links may not be easy, it would appear that this is a challenge which colleges must now address if they are to re-establish a strong presence in vocational education and training.

While the views of employers are crucial in funding and supporting programmes, clearly it is learners that engage their energies in undertaking them. So the decisions of potential learners, both young entrants and those already in the workforce, are important. At the time of writing, a vibrant debate on the funding of higher level learning in England is taking place; and the failure of a functioning market in higher education is finally being addressed with the announcement of a comprehensive review of funding options (May, 2018). It is unlikely, however, that this review will break decisively from the market approach that has driven policy in England in recent decades, particularly given the suggestions that have emerged to use price differentials to nudge learners towards shorter courses. Further calls for parity of esteem between degrees and vocational qualifications seem likely to continue to be ineffective. While potential students perceive that better forms of employment are tied to 'good' degrees, they may take the rational decision to work towards such a degree, aiming to avoid, in their own case, the pitfall of a 30 per cent underemployment rate. So here we return to the role of employers in strengthening learner confidence in sub-degree vocational qualifications. By increasing the rewards attached to jobs that are associated with these qualifications, and improving job satisfaction, they may encourage greater take up of these sub-degree qualifications. As we have noted in Scotland, there is policy interest in promoting fair work and improving the use of skills in employment. Although this is a long-term endeavour and requires resources and local infrastructure, it can be viewed as a positive beginning to addressing these entrenched issues. The challenge for colleges is that many of the crucial issues that influence learner demand are shaped by factors which lie outside their control, and the proposed solutions are long-term.

The extent to which colleges can reassert their role in providing vocational education at the higher levels remains an open question, in part because of the range of long-term structural issues we have reviewed, and in part because it requires a myriad of local responses. For almost all colleges, the contributions they make will be more significant at a local or regional, rather than the national, level. Where they serve local industries and populations which feel the universities are too distant a prospect, literally and metaphorically, they have the opportunity to provide a robust vocational higher level option. Establishing a sustainable vocational offer will involve nurturing relationships with employers, particularly those with a local rather than national profile, in order to contribute to discussions on the level and forms of vocational learning that support sustainable work. Here colleges may need to be cautious and certain, rather than merely nimble and responsive.

Notes

1 Higher National Certificates and Higher National Diplomas are located at the same level as the first year and the second year, respectively, of a full-time undergraduate programme.
2 Foundation Degrees are located at the same level as the second year of a full-time undergraduate programme. FDs require some element of work-based learning.
3 This was a four-year study which undertook a comparison of Scottish and English policy and of practice through gathering empirical evidence from learners, college and university staff and employers.

References

Aldaba (2017) *The Costs of Providing Levels 4 and 5 in Further Education* [Online], Department for Education. Available at www.gov.uk/government/publications/the-costs-of-providing-levels-4-and-5-in-further-education (Accessed 16 January 2018).
Association of Colleges (2017) *Key Facts 2017–18* [Online], Association of Colleges. Available at www.aoc.co.uk/sites/default/files/Key%20Facts%202017-18%20.pdf (Accessed 16 January 2018).

Audit Scotland (2016) *Scotland's Colleges 2016* [Online], Audit Scotland. Available at www.audit-scotland.gov.uk/report/scotlands-colleges-2016 (Accessed 16 January 2018).

BBC (2017) 'Apprenticeship numbers fall by 59% after levy imposed', *BBC* [Online]. Available at www.bbc.co.uk/news/business-42092171 (Accessed 23 November 2017).

CIPD (2018) *Assessing the early impact of the apprenticeship levy – employers' perspective*, Chartered Institute of Personnel and Development [Online]. Available at www.cipd.co.uk/knowledge/fundamentals/people/routes-work/impact-apprenticeship-levy# (Accessed 30 January 2018).

Department for Business, Energy and Industrial Strategy (2017) *Industrial Strategy: Building a Britain Fit for the Future*, Cm 9528, London, DBEIS/HMSO.

DfE (2017) *Evaluation of the FE Reform Programme 2015* [Online], DfE. Available at www.gov.uk/government/uploads/system/uploads/attachment_data/file/652495/Evaluation_of_the_FE_Reform_Programme_2015.pdf (Accessed 16 January 2018).

DfE (2018) *Apprenticeship and Levy Statistics: February 2018, Reported to Date* [Online], DfE. Available at www.gov.uk/government/uploads/system/uploads/attachment_data/file/682464/SFR13_2018_Appandlevystats_Feb_Commentary.pdf (Accessed 22 February 2018).

DfEE (2000) *Foundation Degrees: A Consultation Document*, London, DfEE.

Dromey, J. and McNeil, C. (2017) *Another Lost Decade? Building a Skills System for the Economy of the 2030s* [Online], IPPR. Available at www.ippr.org/publications/skills-2030-another-lost-decade (Accessed 16 January 2018).

FE Week (2017a) 'DfE "watching it closely" as management becomes England's second most popular apprenticeship subject', *FE Week* [Online]. Available at https://feweek.co.uk/2017/10/13/dfe-watching-it-closely-as-management-becomes-englands-second-most-popular-apprenticeship-subject/ (Accessed 13 October 2017).

FE Week (2017b) 'Management apprenticeships debate rages', *FE Week* [Online]. Available at https://feweek.co.uk/2017/11/24/management-apprenticeships-debate-rages/ (Accessed 24 November 2017).

FE Week (2018) 'Revealed: The 12 colleges surviving on government bail outs', *FE Week* [Online]. Available at https://feweek.co.uk/2018/02/09/revealed-the-12-colleges-surviving-on-government-bailouts/ (Accessed 9 February 2018).

Gallacher, J. (2017) 'College education in the college sector: Widening access or diversion? Questions and challenges from the Scottish experience', *Journal of Education and Work*, vol. 30, no. 7, pp. 712–721.

Gallacher, J., Ingram, R., and Reeve, F. (2009) *Work-Based and Work-Related Learning in Higher National Certificates and Diplomas in Scotland and Foundation Degrees in England: A Comparative Study* [Online], GCU/OU. Available at http://oro.open.ac.uk/27241/ (Accessed 16 January 2018).

Gallacher, J., Ingram, R., and Reeve, F. (2012) 'Are vocational qualification vocational?', in Piltz, M. (ed.), *The Future of VET in a Changing World*, Wiesbaden, Springer VS. DOI 10.1007/978-3-531-18757-0

Green, F. and Henseke, G. (2017) *Graduates and 'Graduate Jobs' in Europe: A Picture of Growth and Diversification: Centre for Global Higher Education*, London, UCL Institute of Education.

HEFCE (2017) *Higher Education Providers* [Online], HEFCE. Available at www.hefce.ac.uk/analysis/HEinEngland/providers/colleges/ (Accessed 16 January 2018).

HMG (2015) *English Apprenticeship Our 2020 Vision* [Online], HM Government. Available at www.gov.uk/government/uploads/system/uploads/attachment_data/file/482754/BIS-15-604-english-apprenticeships-our-2020-vision.pdf (Accessed 16 January 2018).

Hodgson, A. and Spours, K. (2017) *FE and Skills across the UK: The Case of England*, Seminar Briefing Paper, UCL Institute of Education.

Hunter Blackburn, L., Kadar-Satat, G., Riddell, S., and Weedon, E. (2016) *Access in Scotland: Access to Higher Education for People from Less Advantaged Backgrounds in Scotland* [Online], Sutton Trust. Available at www.suttontrust.com/research-paper/access-in-scotland-university-participation/ (Accessed 16 January 2018).

Iannelli, C. and Raffe, D. (2007) 'Vocational upper-secondary education and the transition from school', *European Sociological Review*, vol. 23, no. 1, pp. 49–63.

Ingram, R. and Gallacher, J. (2010) 'Vocational and work-related qualifications in Scotland at SCQF level 9 and above', *SQA Policy and New Products Research Report* No. 15, Glasgow, Scottish Qualifications Authority.

Institute for Apprenticeships (2017) *'How to' Guide for Trailblazers*, London, Institute for Apprenticeships.

Institute for Apprenticeships (2018) *Apprenticeship Standards* [Online], IfA. Available at www.instituteforapprenticeships.org/apprenticeship-standards/ (Accessed 16 January 2018).

Keep, E. (2015) 'Unlocking workplace skills: What is the role of employers?', *CIPD Policy Report*, London, Chartered Institute for Personnel and Development.

May, T. (2018) *Prime Minister Launches Major Review of Post-18 Education* [Online], DfE. Available at www.gov.uk/government/news/prime-minister-launches-major-review-of-post-18-education (Accessed 19 February 2018).

McIntosh, S. (2013) 'Hollowing out and the future of the labour market', *Department for Business Innovation and Skills Research Paper* No. 134, London, Department for Business Innovation and Skills.

Milton, A. (2017) *Speech to the Association of Colleges Conference* [Online], DfE. Available at www.gov.uk/government/speeches/anne-milton-speech-to-association-of-colleges-conference (Accessed 16 January 2018).

Parry, G. (2017) *A New Design and Regulatory Framework for Technical Education in England* [Online], Centre for Global Higher Education. Available at www.researchcghe.org/perch/resources/publications/pb4.pdf (Accessed 16 January 2018).

QAA (2004) *Foundation Degree Qualification Benchmark*, Gloucester, Quality Assurance Agency for Higher Education.

RCU (2017) *College Based Higher Education* [Online], Education and Training Foundation. Available at www.et-foundation.co.uk/wp-content/uploads/2017/08/RCU-National-16N003-FINAL.pdf (Accessed 16 January 2018).

Reeve, F., Gallacher, J., and Ingram, R. (2007) 'A comparative study of HNs in Scotland and Foundation Degrees in England: Contrast, complexity and continuity', *Journal of Education and Work*, vol. 20, no. 4, pp. 305–318.

Scottish Apprenticeship Advisory Board (n.d.) *The Scottish Apprenticeship Advisory Board* [Online], Skills Development Scotland. Available at www.skillsdevelopmentscotland.co.uk/what-we-do/partnerships/the-scottish-apprenticeship-advisory-board/ (Accessed 16 January 2018).

Scottish Funding Council (2016) *Infact Database* [Online], Scottish Funding Council. Available at https://stats.sfc.ac.uk/infact/ (Accessed 16 January 2018).

Scottish Funding Council (2017) *College Leaver Destinations 2015–16* [Online], Scottish Funding Council. Available at www.sfc.ac.uk/publications-statistics/statistical-publications/statistical-publications-2017/SFCST072017.aspx (Accessed 30 October 2017).

Scottish Government (2014) *Developing the Young Workforce: Scotland's Youth Employment Strategy* [Online], Scottish Government. Available at www.gov.scot/Publications/2014/12/7750 (Accessed 16 January 2018).

Scottish Government (2015) *Scotland's Economic Strategy* [Online], Scottish Government. Available at www.gov.scot/Publications/2015/03/5984 (Accessed 16 January 2018).

Scottish Government (2017a) *Scottish Funding Council: Guidance 2017–18* [Online], Scottish Funding Council. Available at www.sfc.ac.uk/web/FILES/AboutUs/SFC_Letter_of_Guidance_2017-18.pdf (Accessed 16 January 2018).

Scottish Government (2017b) *Scottish Government 15–24 Learner Journey Review* [Online], www.gov.scot/Topics/Education/post16reform/post16reform/LearnerJourneyReview (Accessed 16 January 2018).

Scottish Qualification Authority (2007) *HN Toolkit: Introduction and Overview*, Glasgow, Scottish Qualifications Authority.

Skills Development Scotland (2017) *Modern Apprenticeship Statistics: Up to the End of Quarter 2, 2017/18* [Online], Skills Development Scotland. Available at www.skillsdevelopmentscotland.co.uk/media/43869/modern-apprenticeship-statistics-quarter-2-2017-18.pdf (Accessed 16 January 2018).

Skills Development Scotland (2018) *Graduate Apprenticeships* [Online], Apprenticeships Scotland. Available at www.apprenticeships.scot/become-an-apprentice/graduate-apprenticeships/ (Accessed 16 January 2018).

Wheelahan, L. and Moodie, G. (2017) 'Vocational education qualifications' roles in pathways to work in liberal market economies', *Journal of Vocational Education & Training*, vol. 69, no. 1, pp. 10–27.

Wilton (2017) *Further Progression: Developing Masters-Level Degree Apprenticeship Programmes* [Online], FE News. Available at www.fenews.co.uk/fevoices/15273-further-progression-developing-masters-level-degree-apprenticeship-programmes (Accessed 16 January 2018).

Wolf, A. (2016) *Remaking Tertiary Education: Can We Create a System That Is Fair and Fit for Purpose?*, London, Education Policy Institute.

Chapter 10

How are 'applied degrees' applied in Ontario colleges of applied arts and technology?

Gavin Moodie, Michael L. Skolnik, Leesa Wheelahan, Qin Liu, Diane Simpson and Edmund G. Adam

Introduction

In 2000, the Ontario Parliament authorised the relevant minister to approve colleges of applied arts and technology to offer baccalaureates provided each is 'a baccalaureate degree in an applied area of study' (Queen's Printer for Ontario, 2017, section 4(5)(a)). But what is 'a baccalaureate degree in an applied area of study', or, more tersely and commonly, what are 'applied degrees'? This chapter describes the ways in which Ontario colleges' baccalaureates are applied, based on the authors' broader investigation of Ontario college baccalaureates. These findings are put in an analytic framework and an historic context, and the chapter then answers its two questions.

The study concludes that there seem to be four characteristics common to many understandings of applied degrees: the curriculum is specific to an occupation rather than a general preparation for work, life or further education; the pedagogy includes more practical work, often at a workplace, than non-applied degrees; the curriculum and pedagogy integrate knowledge fundamental to the practice of an occupation; and the outcome is a qualification relevant to the labour market. Ontario college baccalaureates 'in an applied area of study' seem to have all these characteristics.

Ontario college baccalaureates also teach 'applied knowledge', which may derive from two sources: disciplinary knowledge recontextualised for a field of practice, and a practice's established rules and practices which have been restructured as systematic procedural knowledge. The chapter concludes by suggesting a distinctive role for colleges in codifying, restructuring and systematising rules and procedures of practice, particularly in fields which do not have a strong institution to systematise practice.

We now see how Ontario colleges apply 'applied degrees' in practice.

Ontario college baccalaureates

In 2016 some 13 of Ontario's 24 colleges offered 108 degrees. However, the five colleges with the biggest degree offerings offered 73 per cent of all college degrees and enrolled 86.6 per cent of college baccalaureate students in 2013/2014. College baccalaureate enrolments grew by 237 per cent from 2006 to 2015, but this was off a tiny base and baccalaureate students were only 6.5 per cent of colleges' total enrolments: half of college students were in diplomas in 2015, which had grown by 46 per cent since 2006. College degrees remain a modest 4 per cent of all undergraduate degrees offered in Ontario (Wheelahan et al., 2017, pp. 29–32).

There are marked differences between fields of study for students enrolled in college degrees and all college student enrolments. Applied arts' share of college baccalaureate enrolments (42.6 per cent) is much higher than their share of all college enrolments (32.5 per cent). Businesses' share of baccalaureate enrolments (34.7 per cent) is also well above its share of all college enrolments (27.4 per cent). Ontario college enrolments in degrees in health (4.4 per cent) are substantially lower than in health credentials offered in colleges overall (14.7 per cent). This may be because colleges are not permitted to offer their own nursing degrees which lead to occupational designation as a registered nurse. Colleges offer nursing degrees in partnership with universities, but students are enrolled in university credentials. Colleges' non-baccalaureate health students are mostly diplomas training registered practical nurses and pre-health science programmes which prepare students to enter higher level health programmes.

We examined Ontario college baccalaureate curriculum in two ways. First, we examined the curriculum of baccalaureates of four colleges in three fields of study, in applied arts, business and technology. We compared those with the curriculum of four cognate degrees offered by two Ontario universities that emphasise the applied and experiential nature of their programmes, and with the curriculum of four cognate degrees offered by three traditional Ontario universities. The study compared these cognate degrees' programme maps, objectives and content. The degrees' content was examined by comparing the weight of theoretical and applied knowledge in the curriculum, the structure of the degree, and curriculum breadth. Curriculum breadth was examined by finding whether students were required or had opportunities to undertake learning outside their main discipline. The study examined work integrated learning experiences by finding whether students were required to undertake a cooperative learning or work placement.

College baccalaureates allocated around half of their curriculum to applied studies, compared to from around 12 per cent to 30 per cent at the universities which emphasised the applied and experiential nature of their programmes and from 5 per cent to 30 per cent at the traditional universities. Theoretical studies comprised around 25 per cent of the curriculum in college baccalaureates, from 40 per cent to 60 per cent of the curriculum in experiential universities and from 50 per cent to 80 per cent of the curriculum in traditional universities. Studies outside the main discipline were from 5 per cent to 15 per cent of the colleges' curriculum, from 2 per cent to 40 per cent of the curriculum in experiential universities and from 20 per cent to 45 per cent in traditional universities. Cooperative and work placement programmes were from 12 per cent to 40 per cent of college baccalaureates from 0 per cent to 42 per cent of experiential universities, but were not part of the traditional university baccalaureates examined, though they are part of traditional universities' other baccalaureates such as in medicine, nursing and teacher education (Wheelahan et al., 2017, p. 44).

Secondly, we interviewed 18 Ontario college leaders and 35 faculty members, all of whom were at colleges which offered baccalaureates except two college leaders. Most interviewees said that colleges offer baccalaureates with a distinctive curriculum in being more applied than that of universities, more practical and more directly related to specific occupations rather than employment in general or in a broad field. Many interviewees argued that the key strength of college curriculum was the integration of theory and practice (Wheelahan et al., 2017, p. 47). One faculty member who taught in their college's baccalaureate in a technological field argued the virtues of what they described as their 'just in time curriculum'. Rather than provide in first year all the physics which a student needs for their whole programme and indeed for their career, the faculty member said that each term they provided just enough physics for students to understand the technological principles taught in that term. Here we merely note the claim for just in time curriculum; we are not necessarily endorsing it and argue for the importance of disciplinary knowledge towards the end of this chapter.

Interviewees also reported a distinctive pedagogy for college baccalaureates. Frequently mentioned was college baccalaureates' small class sizes, which many interviewees contrasted favourably with big and anonymous undergraduate university classes. They reported that this allowed more time for discussion and for more intensive teaching and that faculty got to know their students which allowed them to respond to their individual needs. Perhaps equally distinctive but less frequently mentioned is colleges' teaching of students in cohorts. Ontario colleges tend to teach both diplomas and baccalaureate students in cohorts: each cohort remains mostly the same for each course and also for all the programme's years. Interviewees argued that college classes are therefore more cohesive than university programmes which do not teach in cohorts. It is also possible to integrate college programmes closely sequentially and concurrently since faculty can be confident of the sequence of courses which college students take.

Many interviewees reported that colleges include a lot of project work in baccalaureates (but not necessarily in their diplomas) which integrate theory and practice and integrate studies in different courses. For example, one college's degree is built on projects: students complete four projects in two parts over two terms. Projects are said to develop students' ability to solve problems in practice and to develop students' soft skills, ability to work in teams, to be more mobile and move to different roles.

College faculty and leaders also referred to the importance of co-operative education placements and their integration with the programme offered on campus. 'Cooperative education' refers to students' work placements which are integrated with their education (Cooperative Education and Work-Integrated Learning Canada, 2018), also known in other contexts as work integrated learning.

An interviewee reported that co-ops greatly enrich students' subsequent studies on campus since students see the application of their knowledge in practice during their co-op placements, have many questions arising from their co-ops and have renewed interest in learning on campus. A leader of a college which offers baccalaureates added that in their final year, students work with local employers in a capstone project which integrates their different fields of knowledge and integrates theory and practice. Of course, all universities offer laboratory classes and universities are increasingly following the University of Waterloo's leading cooperative education programme. But interviewees argued that in universities, theory and practice are often offered separately, leaving their integration to students. In contrast, they argued, colleges integrate theory and practice much more closely (Wheelahan et al., 2017, pp. 48–49).

Interestingly, no interviewee specifically mentioned colleges' distinctively having authentic assessment which 'involves assessment activities like those commonly used in the world outside of the classroom: work samples, performances, exhibitions and self-evaluation reports' (American Psychological Association, 2016). Nonetheless, Ontario college baccalaureates' use of authentic assessment may be inferred from their heavy reliance on practical and project work.

Types of knowledge and the structuring of practical knowledge

The British sociologist of education Basil Bernstein ([1996] 2000, pp. 9, 52) distinguished between disciplines (which he called 'singulars'), the 'field of external practice' such as engineering and nursing, and what Bernstein called 'regions' which are at the interface between disciplines and fields of practice. Later, we will refer to Long's 'trading zones' and to Valleriani's (2017c, p. 3) description of the social structuring of practical knowledge to elaborate the operation of regions, but for now, we observe that regions include disciplinary knowledge which is recontextualised for the field of practice, such as physics for engineering and biology for nursing. Regions also include 'systematic procedural knowledge' or the 'established rules and practices' (Young, 2006, p. 62) of an occupation such as organising a building site or taking a patient's temperature. Fields of practice also include tacit, uncodified and often uncodifiable knowledge and practices which are acquired in workplaces, usually experientially, without explicit instruction (Young, 2006, pp. 113, 118–119). Examples often cited are the physician's skill of diagnosis and the barrister's skill of advocacy, and other examples are the mechanic's skill of tuning a machine for optimal performance, nurses' skill in managing patients and selling techniques. While uncodifiable knowledge and practices can be incorporated into the curriculum via periods of work experience, they can't be turned into disciplinary knowledge, which is necessarily codified.

We thus have disciplinary theoretical knowledge, some of which is recontextualised for regions; fields' established rules and practices, some of which are codified into regions' systematic procedural knowledge; and fields' tacit uncodi-fiable knowledge and practices. These are illustrated in Figure 10.1.

The critical realist author Andrew Collier ([1997] 2003) distinguishes between abstract sciences, concrete sciences and practice. He describes abstract sciences thus:

> Experiments give rise to what may be called the abstract sciences, since they are each about one set of laws which we have discovered by abstrac-tion. They are not about particular entities of one sort or another. Physics is not specially about the physical world; chemistry is equally about the physi-cal world. Chemistry is not about 'chemicals' in the sense that the chemical industry produces chemicals. It is about the chemical aspect of the whole physical world, including living organisms, for instance.
>
> (Collier, [1997] 2003, p. 38)

Collier ([1997] 2003, p. 38) describes concrete sciences, which are about par-ticular entities, by reference to Husserl's ([1990] 1970, pp. 230–231) *Logical investigations*:

> Now some natural sciences – for instance geography, meteorology, medicine – are about particular entities. They may be called the concrete sciences. When making the distinction between abstract and concrete sciences, Husserl says that abstract sciences 'are nomological in so far as their unifying principle, as well as their essential aim of research, is a law', whereas in concrete sciences 'one connects all the truths whose content relates to one and the same object, or to one and the same empirical genus'.
>
> (Collier, [1997] 2003, p. 38)

Collier ([1997] 2003, p. 41) adds that concrete sciences':

> concepts are arrived at partly by retroduction from practical experience – 'how can we explain the way things seem in practice' – and partly borrowed

Disciplines	Regions	Fields of practice
Theoretical knowledge		
Theoretical knowledge →	Recontextualised disciplinary knowledge	
	Systematic procedural knowledge	←Established rules and practices
		Tacit uncodifiable knowledge and practices

Figure 10.1 Types of knowledge in three domains

from the abstract sciences. By these two methods, the concrete sciences build up a stock of abstract concepts of their own.

(Collier, [1997] 2003, p. 41)

Arguably, Collier's abstract sciences, concrete sciences and practice correspond with the disciplines, regions and fields shown in Figure 10.1. Collier's ([1997] 2003, p. 44) main argument in this article is that:

> as a matter of scientific ethics and good public policy, abstract sciences ought never to be allowed to influence practice directly, but only through the assistance they give to concrete sciences . . .
>   the rationality of the practical application of science depends on following the full sequence abstract sciences → concrete science → practice rather than the abridged sequence abstract science → practice . . .
>
> (Collier, [1997] 2003, pp. 43–44)

That is, Collier argues against the direct application of abstract science or theory to practice that many posit.

An example of regions is what Long (2011, pp. 8, 94–126, 2015, 2017, pp. 223–225) calls 'trading zones' which were common ground in the 16th century, such as arsenals, mines, workshops and cities on which unlearned but skilled practitioners who were trained in workshops exchanged knowledge with unskilled but learned humanists who were trained in universities. Long argues further that participants in trading zones converged: the skilled became more learned, and the learned became more skilled. 'These interchanges helped legitimise the value of the practical and integrate it into the discourse of the learned' (Long, 2015, p. 844). Eisenstein ([1979] 1997, pp. 23, 521, 538, 561) similarly described printing shops as sites where learned authors, editors and translators exchanged knowledge with printshop owners, skilled printers and typesetters.

Valleriani (2017c, pp. 2–3) describes knowledge production mechanisms at three levels which correspond to fields, regions and disciplines:

> These are: (1) the knowledge structure of practical activities; (2) the social structuring of practical knowledge; and (3) the conceptual structures of knowledge. The first, concerns the practical knowledge itself structured following the dictates of the workflow and the series of actions needed to achieve the desired final product. At the other end of the scale, there is the layer of knowledge systems, which in their historical dynamics, tended to expand extensively and reflectively, drawing an analogy with cognitive structures of abstraction and representation (Damerow, 1996, pp. 29–70). In between, there is the network of people working within a framework of practical activities, whose social organization continuously changed, and that were shaped by institutional bodies and within new, increasingly

influential social environments. These analytical layers do not mirror one another in a consistent manner. Rather, they trade with one another and develop dynamics that lead to an association of different aspects of knowledge, that, finally, can also explain how, in a later epoch, scientific knowledge had re-impacted practical activities.

(Valleriani, 2017c, pp. 2–3)

Valleriani (2017a) and his co-authors describe the structuring of practical knowledge in the early modern period in major knowledge-intensive projects which therefore required explicit knowledge management: big construction projects; hydraulic engineering projects such as the drainage of marshland and the construction of canals, harbours and dikes (Klein, 2017, p. 289); military campaigns; journeys of discovery; ship building; mining; smelting; and production of metal, glass, paper, books and beer; amongst others (Valleriani, 2017b, p. vi).

Of course, none of these fields was developed by universities until the 19th century despite, for example, architecture being included in Marcus Terentius Varro's (116–27 BCE) *De novem disciplinis* (The nine disciplines); Vitruvius (c. 80–70 – c. 15 BCE) providing a scholarly foundation for a discipline of the art of building in *De architectura libri decem* (The ten books on architecture); the fact that municipalities, churches and princes commissioned big building projects which demanded architect-builders who had practical and theoretical knowledge; and that accordingly, master builders became prominent and enjoyed high social esteem from the 13th century (Moodie, 2016, p. 66). Neither did architects have a distinct occupational affiliation such as a guild during the early modern period (Merrill, 2017, p. 49).

Valleriani (2017b, p. vii, 2017c, pp. 3–5) and his co-authors (Merrill, 2017, p. 35; Lefèvre, 2017, p. 267) observe that these fields structure knowledge in practice in their workflow, division and organisation of labour, work drawings, models, measuring instruments, tables of measurements, written recipes, formulas, woodblock prints, almanacs, commentaries and practical treatises. Practitioners restructured their knowledge to manage their operations; to share it, mainly for apprenticeships and other forms of education; and to document their trials and experiments (Merrill, 2017, p. 23; Valleriani, 2017c, p. 9). Practitioners restructure rather than merely replicate their knowledge because, for example, when a carpenter teaches an apprentice they don't just work wood, but they explain how to work wood; they convey to the apprentice not know-how, but knowledge about know-how (Büttner, 2017, p. 118). This restructuring of practical knowledge not only codified the knowledge of practitioners, but organised it and gave it an analytical framework with principles and theories incorporated from the scholarly literature (Valleriani, 2017c, pp. 6, 11), which, of course, was in Latin rather than the vernacular of practitioners.

But practitioners did not simply apply scholarly principles to practice. For example, Büttner (2017, pp. 119, 129, 157) describes didactic artillery printed textbooks which illustrate ballistic theory with drawings of trajectories and tables of shots' maximum distance at each cannon elevation. While these texts put gunnery theory within a broader scholarly framework (Valleriani, 2017c, p. 6), they were, however, inconsistent with gunnery practice as recorded in practitioners' mnemonic manuals, which were mostly in manuscript. Texts were used to put practice in an analytic framework, but not necessarily to guide it.

Secondly, Lefèvre (2017, pp. 254, 261) describes Renaissance architects' development of Gothic master builders' stereotomy, two-dimensional drawings projecting three-dimensional shapes which were used as templates to carve intricately shaped masonry. Lefèvre (2017, p. 267) emphasises:

> Third, with respect to the mathematics of Renaissance architects, the interplay of practical geometry and learned geometry in the tradition of Euclid cannot be conceived of as an application of the latter by the former. Rather, architects developed, in the context of stereotomy, a sophisticated practical geometry besides learned geometry, a practical geometry that transgressed the canonic arsenal of geometric entities and eventually gave birth to a new mathematical discipline – descriptive geometry.
>
> (Lefèvre, 2017, p. 267)

Thus, the conventional dualism of theory and practice is simplistic. A fuller understanding includes an intermediate category of recontextualised theoretical knowledge and restructured rules of practice.

What is meant by 'applied degrees'; how are applied degrees applied in practice by Ontario colleges?

There is considerable similarity in the understanding of 'applied degrees' over an extended time and geography, as Skolnik (2016b, p. 364) observed. There seem to be four characteristics common to many understanding of applied degrees:

1   the curriculum is specific to an occupation rather than a general preparation for work, life or further education;
2   the pedagogy includes more practical work, often at a workplace, than non-applied degrees;
3   the curriculum and pedagogy integrate knowledge fundamental to and the practice of an occupation ('blend theory and practice');
4   the outcome is a qualification relevant to the labour market.

Less common in the literature but frequently mentioned by faculty and leaders of Ontario colleges offering baccalaureates is their baccalaureates' distinctiveness in teaching 'applied knowledge' (Wheelahan et al., 2017, pp. 41, 47–48). From our reference to the more theoretical literature, we gather that the 'applied knowledge' taught in applied degrees may include both disciplinary knowledge that has been recontextualised for the field of practice and the field's established rules and practices which have been restructured and systematised for teaching.

Thus, the flow of curriculum for applied degrees is not only from theory to practice, but from practice to more generalised principles. Both types of applied knowledge are necessary if applied degrees are to meet the goals expected of them. Applied baccalaureate students need to acquire knowledge of systematised and generalised rules and practices from the field of practice to be prepared for practice. In addition, all students, including students of applied degrees, need access to disciplinary knowledge because disciplinary knowledge includes the methods to proceed from what a person knows to what they do not know, to generate new knowledge, or to think the unthinkable as Bernstein ([1996] 2000, pp. 29, 114) argued. Access to disciplinary knowledge is also needed to preserve access to higher level programmes. This is particularly important in the vertical or USA-type arrangements of post-secondary education, where most if not all opportunities to proceed to higher level studies are along the academic track. This is in contrast to the parallel or European model, in which applied institutes offer many opportunities for advanced study at least up to master's degrees (Skolnik, 2016a).

Most if not all universities offer practical, laboratory or other applied classes. Universities are increasingly including in their baccalaureates cooperative education, work placements and work integrated learning. However, university laboratory classes are not always well integrated with lectures (Edward, 2002, p. 13; Hucke and Fischer, 2002), and so-called work integrated learning is not always well integrated with education on campus (Martin, 1998). Ontario college staff state that their baccalaureates integrate theory and practice and integrate classroom and workplace-based education. At least some Ontario college baccalaureates aim to do this through a heavy reliance on project work.

The historical examples of the restructuring of practical knowledge are useful to counter the common understanding that the direction of development is from pure disciplinary theory advanced by universities to applied vocational practice transmitted by colleges. It also opens a distinctive role for colleges in codifying, restructuring and systematising rules and procedures of practice. Such a role is likely to be particularly valuable in fields which do not have a strong institution to systematise practice such as an occupational association, trade association, regulatory body or sponsoring government department. But the elaboration of that role is the subject of another study.

References

American Psychological Association (2016) *Authentic Assessment: Principles, Practices, and Issues* [Online], PsycINFO Database Record. Available at http://psycnet.apa.org/record/1992-29762-001 (Accessed 24 March 2018).

Bernstein, B. [1996] (2000) *Pedagogy, Symbolic Control, and Identity: Theory, Research and Critique*, revised Edition, Lanham, MD, Rowman & Littlefield Publishers, Inc.

Büttner, J. (2017) 'Shooting with ink', in Valleriani, M. (ed.), *The Structures of Practical Knowledge*, Gewerbestrasse, Switzerland, Springer, pp. 115–166.

Collier, A. [1997] (2003) 'Unhewn demonstrations', *Radical Philosophy*, no. 81, pp. 22–26, reprinted in Collier, A. (ed.) (2003) *In Defence of Objectivity*, London, Routledge, pp. 37–45.

Co-Operative Education and Work-Integrated Learning Canada (2018) *Co-Operative Education Definition* [Online]. Available at www.cewilcanada.ca/coop-defined.html (Accessed 24 March 2018).

Edward, N. S. (2002) 'The role of laboratory work in engineering education: Student and staff perceptions', *International Journal of Electrical Engineering Education*, vol. 39, no. 1, pp. 11–19.

Eisenstein, E. L. [1979] (1997) *The Printing Press as an Agent of Change: Communications and Cultural Transformations in Early Modern Europe*, vols. 1 and 2, Cambridge, Cambridge University Press.

Hucke, L. and Fischer, H. E. (2002) 'The link of theory and practice in traditional and in computer-based university laboratory experiments', in Psillos, D. and Niedderer, H. (eds.), *Teaching and Learning in the Science Laboratory*, Science & Technology Education Library, vol. 16, Dordrecht, Springer.

Husserl, E. [1990] (1970) *Logical Investigations*, vol. 1, London, Routledge & Kegan Paul.

Klein, U. (2017) 'Hybrid experts', in Valleriani, M. (ed.), *The Structures of Practical Knowledge*, Gewerbestrasse, Switzerland, Springer, pp. 287–306.

Lefèvre, W. (2017) 'Architectural knowledge', in Valleriani, M. (ed.), *The Structures of Practical Knowledge*, Gewerbestrasse, Switzerland, Springer, pp. 247–269.

Long, P. O. (2011) *Artisan/Practitioners and the Rise of the New Sciences, 1400–1600*, Corvallis, Oregon State University Press.

Long, P. O. (2015) 'Trading zones in early modern Europe', *Isis*, vol. 106, no. 4, pp. 840–847.

Long, P. O. (2017) 'Multi-tasking "pre-professional" architect/engineers and other bricolagic practitioners as key figures in the elision of boundaries between practice and learning in sixteenth-century Europe: Some Roman examples', in Valleriani, M. (ed.), *The Structures of Practical Knowledge*, Gewerbestrasse, Switzerland, Springer, pp. 223–246.

Martin, E. (1998) 'Conceptions of workplace university education', *Higher Education Research & Development*, vol. 17, no. 2, pp. 191–205.

Merrill, E. M. (2017) Pocket-size architectural notebooks and the codification of practical knowledge, in Valleriani, M. (ed.), *The Structures of Practical Knowledge*, Gewerbestrasse, Switzerland, Springer, pp. 21–54.

Moodie, G. (2016) *Universities, Disruptive Technologies, and Continuity in Higher Education: The Impact of Information Revolutions*, New York, Palgrave Macmillan.

Queen's Printer for Ontario (2017) *Post-Secondary Education Choice and Excellence Act, 2000*, S.O. 2000, c. 36, Sched [Online]. Available at www.ontario.ca/laws/statute/00p36 (Accessed 24 March 2018).

Skolnik, M. L. (2016a) 'Situating Ontario's colleges between the American and European models for providing opportunity for the attainment of baccalaureate degrees in applied fields of study', *Canadian Journal of Higher Education*, vol. 46, no. 1, pp. 38–56.

Skolnik, M. L. (2016b) 'How do quality assurance systems accommodate the differences between academic and applied higher education?', *Higher Education*, vol. 71, no. 3, pp. 361–378.

Valleriani, M. (ed.) (2017a) *The Structures of Practical Knowledge*, Gewerbestrasse, Switzerland, Springer.

Valleriani, M. (2017b) 'Foreword', in Valleriani, M. (ed.), *The Structures of Practical Knowledge*, Gewerbestrasse, Switzerland, Springer, pp. v–viii.

Valleriani, M. (2017c) 'The epistemology of practical knowledge', in Valleriani, M. (ed.), *The Structures of Practical Knowledge*, Gewerbestrasse, Switzerland, Springer, pp. 1–19.

Wheelahan, L., Moodie, G., Skolnik, M. L., Liu, Q., Adam, E. G., and Simpson, D. (2017) *CAAT Baccalaureates: What Has Been Their Impact on Students and Colleges?* [Online], Toronto: Centre for the Study of Canadian and International Higher Education, OISE-University of Toronto. Available at www.academia.edu/34112325/CAAT_baccalaureates_What_has_been_their_impact_on_students_and_colleges (Accessed 24 March 2018).

Young, M. (2006) 'Reforming the further education and training curriculum: An international perspective curriculum', in Young, M. and Gamble, J. (ed.), *Knowledge, Curriculum and Qualifications for South African Further Education*, Cape Town, Human Sciences Research Council, pp. 46–63., www.hsrcpress.ac.za/

Chapter 11

Problems and challenges of full-time and school-based VET in Germany

Thomas Deissinger

Introduction

In the area of VET (vocational education and training), there is growing pressure that VET should not only produce portable skills for the labour market, but also enable individuals to progress to higher education (HE). The functionality of VET qualifications and underlying pathways is therefore embedded within a more general debate on flexibility and permeability within education systems. This includes the general function of different pathways (e.g. workplace learning in the dual system vs. full-time vocational education in schools or colleges) but also the notion of 'hybrid qualifications' (HQ) and, with it, 'functional diversification' of VET. HQ, in political and pedagogical terms, are obviously rather under-represented in the German VET context, while Anglo-Saxon countries, but also Switzerland or Austria, either place stronger emphasis on 'progression routes', or have deliberately undertaken reforms in this area. In Germany, full-time VET serves a number of functions within the VET system. This variety will be outlined and two essential characteristics of full-time courses in this country will be identified: (1) the fact that they only partly have a skill formation function with respect to occupational labour markets against the preponderance of the dual apprenticeship system, and (2) that their contribution to permeability mostly consists in the provision of the same qualifications as those in general secondary education (e.g. Abitur – the university entrance qualification), which also means that they do not deliver vocationally based HQs in the first place. Against this background, it seems that we also need a specific theoretical understanding of what 'full-time' and/ or 'school-based' means, especially in relation to the dual system and the typical 'occupational' orientation within the German VET system.

The location of full-time VET within the German education system

General overview

Looking at VET as a 'system' requires differentiation between 'structure' and 'function' of the respective system architecture in a given country. Although it seems problematic to use the notion of a well-organised entity for existing social systems in general, or for education systems in particular (including the non-systemic character of the so-called dual system in Germany), it makes sense to stick to the term 'system' for pragmatic reasons. System theory helps us to understand the relationship between sub-systems in a given society, their interaction, their specific working principles and the way in which they reveal a 'difference' between themselves and their environment (Luhmann and Schorr, 1979). When looking at VET as a system, the various levels on which it works become relevant. VET systems are not solely depictable on the 'macro level' (normally associated with institutions, structural features and responsibilities of the various stakeholders), but need be understood in their specific pedagogical and/or didactical quality. Kell (2006) differentiates between four system levels, i.e. 'macro', 'exo', 'meso' and 'microsystem'. In the case of VET, 'macro' and 'micro' stand for the structural framework and the learning processes, while 'exo' indicates that there are strong determining systems 'around' the VET systems, in particular the employment system and the (higher) education system. Finally, 'meso' refers to the institutions in which vocational learning processes takes place, e.g. schools or companies or partnerships of these two (Kell, 2006, p. 460). It is evident that the links and the interdependences between these system levels give a VET system a distinctive shape and quality in relation to other educational sub-systems.

Young people not going to university in Germany traditionally undertake apprenticeships in the dual system which is characterised by the notion of 'recognised qualifications' based on the Vocational Training Act (Greinert, 1994; Deissinger, 1996). The dual system is a major pathway into skilled employment and also a crucial element of workforce development for many companies. Being virtually an apprenticeship system its core element is qualifying young people in an 'occupation' (Deissinger, 1998, 2010; Deissinger and Breuing, 2014), although it also opens up formalised progression to further training (such as the 'Meister'). There are a number of historical and cultural reasons for calling it the 'centrepiece of vocational education and training in the Federal Republic' (Raggatt, 1988, p. 166), which can still be seen when looking at the statistics of VET. In 2015, some 1.4 million young people were receiving initial training in the dual system, while some 1.1 million attended to a vocational school outside the apprenticeship system (Statistisches Bundesamt, 2017a, p. 26; Statistisches Bundesamt, 2017b, p. 18).

Besides state regulation the dual system also contains the sphere of 'public responsibility', with trade unions, employer organisations and chambers acting as stakeholders and, in the case of chambers, supervising and examining bodies. This principle of self-government goes back to the ancient guild system. As it never wholly disappeared in the process of industrialisation, it has basically survived as a cultural pattern. The Craft Act of 1897 contributed to the foundations of the corporatist framework still typical of the dual system (Deissinger, 1996) as it led to a revival of the guild system and stipulated chambers as self-governing organisations for the craft sector. Therefore, in Germany, there is a 'long-standing and highly regulated participation of business/industry in training' in the initial training sector, which is certainly 'an outstanding feature of the German system' (Noah and Eckstein, 1988, p. 62). At the same time in schools, this system architecture differs fundamentally from full-time VET: firstly, companies are not involved systematically in VET; and, secondly, governmental regulation is mostly located on the federal state level, due to the German constitution which forbids involvement of the federal government in educational affairs.

One of the indicators of a gradual weakening of the position of company-based training within Germany's educational architecture is the rise of young people entering special transition programmes (Übergangssystem) or opting for vocational courses in full-time VET which traditionally have been a more or less ancillary system to the dual system when it comes to skill formation (Deissinger, 2007; Dobischat et al., 2009; Seeber and Michaelis, 2015). Both in comparison with entries into HE and with participants in non-company-based formal training, the dual system has always been considered to be the main destination for school leavers. However, this situation has changed, since more students in Germany now enter HE than new apprentices in the dual system or students in full-time VET. In 2016, some 480,000 apprentices embarked on their training in the dual system while some 511,000 young people began their studies in HE (BMBF, 2017, p. 45).

The following chart (see Figure 11.1) shows the positioning of full-time VET within the education system in Germany.

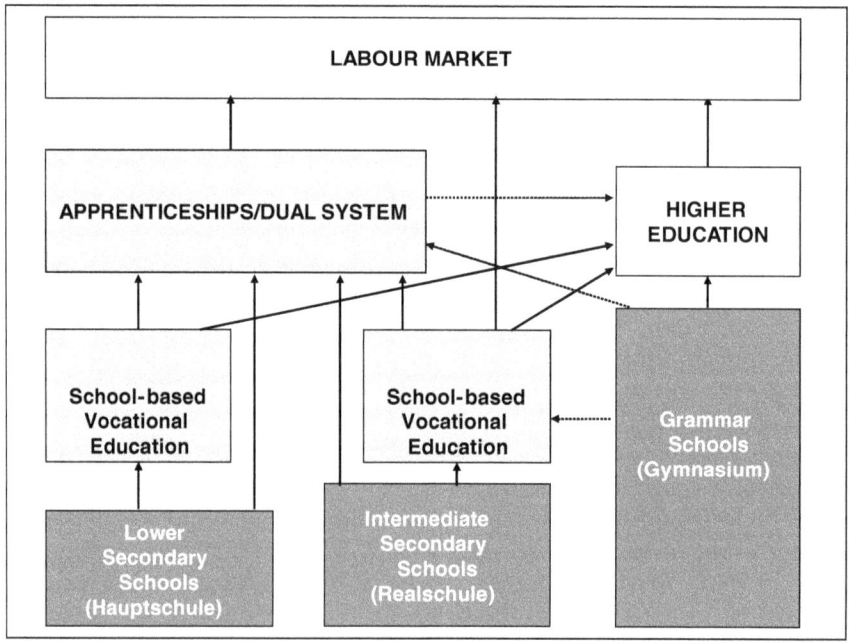

Figure 11.1 The German education system's own chart, for a comparable source see e.g. MKJS Baden-Württemberg, 2014, p. 6f.

Progression routes in the chart indicate three *major modes of 'student traffic'* (Harris et al., 2005):

* Moving from general secondary education to VET
* Moving within the VET system between full-time VET and the dual system
* Moving from the VET system to higher education.

The *dotted lines* indicate that these are *non-traditional traffic routes*: this means that only a small number of school leavers from the grammar schools find their way straight to the apprenticeship system, while this way is quite common from the highest level of the full-time VET sector (vocational high school), which provides the full university entrance qualification. Also, moving from the apprenticeship system into HE is only possible once graduates of dual training already possess a university entrance qualification – although they can embark on studies at a university of applied sciences with the so-called 'Fachhochschulreife' (which is mainly achieved in the VET sector, not in general education). The *continuous lines* stand for the *conventional pathways*, which include direct entry into apprenticeships from lower and intermediate general education, as well as progressing from higher secondary VET in schools into HE. All these pathways nowadays have come under pressure with academic drift (Deissinger and Ott, 2016; Deissinger and Gonon, 2016), i.e. the aspirations of young people and their parents to enter a grammar school after year four (i.e. at the age of ten). In Germany, academisation can be observed as early as in the 1960s. Between 1965 and 1990, the share of school leavers with an Abitur rose from some 7 per cent to 27 per cent (Jacob and Solga, 2015, p. 163). The recent academic drift particularly materialises in the concept of the Gemeinschaftsschule in the federal state of Baden-Württemberg (a kind of comprehensive secondary school merging the lower and the intermediate secondary school) where objectives such as permeability (Durchlässigkeit) and equality of opportunities (Chancengleichheit) are the underlying pedagogical and, more to the point, political motives (Bohl and Meissner, 2013). Also, transferring from primary school to secondary school is much more open than in former decades and 'meritocratic' attitudes of parents have become stronger, which explains recent educational reforms which have been unfavourable to the lower secondary schools (Neugebauer, 2010).

We will discuss this later in this paper, as it is closely associated with the high level of diversity within the full-time VET system. This latter certainly is complicated by the fact that the federal states in Germany regulate school-based VET so that one may assume that the country has an even more diversified structure than what has developed in institutional terms due to a kind of double function of VET as it is perceived in the German context. This means that VET is not exclusively awarding labour market relevant qualifications, but also serves educational aspirations of young people who want to proceed to a higher level in the educational hierarchy (Deissinger et al., 2006).

Classification of full-time vocational schools and school-based training outside the dual system

Against this background, we can point out what may be called the *functional diversity of full-time VET* (Zabeck, 1985; Deissinger et al., 2006; Feller, 2002, 2004; Dobischat et al., 2009; Seeber and Michaelis, 2015). It is possible to distinguish *six sub-types of vocational schools/courses* in Germany (with only the first constituting the dual apprenticeship system):

I   Part-time vocational schools which provide underpinning theoretical knowledge and general education for apprentices in the dual system (Berufsschulen)
II Full-time schools that qualify young people in so-called 'school occupations', mainly 'assistant occupations', based on federal state law (Berufsfachschulen, Berufskollegs) – These types of schools account for 6.7% of entrants to school-based VET in Germany and an additional 10.2% who obtain a HQ (BiBB, 2017, p. 197)
III Full-time schools that provide skill formation for young people via so-called 'school occupations' based on the Vocational Training Act (Berufsfachschulen) – these types of schools account for just 2.1% of entrants to school-based VET in Germany (BiBB, 2017, p. 197)
IV School-based formalised training leading to a nationally recognised qualification in the health and human services sector (hospital nurses, nurses for the elderly, physiotherapists) (Schulen des Gesundheitswesens) – this is the largest category of school-based training and accounts for 81% of VET entrants in the school-based system (BiBB, 2017, p. 197)
V   Full-time courses within the 'transition system' (mostly aiming at vocational preparation and/or bridging general education and apprenticeships) (Berufsvorbereitungsjahr and similar courses)[1]
VI Full-time vocational schools that lead to educational qualifications (lower secondary school standard, intermediate secondary school standard, university of applied sciences entry qualification, general university entry qualification, e.g. in Wirtschaftsgymnasien) – these schools/courses partly provide for the academic aspirations of young people, though they also may lead into an apprenticeship.

The categories indicate that 'full-time VET' in Germany is a term which only partly describes the character of these educational institutions correctly. In fact, it is necessary to distinguish *two major types overarching the above-mentioned categories*. Only a proportion of courses (namely categories II, III and IV) work as full-time VET in the sense that the objective of attendance is actually training and with it achieving a labour market relevant qualification. I therefore suggest to name category VI *'full-time VET in a narrow sense'*, since courses here neither contain substantial practical periods nor the participation of companies as young people reach out for higher school qualifications. In contrast, *'full-time*

VET in a wider sense' means (categories II, III and IV) that schools play a dominant role in the skill formation process, or that learning exclusively takes place
in the classroom and in workshops or workplaces in the school building, or that
it is physically and institutionally linked up with a VET school (e.g. a hospital).

Apart from these school-based courses, the transition system (category V)
which 'offers young people an opportunity to improve their individual chances
of gaining training' (Federal Ministry of Education and Research, 2017, p. 60)
is a heterogeneous catch-all for those striving to become an apprentice, but also
for school leavers who are uncertain about their futures and drop-outs from
school. Here, migrants and young men make up the majority of participants.
Another feature of the transition system is that there is school-based provision, company-based internships (called 'entry qualifications') and vocational
preparation and orientation courses offered by private training providers. The
number of young people entering this sub-system of VET has risen between
2015 and 2016, also due to the widening of programmes for young refugees and
asylum seekers. It is especially the school-based 'vocational preparation year' or
'pre-vocational year' that has become more important recently. However, as a
category, it is not really an unequivocal part of full-time VET (Federal Ministry
of Education and Research, 2017, p. 60; for more details on the transition system, see also Schmidt, 2011).

The health sector (category IV) with its non-academic health and care occupations (Zöller, 2012) is a particularly interesting example of the second major
type. The reason is that most of these occupations formally neither belong to
the dual system (although the training is dual/alternating) nor to the 'normal'
pathways of progression in full-time vocational schools leading to educational
qualifications (e.g. the Abitur). These schools are only partly a sub-category
of the full-time VET system, under the auspices of the federal states, due to
the fact that training in these occupations is not exclusively school-based, as the
participation of organisations, e.g. hospitals, is required – which means this
sub-system resembles, at least partly, the learning configuration of the dual
apprenticeship system. However, in the official statistics, health, health-related
and human services occupations are not always different from category II.
This corresponds with the fact that roughly half of the student population of
these institutions get their training in 50 occupations under federal state law,
including, e.g. nurse assistants or child care specialists/nursery nurses, while
only 17 occupations are based on nationally uniform regulations and curricula. Training times stretch from 12 to 36 months (the latter mainly for
the nationally regulated health occupations such as nurse or physiotherapist)
(BiBB, 2017, p. 200). In fact, health, health-related and human services occupations are distributed in various ways among three sub-sectors of school-
based VET (Bonse-Rohmann, 2015; Zöller, 2012; Feller, 2004): full-time VET
in Berufsfachschulen (mostly based on federal state law); special health schools
(normally attached to hospitals); and well-established health-related occupations (health provision) trained in the dual system (Zöller, 2012, p. 7). In the

latter category, we find occupations such as the medical assistant (to medical doctors), which is one of the most frequently selected occupations among young women (BMBF, 2017, p. 34).

Categories II, III and IV represent the essential sub-systems in full-time VET outside the dual system. This is especially the case for social and child care, as well as for beauticians, which represent a sub-category under the auspices of the federal states and the respective school laws (Friese, 2017, pp. 35). However, it is sometimes quite difficult to relate numbers of students entering the various courses to these different streams of VET, especially when we look at full-time VET based on federal state law and the transition system, since there are intersections between the two, e.g. the vocational full-time school building upon the lower secondary school certificate and leading young people to an intermediate school qualification (Berufsfachschule). This category of school also is the one with the most heterogeneous course structure (Feller, 2002; Feller, 2004).

The three following charts/tables depict the rough shares and the underlying streams of (mostly) full-time VET in Germany under the heading 'Berufsfachschulen'. The common feature of those among these schools that deliver portable qualifications for employment is that they either are not offered in the dual system or belong to a specific 'family' of occupations, such as health, health-related and human services occupations. Besides, as already mentioned, there are some occupations, called 'assistant qualifications' which traditionally are trained in vocational full-time schools. Another sub-group consists of occupations that can also be trained in the dual system, e.g. beautician (Feller, 2004, p. 49); see Figure 11.2.

In terms of numbers, Tables 11.1, 11.2 and 11.3 illustrate the most frequently trained occupations in full-time VET, either based on national or federal state law. One can conclude from these figures that there is quite a large segment of school-based occupations outside the dual system, while the sector of health, health-related and human services occupations is a kind of 'dual system' outside the apprenticeship system, which is treated as a separate sphere of VET (because it is school-based but not full-time) and which we will touch on but not discuss in more detail in this chapter. In contrast to these occupations those based on the Vocational Training Act or the Craft Regulation Act (normally training occupations in the dual system) are quite negligible (with falling numbers in the past few years and due to a more accessible training market in the apprenticeship system).[2] This latter fact once again underlines the overall importance of the dual system, providing training in nearly all of the state recognised training occupations, and reveals that full-time VET in many of its sub-categories has a compensatory (transitional) or complementary function in relation to apprenticeships (Deissinger, 2010). It needs to be recalled that the apprenticeship system with its 330 training occupations takes up nearly 500,000 young people annually which accounts for some 1.4 million young people in training (BMBF, 2017, p. 45).

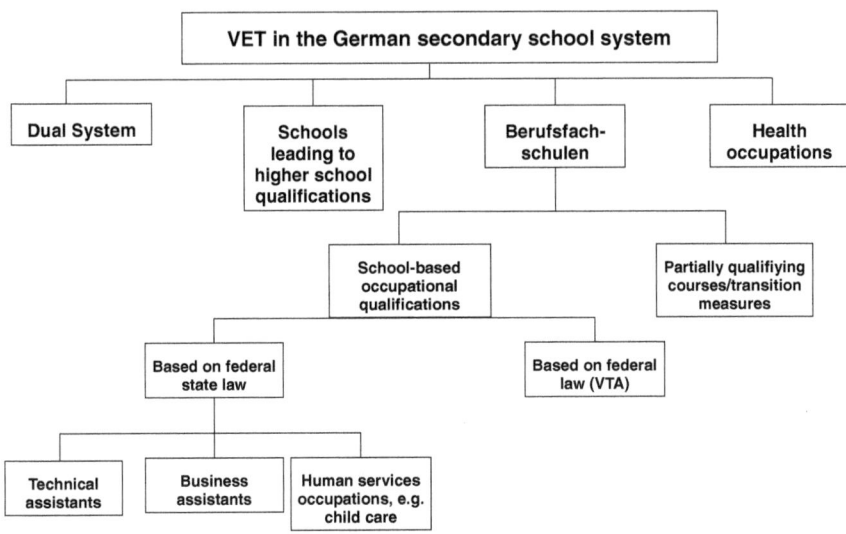

Figure 11.2 Full-time VET and school-based VET in 'Berufsfachschulen' own chart based on Feller, 2002, p. 140

It needs to be added that the meaning of 'federal law' stretches beyond the scope of the Vocational Training Act or the Craft Regulation Act (the joiner, e.g., may be trained full-time though numbers are very low), but – in the case of health occupations – is associated with the Health Care Act (Krankenpflegegesetz) which requires a specific pattern of training of normally three years in the case of nurses (now called Gesundheits–und Krankenpfleger/in).[3] Another notable feature is that those school occupations (e.g. business assistant) that are not health-related or which do not offer alternative training through the dual system under the same denomination (e.g. office management assistant) are comparatively weak in terms of numbers. It can also be seen that many school occupations are dominated by female students. Generally, the share of VET taking place in schools in relation to the dual apprenticeship system has been stable since 2005. In 2016, it roughly stands at 30 per cent against 70 per cent but differs enormously between individual federal states: in most of the East German states, there is more occupational training in schools than on average countrywide. On the other hand, states such as Bavaria or Hamburg have lower shares, which generally spread between 18.8 per cent in Bremen to 43 per cent in Berlin. The health sector is the largest sub-category of school-based occupational training, reaching from roughly 70 per cent in Rheinland-Pfalz up to nearly 99 per cent of school-based vocational trainees in the Saarland (BiBB, 2017, p. 198).

Table 11.1 Major sectors with school-based entrants in 2016

	Entrants to VET programmes	Percentage of students who are female
School occupations based on federal state law without health sector	14,463	55.6
School occupations based on federal law	4,448	59.4
Health, health-related and human services occupations (federal and federal state law)*	174,380	77.9
School-based occupations leading to a hybrid qualification	21,897	40.8
Total	215,288	-

Source: based on data from BIBB (2017)

Table 11.2 Most important occupations in school-based VET in 'Berufsfachschulen' 2015/16 based on *federal law* (including some of the major health-related occupations)

Occupation	Entrants in 2015/16	Percentage of students who are female
Elderly care worker*	23,612	74.8
Nurse (m/f)*	22,892	79.2
Physiotherapist	8,346	60.6
Pharmaceutical assistant	3,756	89.5
Ergotherapist	3,610	88.8
Beautician**	1,106	99.7
Office management assistant**	926	55.1

NB: * health occupation, not strictly full-time, but basically dual/** also trained in the dual system

Source: based on data from BIBB (2017)

Table 11.3 Most important occupations in school-based VET in 'Berufsfachschulen' 2015/16 based on *federal state law* (including some of the major health-related occupations)

Occupation	Entrants in 2015/16	Percentage of students who are female
Nursery nurse*	24,750	80.9
Social care assistant	17,055	78.1
Social pedagogical assistant	12,723	83.7
Elderly care assistant*	7,718	77.9
Information engineering assistant	3,548	5.5
Nurse assistant*	3,486	77.1

NB: * health or related occupations not strictly full-time, but basically dual

Source: based on data from BIBB (2017)

The marginal relevance of hybrid qualifications

Category VI among the VET schools in Germany leads us to take a closer look at educational qualifications within the VET system and also HQs. Schools in this category are quite strong in some federal states and focus on progression as far as HE. In 2015/16, the number of students in vocational schools in Germany (including apprentices in the dual system) stood at some 2.5 million, among which Berufsfachschulen in general accounted for the largest proportion besides the part-time vocational school (some 17.3%). Apart from the occupational courses in some of these schools, full-time VET (in a narrow sense) here functions as a catalyst for the 'pathway of the second chance' for young people without higher school certificates, which often means helping school leavers to enter the dual system more smoothly after attending a vocational course at a Berufsfachschule or a Berufskolleg. It is of considerable interest that nearly all certificates opening access to universities of applied science (Fachhochschulreife) are achieved in full-time vocational schools. Also, in 2016, more than 56,000 Abitur certificates (full university entrance qualifications) were obtained in vocational full-time schools nationwide (which accounts for some 16 per cent of all certificates of this kind) (Statistisches Bundesamt, 2017c, p. 3ff.). In this context, schools such as Berufsoberschulen (leading to a general university entrance qualification), Fachoberschulen and Berufskollegs (advanced vocational schools leading to admission to universities of applied science) and vocational high schools (leading to a general university entrance qualification) are the most relevant institutions when it comes to opening progression routes (Schindler, 2014). There is however a link with the dual system, too, since HE entrance qualifications in Germany are often used to access a high level apprenticeship placement, e.g. in banking, insurance or other attractive commercial occupations (Pilz, 2009).

Therefore, there is in fact a significant contribution of full-time VET to academisation, since it is possible to proceed from one stage in the VET school system (e.g. lower secondary school certificate) to the next one (e.g. intermediate secondary school certificate). In 1975, there were just some 5,155 graduates from vocational high schools in the federal state of Baden-Württemberg who obtained an Abitur, but in 2016, their number had risen to 18,646. Lower secondary school qualifications rose in a similar way, i.e. from nearly zero in 1975 to 3,806 in 2016, while intermediate school qualifications have been declining since 1985, from 13,063 to 9,705 due to a more open general secondary school system.[4] However, academisation in this context does not necessarily mean setting up HQ as a key way of establishing permeability between vocational and higher education.

In Germany, the concept of 'hybridity' or 'hybrid' or 'double qualifications', respectively, is historically associated with the educational reform in the late 1960s and especially the 1970s. Inspired by the Social Democrats, one of the educational objectives emanating from the policy discourse was to integrate, both in organisational and curricular terms, VET and general education and to assign parity of esteem to culturally and pedagogically different educational pathways. The term 'Doppelqualifikationen' (double qualifications) was used particularly within the scope of this ambitious reform period, and it marks certainly one of the most fundamental debates in the area of vocational education theory in Germany, since it was linked to political objectives such as 'equality of opportunities', 'emancipation', 'democratisation' and, above all, a more state-orientated and school-based type of vocational learning (Zabeck, 2009, p. 659). The term itself was initially introduced by the Bund-Länder Commission for Educational Planning and Research Promotion (BLK) in 1974 (Zimmermann, 1982, p. 1). Subsequently, the expression 'Doppelqualifikation' became an important component of the educational debate in Germany (Bojanowski, 1996, p. 533; Kutscha, 2003).

When it comes to HQs today, we need to distinguish between those acquired in the dual system and those obtainable in a vocational full-time school, such as a Berufsfachschule or a Berufskolleg (vocational college in the following). HQs in the dual system are nearly non-existent in the German VET system (Deissinger et al., 2013b) – which is quite different from Switzerland, where the 'vocational Baccalaureat' has proved to become a popular amendment to occupational qualifications, a situation in this country which underlines the even more significant role the dual system plays in the Swiss society (Deissinger and Gonon, 2016). However, there is a (small) segment within the vocational full-time school system in Germany which delivers HQ (Deissinger et al., 2013b). These institutions offer 'combinations of accredited general (academic) and vocational learning and attainment that formally qualify for entrance to higher education and the labour market' (Deissinger et al., 2013a, p. 8). HQs, especially in Germany, may be considered as a tool leading to a kind of generalisation of vocational education. Their relevance and importance is underlined by their function within the education system to open up vocational pathways into HE (though in most of the cases, only into the universities of applied science).

According to the official German training statistics (BiBB, 2017), school-based HQs are reported to be the second strongest category among school-based VET courses and qualifications behind the health sector, although the number of new entrants declined from some 29,000 in 2005 to some 22,000 in 2016 and eight out of 16 federal states do not offer HQs at all (BiBB, 2017, pp. 194, 198). One reason is that the vocational colleges (Berufskollegs) in Baden-Württemberg are now counted in another category, i.e. as 'schools leading to a higher school qualification'. This means that since 2008, the entrance qualification for HE has become the 'regular' qualification in these schools (Breuing et al., 2017; Deissinger and Breuing, 2016).

Against this background, the Berufskolleg (BK) is an interesting example of school-based hybridity in Germany (Deissinger, 2007; Deissinger et al., 2006; Deissinger and Ruf, 2006). The Berufskolleg may be described as a secondary post-compulsory institution and an alternative to the later years of the grammar school in general education. It is open to students, normally aged between 16 and 18, with a medium-level school-leaving qualification. Students enter either from the two-year vocational full-time school (Berufsfachschule), which takes up graduates from the lower secondary schools normally aged 15 or 16, or from the tenth year of the lower secondary schools (Werkrealschule) or from the two higher streams in the general education system (Gymnasium or Realschule). The vocational college is offered in a number of occupational fields but the largest proportion can be assigned to the commercial vocational college (Statistisches Landesamt Baden-Württemberg, 2017, p. 3). The commercial vocational college II (BK II), where the commercial assistant qualification is obtainable, is a good example for the polytechnic/university of applied sciences entrance qualification being combined with the assistant certificate. The BK II is based on the commercial vocational college I (BK I). Both the BK I and the BK II last one year each. Only students who have finished the BK I successfully (with adequate average grades) are allowed to attend the BK II. Until some ten years ago, students who had attended the elective mathematics class at the BK I could go for an entrance qualification for universities of applied sciences which then led to an HQ after completion of the BK II after attending even more additional subjects (for more details, see Deissinger et al., 2013b; Deissinger, 2007).

Within the scope of a comparative Leonardo research project on HQ in Germany, Austria, England and Denmark (Deissinger et al., 2013a), we found that 'academic aspirations' of students with an intermediate secondary school leaving certificate are best satisfied by the vocational college. Another very important motive of students for the attendance of a vocational college seems enhancing their own prospects of successfully entering apprenticeship training. Most graduates of this vocational full-time school traditionally aspire to take up subsequent vocational training in a company, i.e. through the dual system. On the other hand, the vocational college does not stand for leading young people to the achievement of a portable labour market relevant occupational qualification outside the dual system. This becomes clear when looking at the relevance of this function of the vocational college from the point of view of students (Deissinger et al., 2013a) The major reason certainly is that assistant qualifications are not acknowledged by companies, be it for subsequent training or for recognition of prior training. These empirical findings were confirmed by a smaller follow-up study, which even more came out with the fact that the most important motivation to attend a vocational college consists in the option to go to a university of applied science, closely followed by taking up a commercial apprenticeship in the dual system (Breuing et al., 2017).

Interview partners in the comparative Leonardo project argue that there is generally only 'modest interest' in HQs on the part of young people which could be a major obstacle for intensifying and widening HQ pathways within the dual system (this was especially an aspect put forward by teachers and headmasters). It is held that apprentices who prepare for HE while following a VET programme obviously face an additional workload, which can become too high a burden for apprentices. Another interesting argument points to the fact that apprentices normally are happy with their vocational perspective, especially when considering that continuing training can lead to a technician or a master craftsman qualification, and people can open up a business without passing through an academic pathway (Deissinger and Breuing, 2014). The strong position of the craft sector in the dual system (with a quarter of all apprentices) certainly explains this common understanding of occupational careers. Other arguments brought forward against HQs in the interviews were: the lack of information about HQ, complaints about the reliability and transparency due to the major say of federal states in educational matters, the fear of rising public expenditure for VET due to HQ and the fear on the side of companies of losing trained employees after completion of their apprenticeships (for more details, see Deissinger et al., 2013b, p. 130).

HQs in Germany and their underlying educational programmes are on the one hand located in the vocational context, but on the other hand remain mostly separated from apprenticeship training (Frommberger, 2012, p. 187), which emphasises their 'scientific' character. Therefore, hybridity which is not linked to vocational training in a narrow sense, as is the case in Germany, has a stabilising impact on the dual system. Companies in Germany, at least in some major occupational fields, clearly prefer recruiting high quality school leavers from upper secondary education to other applicants for an apprenticeship. Graduates from the Berufskolleg in Baden-Württemberg now increasingly belong to this group, and they are perceived by employers as having a strong aspiration towards a company-based career (Deissinger and Ruf, 2006).

Reasons why HQs (still) have a comparatively inferior status in the German VET system (Deissinger et al., 2013b, p. 135) may be summarised as follows:

• The apprenticeship system is still the major and most accepted route into employment for non-academically inclined school leavers, and demand for apprentices on the side of employers is high.
• The school-based (full-time) VET system is seen as offering a number of opportunities for young people coming from the lower and middle tracks of the school system to proceed as high as to universities or (in even more cases) to the (formerly so-called) polytechnics or universities of applied sciences.
• Besides, there now exists an attractive 'dual system' on the academic level, namely the so-called 'vocational academies' or (as they now are called) 'universities of cooperative education' or 'dual universities' (Hippach-Schneider and Schneider, 2016; Deissinger, 2000; Deissinger and Ott, 2016, p. 275).
• Since the HE system is only coupled with school-based VET, and pathways from work to HE have been created recently to compensate for the missing links between the vocational and the academic sphere, there does not seem to exist a strong inclination on the side of politicians to establish more 'direct' progression routes.

Conclusion

An article focussing on the differences between school-based VET in Australia and Germany identified some interesting differences between the two countries, but also noted some similarities (Deissinger et al., 2006). Both countries are facing common problems with the traditional apprenticeship model, which include the difficulty of attracting young people into specific occupations and also the reluctance of some employers to make the necessary investment in the system. In order to increase the labour market chances of young people and to address skill needs, both countries have installed initiatives at both federal and national levels to improve enrolments. In this context, one way of addressing the lack of apprentice places has been to offer vocational courses full-time although this alternative lacks legitimacy in the eyes of companies. While in Germany the apprenticeship model still functions as the core of the VET system, gaining vocational qualifications in schools or colleges is a widespread possibility in Anglophone countries, including the interesting option to start with VET in general education (Polesel and Clarke, 2011). In Germany, as we have explained in this chapter, full-time VET mostly aims at obtaining educational qualifications leading young people into progression routes as far as HE, whereas school-based training in Germany (which does not need to be full-time in a narrow sense of the word) only covers specific groups of occupations, such as health, child care/nursery nurses and the so-called 'assistant occupations'. The deeply entrenched nature of the dual system in Germany seems one of the reasons behind this system logic. One of the disadvantages of full-time VET certainly is its 'confusing' system architecture, with different formal responsibilities. However, some of the occupational courses are highly relevant for the German labour market. This is especially the case for services occupations in specific segments of the economy, such as health and child care. In terms of assessing the quality and relevance of the German full-time VET system, it seems necessary to point out this invaluable social and economic contribution of VET outside the dual system, together with those schools that make sure that young people do not get stuck in dead end educational roads. However, the fact that there is an ambivalence in the German VET system or, in other words, an ostensible multi-functionality also seems responsible for the relatively weak status of HQ in this country. It is above all the school-based VET system which still seems to oscillate between a clear qualification orientation and the role of schools to bridge the gap between VET and HE.

Notes

1 In 2016, nearly 300,000 young people had to enter a 'measure' in the transition system. Some of these measures traditionally are offered by vocational schools, including the first year of courses in Berufsfachschulen (not fully qualifying) or the Vocational Preparation Year (BMBF, 2017, p. 45; Statistisches Bundesamt, 2017b, p. 24f.).

2 Between 2005 and 2016, the number of entrants fell from some 11,500 down to some 4,500 young people (BiBB, 2017, p. 194f.).

3 See www.gesetze-im-internet.de/krpflg_2004/BJNR144210003.html (Accessed: 12/02/18).
4 See www.statistik-bw.de/BildungKultur/SchulenAllgem/abgaenger_mehrjaehrig.jsp?path=/ BildungKultur/SchulenBerufl/ (Accessed: 13/02/18).

References

Bohl, T. and Meissner, S. (2013) *Expertise Gemeinschaftsschule. Forschungsergebnisse und Handlungsempfehlungen für Baden-Württemberg*, Weinheim, Beltz.

Bojanowski, A. (1996) 'Modelle zur Doppelqualifikation', in Dedering, H. (ed.), *Handbuch zur arbeitsorientierten Bildung*, München, Oldenbourg, pp. 533–559.

Bonse-Rohmann, M. (2015) 'Strukturen, Orientierungen und neuere Entwicklungen der Lehrerinnen-und Lehrerbildung in den beruflichen Fachrichtungen Gesundheit und Pflege', in Pundt, J. and Kälble, K. (eds.), *Gesundheitsberufe und gesundheitsberufliche Bildungskonzepte*, Bremen, Apollon University Press, pp. 165–197.

Breuing, K., Deissinger, Th., and Heck, J. (2017) 'Subjektive Theorien von Schüler/-innen des Kaufmännischen Berufskollegs mit Übungsfirma (BK-ÜFA) in Baden-Württemberg mit Blick auf Kompetenzerleben und berufliche Aspirationen', *Wirtschaft und Erziehung*, vol. 69, no. 2, pp. 63–68.

Bundesinstitut für Berufsbildung (BiBB) (2017) *Datenreport zum Berufsbildungsbericht 2017*, Bonn, BiBB.

Bundesministerium für Bildung und Forschung (BMBF) (2017) *Berufsbildungsbericht 2017*, Bonn, BMBF.

Deissinger, Th. and Ott, M. (2016) 'Tertiarisation of vocational education and training and its implications: Problems and issues in Germany and France', in Bohlinger, S., Dang, T. K. A., and Glatt, M. (eds.), *Education Policy: Mapping the Landscape and Scope*, Frankfurt a.M., Peter Lang, pp. 267–296.

Deissinger, Th. (1996) 'Germany's vocational training act: Its function as an instrument of quality control within a tradition-based vocational training system', *Oxford Review of Education*, vol. 22, no. 3, pp. 317–336.

Deissinger, Th. (1998) *Beruflichkeit als "organisierendes Prinzip" der deutschen Berufsausbildung*, Markt Schwaben, Eusl.

Deissinger, Th. (2000) 'The German "Philosophy" of linking academic and work-based learning in higher education: The case of the "vocational academies"', *Journal of Vocational Education and Training*, vol. 52, no. 4, pp. 609–630.

Deissinger, Th. (2007) '"Making schools practical": Practice firms and their function in the full-time vocational school system in Germany', *Education and Training*, vol. 49, no. 5, pp. 364–379.

Deissinger, Th. (2010) 'Dual System', in Peterson, P., Tierney, R., Baker, E., and McGaw, B. (eds.), *International Encyclopedia of Education*, 3rd Edition, vol. 8, Oxford, Elsevier, pp. 448–454.

Deissinger, Th. and Breuing, K. (2014) 'Recruitment of skilled employees and workforce development in Germany: Practices, challenges and strategies for the future', in Short, T. and Harris, R. (eds.), *Workforce Development: Strategies and Practices*, Singapore, Springer, pp. 281–301.

Deissinger, Th. and Breuing, K. (2016) 'Übungsfirmen an beruflichen Schulen in Deutschland am Beispiel des Berufskollegs Baden-Württemberg: ihr Beitrag zur Praxisorientierung', in Fortmüller, R. (ed.), *Entrepreneurship Erziehung und Gründungsberatung – Beiträge zur Entrepreneurship Erziehung und Gründungsberatung aus ukrainischer, russischer und europäischer Perspektive*, Wien, Manz, pp. 51–60.

Deissinger, Th. and Gonon, Ph. (2016) 'Stakeholders in the German and Swiss vocational educational and training system: Their role in innovating apprenticeships against the background of academisation', *Education and Training*, vol. 58, no. 6, pp. 568–577.

Deissinger, Th. and Ruf, M. (2006) *Übungsfirmen am Kaufmännischen Berufskolleg in Baden-Württemberg. Praxisorientierung vollzeitschulischer Berufsbildung zwischen Anspruch und Wirklichkeit*, Paderborn, Eusl.

Deissinger, Th., Smith, E., and Pickersgill, R. (2006) 'Models of full-time and part-time vocational training for school-leavers: A comparison between Germany and Australia', *International Journal of Training Research*, vol. 4, no. 1, pp. 30–50.

Deissinger, Th. et al. (2013a) *Hybrid Qualifications: Structures and Problems in the Context of European VET Policy*, Bern, Peter Lang.

Deissinger, Th. et al. (2013b) 'Progression from VET into higher education via hybrid qualifications in Germany: Context-policy-problem issues', in Deißinger, Th., Aff, J., Fuller, A., and Jorgensen, C. H. (eds.), *Hybrid Qualifications: Structures and Problems in the Context of European VET Policy*, Bern, Peter Lang, pp. 111–145.

Dobischat, R., Milolaza, A., and Stender, A. (2009) 'Vollzeitschulische Berufsbildung – eine gleichwertige Alternative zur dualen Berufsausbildung', in Zimmer, G. and Dehnbostel, P. (eds.), *Berufsausbildung in der Entwicklung – Positionen und Leitlinien*, Bielefeld, W. Bertelsmann, pp. 127–151.

Federal Ministry of Education and Research (2017) *Report on Vocational Education and Training*, Bonn, BMBF.

Feller, G. (2002) 'Leistungen und Defizite der Berufsfachschule als Bildungsgang mit Berufsabschluss', in Wingens, M. and Sackmann, R. (eds.), *Bildung und Beruf. Ausbildung und berufsstruktureller Wandel in der Wissensgesellschaft*, Weinheim, Juventa, pp. 139–157.

Feller, G. (2004) 'Ausbildungen an Berufsfachschulen – Entwicklungen, Defizite und Chancen', *Berufsbildung in Wissenschaft und Praxis*, vol. 33, no. 4, pp. 48–52.

Friese, M. (2017) 'Care work. Eckpunkte der Professionalisierung und Qualitätsentwicklung in personenbezogenen Dienstleistungsberufen', in Weyland, U. and Reiber, K. (eds.), *Entwicklungen und Perspektiven in den Gesundheitsberufen – aktuelle Handlungs-und Forschungsfelder*, Bielefeld, W. Bertelsmann, pp. 29–49.

Frommberger, D. (2012) 'Von der Berufsbildung in die Hochschulbildung (Dritter Bildungsweg). Eine berufs-und wirtschaftspädagogische Einordnung unter besonderer Berücksichtigung aktueller Rahmenwerke zur Förderung von Übergängen und Durchlässigkeit', *Zeitschrift für Berufs-und Wirtschaftspädagogik*, vol. 108, no. 2, pp. 169–193.

Greinert, W.-D. (1994) *The "German System" of Vocational Training: History, Organization, Prospects*, Baden-Baden, Nomos.

Harris, R., Sumner, R., and Rainey, L. (2005) *Student Traffic: Two-Way Movement between Vocational Education and Training and Higher Education*, Adelaide, NCVER.

Hippach-Schneider, U. and Schneider, V. (2016) *Tertiary Vocational Education in Europe: Examples from Six Education Systems*, Bonn, Federal Institute for Vocational Education and Training.

Jacob, M. and Solga, H. (2015) 'Germany's vocational education and training system in transformation: Changes in the participation of low-and high-achieving youth over time', *European Sociological Review*, vol. 31, pp. 161–171.

Kell, A. (2006) 'Organisation, Recht und Finanzierung der Berufsbildung', in Arnold, R. and Lipsmeier, A. (eds.), *Handbuch der Berufsbildung*, Wiesbaden, VS Verlag, pp. 453–484.

Kutscha, G. (2003) 'Zum Verhältnis von allgemeiner und beruflicher Bildung im Kontext bildungstheoretischer Reformkonzepte – Rückblick und Perspektiven', *Zeitschrift für Berufs-und Wirtschaftspädagogik*, vol. 99, no. 3, pp. 328–349.

Luhmann, N. and Schorr, K.-E. (1979) *Reflexionsprobleme im Erziehungssystem*, Stuttgart, Klett-Cotta.

Ministerium für Kultus, Jugend und Sport Baden-Württemberg (2014) Bildungswege in Baden-Württemberg, Stuttgart, MKjS.

Neugebauer, M. (2010) 'Bildungsungleichheit und Grundschulempfehlung beim Übergang auf das Gymnasium: Eine Dekomposition primärer und sekundärer Herkunftseffekte', *Zeitschrift für Soziologie*, vol. 39, no. 3, pp. 202–214.

Noah, H. J. and Eckstein, M. A. (1988) 'Business and industry involvement with education in Britain, France and Germany', in Lauglo, J. and Lillis, K. (eds.), *Vocationalizing Education: An International Perspective*, Oxford, Pergamon Press, pp. 45–68.

Pilz, M. (2009) 'Why abiturienten do an apprenticeship before going to university: The role of "double qualifications" in Germany', *Oxford Review of Education*, vol. 35, no. 2, pp. 187–204.

Polesel, J. and Clarke, K. (2011) 'The marginalisation of VET in an Australian secondary school', *Journal of Vocational Education and Training*, vol. 63, no. 4, pp. 525–538.

Raggatt, P. (1988) 'Quality control in the dual system of West Germany', *Oxford Review of Education*, vol. 14, no. 2, pp. 163–186.

Schindler, S. (2014) *Wege zur Studienberechtigung – Wege ins Studium? Eine Analyse sozialer Inklusions-und Ablenkungsprozesse*, Wiesbaden, VS Verlag.

Schmidt, C. (2011) *Krisensymptom Übergangssystem: Die nachlassende soziale Inklusionsfähigkeit beruflicher Bildung*, Bielefeld, W. Bertelsmann.

Seeber, S. and Michaelis, C. (2015) 'Zur Entwicklung des Schulberufssystems: eine Analyse im Kontext demographischer Veränderungen und arbeitsmarktbezogener Herausforderungen', *Recht der Jugend und des Bildungswesens*, vol. 63, no. 3, pp. 271–290.

Statistisches Bundesamt (2017a) *Bildung und Kultur. Berufliche Bildung*, Fachserie 11, Reihe 3, Wiesbaden.

Statistisches Bundesamt (2017b) *Bildung und Kultur. Berufliche Schulen*, Schuljahr 2015/2016, Fachserie 11, Reihe 2, Wiesbaden.

Statistisches Bundesamt (2017c) *Bildung und Kultur. Schnellmeldungsergebnisse zu Studienberechtigten der allgemeinbildenden und beruflichen Schulen – vorläufige Ergebnisse*, Abgangsjahr 2016, Fachserie 11, Reihe 1 und 2, Wiesbaden.

Statistisches Landesamt Baden-Württemberg (2017) *Statistik aktuell*, Stuttgart. Available at www.statistik-bw.de (Accessed 24 March 2018).

Zabeck, J. (1985) 'Berufliche Bildung', in Görres-Gesellschaft (ed.), *Staatslexikon Recht – Wirtschaft – Gesellschaft*, 7th Edition, Freiburg, Herder, pp. 669–683.

Zabeck, J. (2009) *Geschichte der Berufserziehung und ihrer Theorie*, Paderborn, Eusl.

Zimmermann, H. (1982) *Doppeltqualifizierende Bildungsgänge. Gesellschaftliche Ursachen für die politische Thematisierung als Reformvorhaben: Probleme, Formen und Perspektiven der Realisierung*, Weinheim, Beltz.

Zöller, M. (2012) 'Qualifizierungswege in den Gesundheitsberufen und aktuelle Herausforderungen', *Berufsbildung in Wissenschaft und Praxis*, vol. 41, no. 6, pp. 6–10.

Part IV

Relationships between further and higher education

Chapter 12

Seeking distinction and addressing inequalities

An analysis of new times for college-based higher education in England

Ann-Marie Bathmaker

Introduction

This chapter examines new times for English further education (FE) colleges in the second decade of the 21st century, focusing specifically on college provision of higher education (HE). What were once termed 'non-university' forms of HE (Teichler, 1988) have long formed part of the landscape of HE, seen as an economically viable means of expanding HE, as well as widening access to a more diverse population (Osborne, 2005). The 2010s have seen intense policy interest among countries across the globe in these more technical and vocational forms of higher level education, as demonstrated in the 2014 OECD review *Skills Beyond School* (OECD, 2014).

In England, technical education at all levels is a key priority identified in the 2017 Industrial Strategy White Paper, which declares bold aspirations for the future:

> We want our technical education system to be as prestigious as higher education in this country, and for it to rival the best systems in the world.
>
> (HM Government, 2017b, p. 102)

A major policy reform programme for technical education (BIS and DfE, 2016a; BIS and DfE, 2016b) sits alongside significant reforms to the whole of the HE system which aim to promote 'quality, competition, choice and diversity across degree level qualifications' (BIS, 2016, p. 26). There is also growing pressure for change to the student funding system for both bachelor's degrees and other forms of HE (Wolf, 2015, 2016). This policy 'ensemble' (Ball, 1993) has major implications for college HE in England.

Overview of this chapter

The first section of the chapter outlines the opportunities and challenges for HE provision that sits at the nexus of HE and VET. The chapter then goes on to present a brief picture of college HE in England at the present time. This is followed by a discussion of policy changes in England in the second half of the 2010s and what issues are raised by these reforms for college HE. Finally, the chapter draws out the implications for distinction and addressing inequalities for colleges in new times.

Opportunities and challenges at the nexus of higher education and VET

In the 21st century, increasing participation in education and training at higher levels is seen as a key mechanism in 'knowledge' economies both to increase national productivity and to raise the economic participation of disadvantaged equity groups (OECD, 2012, 2014; Piketty, 2014). The development of human capital is deemed vital for individuals and for economies, as emphasised by Becker (2006, p. 292):

> This is the 'age of human capital' in the sense that human capital is by far the most important form of capital in modern economies. The economic successes of individuals, and also of whole economies, depends on how extensively and effectively people invest in themselves.

The OECD, in its work on education, stresses human capital as a key driver for tertiary education policy:

> The widespread recognition that tertiary education is a major driver of economic competitiveness in an increasingly knowledge-driven global economy has made high-quality tertiary education more important than ever before. The imperative for countries is to raise higher level employment skills, to sustain a globally competitive research base and to improve knowledge dissemination to the benefit of society.
>
> (OECD, 2008, p. 8)

However, college HE and higher vocational education are located in an ambiguous in-between space (Bathmaker, 2015), at the nexus of separate policy and organisational fields that deal with higher education and vocational education and training (VET) respectively, evident for example in the Bologna (HE) and Copenhagen (VET) processes in the European Union (Powell and Solga, 2010), and further evident in the work of the OECD. The OECD's international review of higher level education in the first decade of the 21st century (OECD, 2008) was deliberately entitled *Tertiary Education for the Knowledge Society* to embrace a diversified HE system that includes 'new types of institutions such as polytechnics, university colleges, or technological institutes' (OECD, 2008, p. 8). In a more recent report however, published in 2014, these new types of institution form part of a programme of reviews of vocational education and training. This later review focuses explicitly on the world of 'post-secondary vocational education and training', with the title *Skills Beyond School*, and the OECD argues that:

> Many professional, technical and managerial jobs require no more than one or two years of career preparation beyond upper secondary level, and some countries have as much as one-quarter of the adult workforce with this type of short-cycle qualification.
>
> (OECD, 2014, p. 21)

While bringing what the OECD calls 'the hidden world of professional education and training' (2014, p. 21) into the public gaze may have important and possibly beneficial effects for the role and status of higher level vocational education, the opportunities and challenges that are created through the shifting positioning of this provision become apparent in research that looks at the evolution of higher vocational education in different countries.

In the 2000s, the possibility of a 'tertiary moment' suggested by the OECD report of 2008 was considered in a collection of studies, based on mainly Anglo-phone countries (Gallacher and Osborne, 2005; Layer, 2005a; Osborne et al., 2004). In a summary of the trends in sub-bachelor college HE (also referred to as short-cycle HE) to be found in these studies, Gallacher and Osborne (2005, p. 196) identify three functions served by college HE: firstly providing vocationally oriented higher education; secondly, increasing participation in HE, particularly through provision that is closely linked to the needs of employers and business; and, thirdly, widening participation to groups who have traditionally been under-represented in HE. They caution that much of this provision 'has traditionally been relatively low status' (p. 195). They also note that there is a tension between the role of short cycle sub-bachelor HE as an exit qualification and, alternatively, its purpose as a progression route to a full bachelor's degree.

For Layer (2005b, p. 199), the question is whether such provision can provide both 'equity' and 'excellence'; that is, can college HE meet equity goals of widening participation at the same time as aiming to provide vocationally oriented HE, whose quality has parity with academic HE? In a comment prescient for current policy in England, Layer is sceptical that these goals can be achieved through market competition: 'If left to market forces there is no clear undertaking that 'equity', 'excellence' or both will be sustainable' (p. 199).

Over the past decade, two significant trends can be discerned that provide insights into the evolving dilemma of equity and excellence raised above. One involves college HE, which is distinctive through its focus on widening participation. This is found in particular in the American community colleges and their global counterparts (though it should be acknowledged that these are not all of a piece – see, for example, Webb et al. (2017) and Wheelahan (2016). Jephcote and Raby (2012, p. 350) emphasise the role that these colleges play 'at the forefront of providing educational opportunities for non-traditional students and facilitating their progression into continuing and higher educational options'. They identify key characteristics of this provision as serving the local environment, offering a 'second chance' for non-traditional students who have long been excluded from higher education and providing the only post-secondary education that many students can obtain.

The problem that such institutions face is that in a hierarchically stratified HE system, they become positioned as inferior to university HE (Bathmaker, 2016), catering to the mass population, while universities are reinterpreted for the elite. Despite catering for a more diverse population, their success is regularly judged against university HE in terms of student outcomes – the level and number of qualifications gained, and the numbers progressing to and completing degree level education. Jephcote and Raby (2012, p. 361) comment that: 'These are harsh ways of judging the performance of a sector which embraces those from non-traditional and disadvantaged backgrounds, who have greater obstacles to overcome'.

The second trend involves the growth of distinctive and prestigious forms of higher vocational education. These have historically occurred in dual systems (Scott, 1995) that have a clearly separate field of VET, but now involve the introduction of hybrid forms of work-based academic education, which combine elements of vocational training and higher education, often in new hybrid institutions. This trend has been a key development in the German speaking DACH countries (Germany, Austria and Switzerland), where there is a strong tradition of commitment from employers working in partnership with education. Graf's (2013) detailed analysis of these developments concludes that these new hybrid institutions 'signify a new premium sector, for example in terms of social prestige and labour market prospects' (p. 17). The challenge however, found both here (Baethge and Wolter, 2015) as well as in analogous systems in other European countries such as Denmark (see, for example, Jørgensen, 2017), is that the development of prestigious, hybrid programmes makes equity goals more difficult. Their prestige and distinction may serve to attract into vocational HE those who might have pursued university HE, but this can be to the disadvantage of learners who previously followed these vocational routes, leading to competitive selection processes that do not favour those who benefit from open access widening participation practices (Bathmaker, 2017).

The next section of the chapter now turns to college HE in England and offers a brief statistical picture of college-based HE in the 2010s. What this picture suggests is that the distinctiveness of college HE in England is closely intertwined with its role in addressing inequalities through providing wider access to HE and progression routes to the bachelor level and serving local communities including mature students. In this, it is much more in line with the community college model outlined above than the distinctive and specialist models which are developing in German speaking countries. Where the former, including the introduction of the short-cycle Foundation Degree, was possibly the preferred direction of travel in the 2000s as part of the New Labour government's (1997–2010) widening participation policies, UK policymakers in the current Conservative government appear keen to emulate the dual specialist model exemplified by the DACH countries through a distinct and separate route and the introduction of new National Colleges and Institutes of Technology, which are explained further below.

College HE in England in the 2010s

College provision of HE forms an enduring element of the work of FE colleges in England, which can be traced back over more than 60 years. In 2017–18, 218 out of 288 colleges offered HE (AoC, 2017),[1] though provision in most colleges is quite small (less than 100 students), and there are only a limited number of large providers of HE. The college contribution represented just under 10 per cent of all HE in England in 2015/16 (ETF and RCU, 2017, p. 5). Since the early 2000s, this college contribution has been positioned in policy as playing two important roles: providing higher level vocational education that connects closely to workplace requirements, and widening participation to those traditionally under-served or excluded from HE (BIS, 2011a, 2011b). But provision is very diverse; it is not exclusively higher *vocational* education, and it includes a range of programmes at different levels, including sub-bachelor qualifications (such as Foundation Degrees and Higher National Diplomas (HNDs)) and full bachelor's degrees, as well as higher and degree apprenticeships.

It is at the same time distinctive in comparison to university HE in a number of ways: colleges offer more opportunities for sub-degree study; they provide part-time study, and they cater for more students from local areas with low HE participation rates, as well as older students. In 2015–16, over half of all students in college HE (56%) were taking sub-bachelor qualifications; Foundation Degrees represented over 40 per cent of participation, and a further 16 per cent were studying for either HNDs or Higher National Certificates (HNCs) (ETF and RCU, 2017, p. 17). By comparison, bachelor provision comprised 30 per cent of full-time and only 4 per cent of part-time numbers in the same period (ETF and RCU, 2017, p. 12). Alongside these courses, higher level apprenticeship programmes have grown in size, with numbers doubling from just over 7,000 in 2013/14 to more than 16,000 in 2015/16 (though higher level and degree apprenticeships still only accounted for 5 per cent of all apprenticeships).

Despite a collapse in part-time numbers (between 2008–09 and 2012–13 numbers fell by 134,000), colleges continue to be important providers of part-time courses. In 2015/16 out of the total of 151,360 HE students in FE colleges, just under half were part-time students. Amongst full-time students, just over half (53%) were registered for a sub-bachelor's degree (37.8% Foundation degrees; 15% HNDs), but a much smaller proportion (19.3%) amongst those studying part-time (15.5% Foundation Degrees; 3.7% HNDs).

Colleges recruit on average more than 78 per cent of their HE students from the local region, and a considerable proportion of these live in HE 'cold spot' areas, where there is no university provision of HE. In 2015/16, over 16,000 college full-time HE students lived in cold spot areas, representing more than a fifth of the total full-time cohort, with just under a fifth (19%) of part-time HE students coming from 'cold spots' (ETF and RCU, 2017, pp. 8–9). A further area of distinctiveness involves the participation of older students. The majority of part-time students and just over a third of full-time students studying HE in FE colleges were aged 25 or over in 2015/16 (ETF and RCU, 2017, p. 6). However, these areas of distinctiveness are also areas of uncertainty and risk for colleges. There is a long-term decline in the numbers taking sub-bachelor's level qualifications and, more recently, a stark decrease in the number of part-time students.

The changing policy environment

In the late 2010s, the policy landscape is one of radical change, and the position of college HE at the nexus between higher and vocational education (Powell and Solga, 2010) means that college provision faces reform not just as a result of HE policy, but what Ball (1993) refers to as an 'ensemble' of related policies. This ensemble constitutes a combination of HE reforms, technical education reforms, changes to student funding, and area reviews of FE colleges.

In 2016, a *Post-16 Skills Plan* (BIS and DfE, 2016b), which focuses on technical education, and a White Paper *Success as a Knowledge Economy* (BIS, 2016), which introduces HE reforms, were published within two months of each other, proposing a 'technical education revolution' (Greening, 2017), alongside a shake-up of the whole HE system. At the same time as the reforms put forward in these policy documents, a series of area reviews of post-16 education provision in England took place between 2015 and 2017. In a context of ever tighter government funding, with colleges facing severe financial difficulties, these reviews involved a new phase of FE college mergers, intended to create 'fewer, often larger, more resilient and efficient providers' (BIS, 2015a, p. 3). One of the suggested ways in which colleges were encouraged to envisage their future involved '[a] more significant role in supporting skills development at level 4 and beyond' (Further Education Commissioner Letter, 2015).

The technical strand of reform follows the recommendations of a review led by Lord Sainsbury into technical education (BIS and DfE, 2016a) and endorsed in the government's Post-16 Skills Plan (BIS and DfE, 2016b). These reforms introduce two distinct and separate routes post-16: a technical and an academic option. According to the Plan:

> The technical option will prepare individuals for skilled employment which requires technical knowledge and practical skills valued by industry.
>
> (2016b, p. 7)

While current attention is focused on new 'T levels' offered in 15 occupational areas that are intended to be equivalent to academic 'A levels' (DfE, 2017a), the technical option is projected to extend through to levels 4, 5 and 6 (equivalent to ISCED levels 5 and 6). The plans for these higher levels are however much less clear, with a further review, announced by the Department for Education (DfE) at the end of October 2017.[2] The higher levels do not involve new qualifications in the first instance. A new Institute for Apprenticeships and Technical Education will keep a register of qualifications at levels 4 and 5 that are deemed eligible for public subsidy (such as student loans), and to begin with, the Plan explains, they will be drawn from 'existing technical qualifications which are considered to do the best job of meeting national standards'. (BIS and DfE, 2016b, p. 26) As with other levels in the technical option, these higher levels include work-based apprenticeships, as well as college-based programmes, with higher level apprenticeships intended to form part of the 3 million apprenticeship starts promised by 2020 (BIS, 2015b).

For college HE, these changes to qualifications pathways are not the only significant change. Two new types of institutions offering higher technical education – National Colleges and Institutes of Technology – have been introduced. National Colleges were first proposed under the previous government in a speech by Vince Cable in 2014 (Cable, 2014), and five colleges came into operation in 2017, each specialising in one key sector: nuclear, digital skills, high-speed rail, onshore oil and gas and the creative and cultural industries. The Skills Plan states that these colleges will 'lead the design and delivery of technical skills training at levels 4–6' in their specialist area (BIS and DfE, 2016b, p. 34).

Institutes of Technology (IoTs), on the other hand, were first put forward in 2015 in the Productivity Plan published by HM Treasury (HM Treasury, 2015), which proposed that some existing FE colleges would be invited to become IoTs and specialise in providing higher level technical education in areas of local economic priority. The Skills Plan confirmed the introduction of IoTs, stating that they were looking for collaborative ventures that would involve 'innovative ways of working across higher education, further education, private providers and industry'. (BIS and DfE, 2016b, p. 35) The subsequent Institutes of Technology prospectus (DfE, 2017b), states that IoTs will be: 'A prestigious and high quality employer-led institution delivering higher level technical education with a clear route to high-skilled employment'. (DfE, 2017b, p. 6)

Turning to the HE part of the policy ensemble, reforms here centre around the proposals announced in the 2016 White Paper on higher education *Success as a Knowledge Economy* (BIS, 2016). They introduce wide-ranging changes to the HE system as a whole, including significant developments that affect college HE. Central to the White Paper is 'creating a competitive market', with 'greater choice' at 'lower cost' and with 'greater competition between high quality new and existing providers in the HE sector' (BIS, 2016, p. 8).

The new Office for Students creates a single regulator for the whole HE sector, replacing both the Higher Education Funding Council for England and the Office for Fair Access. The new regulator's work will include the HE work of further education colleges as well as higher education institutions, alternative providers and new entrants (BIS, 2016, p. 63). This, it is claimed, will create 'a level playing field for all providers' (p. 24) in order to create greater competition.

The White Paper proposes much greater flexibility to gain degree awarding powers for both foundation and bachelor's degrees and awarding powers granted for specific rather than all subjects. Furthermore, the Paper promotes the development of different modes of study to the traditional three- and four-year bachelor's degree, including a two-year, accelerated bachelor's degree; studying part-time; in modules; from a distance; or in a degree apprenticeship, embedded with an employer. Student choice as outlined here thus involves a further range of options for HE study, in addition to choosing between the technical and academic options proposed in the Post-16 Skills Plan. To fund HE study, maintenance loans as well as tuition fee loans are to be made available for part-time as well as full-time study in order to tackle the long-term decline in part-time numbers.

There is a further dimension to this policy ensemble, which highlights the considerable tension between these parallel but separate reforms to HE and vocational/technical education. There is increasing pressure from key policy influencers, most prominently Lord Sainsbury and Baroness Wolf, who advance the argument that too much emphasis has been placed on the expansion of bachelor's-level HE, at too great a cost and with diminishing labour market returns to individuals. Wolf in particular has published a series of reports (Wolf, 2015, 2016) which argue that financial incentives and administrative structures wrongly promote bachelor's degrees at the expense of higher level vocational education:

> In post-19 education, we are producing vanishingly small numbers of higher technician level qualifications, while massively increasing the output of generalist bachelors degrees and low-level vocational qualifications. We are doing so because of the financial incentives and administrative structures that governments themselves have created, not because of labour market demand, and the imbalance looks set to worsen yet further. We therefore need, as a matter of urgency, to start thinking about post-19 funding and provision in a far more integrated way.
>
> (Wolf, 2015, p. 76)

Elsewhere, concerns about funding have become highly visible in relation to HE tuition fees, and in February 2018, the Conservative Prime Minister Theresa May announced a year-long review of tertiary education in response to concerns about graduate debt and returns to their education:

> Making university truly accessible to young people from every background is not made easier by a funding system which leaves students from the lowest-income households bearing the highest levels of debt, with many graduates left questioning the return they get for their investment.
>
> (O'Malley 2018, unnumbered)

What are the prospects for college HE?

While there is a policy drive through technical education reform to address once again the long-standing problems facing vocational education in England, the policy debate over HE, including college HE, is currently waged almost exclusively on the terrain of the demand for higher level and graduate skills, the returns to higher level qualifications and therefore which forms of HE are worth investing in for government and for individuals. In the wider socio-economic context, this connects to major concerns about the UK's 'long-standing productivity deficit compared to other advanced economies' (Anderson and Education Policy Institute, 2017, p. 17) and, in the light of the UK's imminent exit from the European Union, what is viewed as a productivity crisis. For college HE, there are considerable risks and uncertainty in this context which are intensified by the determined drive to promote market competition by the Conservative Government.

A key objective for the programme of post-16 area-based reviews of college provision was to ensure '[c]lear, high quality professional and technical routes to employment, alongside academic routes, which allow individuals to progress to high level skills valued by employers' (BIS, 2015a, p. 2). What is not clear, however, is what is meant by 'high level skills', particularly ones that are 'valued by employers', and this matters. For while there are regular claims of increasing labour market demand for high skills (Anderson and Education Policy Institute, 2017), there are conflicting prognoses for the future of intermediate, middle-skilled jobs.

Sissons (2011) and Holmes and Mayhew (2012) talk of an hourglass economy, with an increasing polarisation of the UK labour market since the 2008 recession and the hollowing out of middle-wage jobs. Sissons points out that although the economy has begun to create jobs, a significant number of these have been in low-wage occupations (elementary occupations and sales and customer services) and at the top end with professional growth, but there is declining employment among middle-wage occupations.

This analysis contrasts with reports that forecast job redesign and pockets of opportunity within sectors including agriculture, skilled trades and construction (Bakhshi et al., 2017). These differing analyses of the labour market along with ambiguous definitions of 'higher skills' 'below graduate level' are played out in UK policy. The Industrial Strategy Green Paper (2017) claims:

> We have a shortage of **high-skilled technicians below graduate level**. Reflecting the historic weakness of technical education in the UK, only 10% of adults hold technical education as their highest qualification, placing us 16th out of 20 OECD countries.
>
> (HM Government, 2017a, p. 38)

Yet HEFCE, the (former) funding council for HE in England, states that there is:

> considerable confusion in the marketplace as to what intermediate techni-
> cal skills are, how they are of value in the current economy, and, perhaps
> most importantly, how they will be of value in the future.
>
> Employers and stakeholders – but mainly the former – exhibit uncertainty
> as to what intermediate technical education is, and what its value is to them.
>
> (Pye Tait Consulting/HEFCE 2016: 10)

In addition to questions about the demand for higher level skills, which as
the comments above indicate sit in an ambiguous place between intermediate and high skills, there are issues concerning the returns to different levels of
skill. Here too there are differing ways in which the available evidence can be
viewed. The DfE reported in 2016 that the returns to a 'high' skills qualification
in England appeared to be declining:

> The median earnings five years post graduation for those graduating in
> 2003/04 was £26,000 compared to £25,500 for those who graduated in
> 2008/9.
>
> (DfE, 2016, p. 10)

> 1 in 4 graduates from 2003/4 was earning £20,000 or less ten years after
> graduation.
>
> (DfE, 2016, p. 11)

However, the lifetime benefit associated with studying for different types of
qualifications reported in by the Department for Business Innovation and
Skills (BIS, 2011c) showed that the premium for obtaining a bachelor's degree
remained considerably higher, compared with a Foundation Degree and other
forms of HE (see Table 12.1):

Table 12.1 Lifetime benefit associated with studying for different types of qualifications

Degree level	Net present value
Bachelor's degree	£108,121
Foundation Degree	£51,402
HE diploma	£69,465
Other HE	£31,611

Source: Data taken from BIS (2011c).

In addition to these pressures related to demand for skills and returns to
qualifications, college HE is further affected by a determined commitment to
market-led reform in all spheres of current UK policy as emphasised in the
Industrial Strategy White Paper (HM Government, 2017b, p. 21):

We believe in the power of the competitive market – competition, open financial markets, and the profit motive are the foundations of the success of the UK. Indeed the best way to improve productivity is to increase exposure to competition.

Market-led reforms for higher and technical education mean that further education colleges are not necessarily the provider of choice or the preferred provider for any developments, whether that be college-based sub-bachelor higher level education or higher and degree apprenticeships. They are part of an increasingly crowded HE marketplace (Saichaie and Morphew, 2014), where government HE policy looks to 'alternative' providers, which include new and private providers as well as existing further education colleges, while technical education policy introduces Institutes of Technology and National Colleges (BIS, 2016).

What are the implications for distinction and addressing inequalities?

Under New Labour (1997–2010), further education colleges were intended to play a role in widening participation through distinctive forms of sub-bachelor's degree provision, but also with an emphasis on the opportunity for progression to a full bachelor's degree. A key strength of college HE at this time was permeability and progression, allowing successful movement between more academic and more vocationally oriented routes, and between college-based HE and provision in higher education institutions. When the Coalition Government came to power in 2010, policies of widening participation and 'college for all' leading to bachelor's degrees came under critical scrutiny. Since the election of a Conservative Government in 2015, key policy proposals for technical education reform (BIS and DfE, 2016a, 2016b) on the one hand, and plans to increase market competitiveness in the HE sector (BIS, 2016), on the other, suggest a shift in the role and purpose of college HE in the eyes of national policymakers. Firstly, colleges are potentially central to a new technical education pathway that is distinct and separate from an 'academic' pathway and provides a route through from the lowest level of qualification to graduate and postgraduate levels (BIS and DfE, 2016b). Secondly, there has been a shift in emphasis in HE policy, from open-access policies of widening participation intended to open up HE to those groups under-served by traditional university education to a focus on (labour) market mobility, whereby choice of higher level provision is to be determined by market demand and success judged by the labour market returns to qualifications.

So how are questions of distinction and addressing inequalities likely to fare in the context of policy imperatives that focus on markets, competition and choice? In a marketised system of HE, policies that prioritise competition and require 'choice' encourage hierarchies of distinction, and in the hierarchically stratified field of HE, 'distinction' is likely to remain determined by more powerful 'academic' players, leading to vertical stretching of stratification (Marginson, 2016), rather than increased parity through distinction for both academic and higher vocational forms of HE. The diversity of college HE in England can be seen as evidence of how colleges have sought to position themselves in the context of a regularly shifting policy landscape, by changing and adjusting their offer rather than limiting themselves to a specific and distinctive vocational role.

Nevertheless, as in the past, colleges in England will continue to mediate policy. While their work is necessarily affected by strategic decisions concerning funding and financial viability, how they mediate policy is also affected by the way they decide to construct their mission in relation to widening participation and the needs of the communities they serve (Avis and Orr, 2016, p. 51). These different drivers suggest colleges are likely to continue to offer a diversity of HE provision, which addresses inequalities through catering to a diversified population, but which may also involve new, distinctive higher vocational provision, in response to current policy reforms. What is likely to prove more elusive is a technical education revolution that resolves the long-standing and complex problems for colleges in England of labour market demand for higher level vocational education, the returns to these qualifications and the dominant place of academic provision.

Notes

1 Seventy-three of the 288 colleges in England are 6th form colleges teaching 16–18-year-old students, many of which are unlikely to offer HE courses.
2 See the Department for Education anouncement 'Level 4 & 5 technical education to be reviewed', www.gov.uk/government/news/level-4-5-technical-education-to-be-reviewed

References

Anderson, R. and Education Policy Institute (2017) *Educating for Our Economic Future* [Online], Education Policy Institute. Available at https://epi.org.uk/publications-and-research/educating-economic-future/ (Accessed 30 January 2018).

Association of Colleges (AoC) (2017) *College Key Facts 2017/18*, London, Association of Colleges.

Avis, J. and Orr, K. (2016) 'HE in FE: Vocationalism, class and social justice', *Research in Post-Compulsory Education*, vol. 21, no. 1–2, pp. 49–65.

Baethge, M. and Wolter, A.(2015) 'The German skill formation model in transition: From dual system of VET to higher education?', *Journal for Labour Market Research*, vol. 48, no. 2, pp. 97–112.

Bakhshi, H., Downing, J. M., Osborne, M. A., and Schneider, P. (2017) *The Future of Skills: Employment in 2030*, London, Pearson and Nesta.

Ball, S. J. (1993) 'What is policy? Texts, trajectories and toolboxes', *Discourse, Studies in the Cultural Politics of Education*, vol. 13, no. 2, pp. 10–17.

Bathmaker, A. M. (2015) 'Thinking with Bourdieu: Thinking after Bourdieu: Using "field" to consider in/equalities in the changing field of English higher education', *Cambridge Journal of Education*, vol. 45, no. 1, pp. 61–80.

Bathmaker, A. M. (2016) 'Higher education in further education: The challenges of providing a distinctive contribution that contributes to widening participation', *Research in Post-Compulsory Education*, vol. 21, no. 1–2, pp. 20–32.

Bathmaker, A.M. (2017) 'Post-secondary education and training, new vocational and hybrid pathways and questions of equity, inequality and social mobility: introduction to the special issue', *Journal of Vocational Education & Training*, vol. 69, no. 1, pp. 1–9.

Becker, G. (2006) 'The age of human capital', in Lauder, H., Brown, P., Dillabough, J. A., and Halsey, A. H. (eds.), *Education, Globalisation and Social Change*, Oxford, Oxford University Press, pp. 292–294.

Cable, V. (2014) *Where Next for Further and Higher Education? Cambridge Public Policy Lecture on the Future for Higher and Further Education Institutions, Teachers and Students Presented in Cambridge on 23 April 2014* [Online]. Available at www.gov.uk/government/speeches/where-next-for-further-and-higher-education (Accessed 20 December 2017).

Department for Business, Innovation and Skills (BIS) (2011a) *Higher Education: Students at the Heart of the System*, London, HMSO.

Department for Business, Innovation and Skills (BIS) (2011b) *New Challenges, New Chances: Further Education and Skills System Reform Plan: Building a World Class Skills System* [Online], London, HMSO. Available at www.gov.uk/government/uploads/system/uploads/attachment_data/file/145452/11-1380-further-education-skills-system-reform-plan.pdf (Accessed 20 June 2015).

Department for Business, Innovation and Skills (BIS) (2011c) 'The returns to higher education qualifications', *Research Paper* No. 45, London, Department for Business, Innovation and Skills.

Department for Business, Innovation and Skills (BIS) (2015a) *Reviewing Post-16 Education and Training Institutions*, BIS/15/433, London Department for Business, Innovation and Skills.

Department for Business, Innovation and Skills (BIS) (2015b) *English Apprenticeships: Our 2020 Vision*, BIS/15/604, London, Department for Business, Innovation and Skills.

Department for Business, Innovation and Skills (BIS) (2016) *Success as a Knowledge Economy: Teaching Excellence, Social Mobility and Student Choice*, Cm 9258, London, HMSO.

Department for Business, Innovation and Skills (BIS) and Department for Education (DfE) (2016a) *Report of the Independent Panel on Technical Education (The Sainsbury Report)* [Online]. Available at www.gov.uk/government/uploads/system/uploads/attachment_data/file/536046/Report_of_the_Independent_Panel_on_Technical_Education.pdf (Accessed 30 September 2016).

Department for Business, Innovation and Skills (BIS) and Department for Education (DfE) (2016b) *Post-16 Skills Plan*, Cm 9280, London, HMSO.

Department for Education (DfE) (2016) *Employment and Earnings Outcomes of Higher Education Graduates: Experimental data from the Longitudinal Education Outcomes (LEO) dataset*. SFR36/2016, Department for Education [Online]. Available at https://assets.publishing.service.gov.uk/government/uploads/system/uploads/attachment_data/file/543794/SFR36-2016_main_text_LEO.pdf (Accessed December 2016)

Department for Education (2017a) *Post-16 Technical Education Reforms: T Level Action Plan* [Online], DFE-00274-2017. Available at www.gov.uk/government/publications (Accessed 20 December 2017).

Department for Education (2017b) *Institutes of Technology Prospectus* [Online]. Available at www.gov.uk/government/uploads/system/uploads/attachment_data/file/663691/DfE_IOT_Prospectus_Nov17.PDF (Accessed 20 December 2017).

Education and Training Foundation (ETF) and RCU Market Research Service (RCU) (2017) *College Based Higher Education* [Online], ETF. Available at www.et-foundation.co.uk/wp-content/uploads/2017/08/RCU-National-16N003-FINAL.pdf (Accessed 20 December 2017).

Further Education Commissioner Letter (2015) *Area Reviews and the Reshaping of the College Sector* [Online]. Available at www.gov.uk/government/uploads/system/uploads/attachment_data/file/473452/area-reviews-and-reshaping-college-sector-FE-commissioner-letter.pdf (Accessed 24 March 2018).

Gallacher, J. and Osborne, M. (2005) 'The role of short-cycle higher education in the changing landscape of mass higher education: Issues for consideration', in Gallacher, J. and Osborne, M. (eds.), *A Contested Landscape: International Perspectives on Diversity in Mass Higher Education*, Leicester, National Institute of Adult Continuing Education, pp. 195–212.

Graf, L. (2013) *The hybridization of vocational training and higher education in Austria, Germany and Switzerland*, Opladen, Berlin and Toronto, Budrich UniPress Ltd.Greening, J. (2017, July 6) *Speech at the Business and Education Summit of the British Chambers of Commerce Business and Education Conference* [Online]. Available at www.gov.uk/government/speeches/justine-greening-speech-at-the-business-and-education-summit (Accessed 20 January 2018).

HM Government (2017a) *Building Our Industrial Strategy: Green Paper* [Online], HMG. Available at www.gov.uk/government/uploads/system/uploads/attachment_data/file/611705/building-our-industrial-strategy-green-paper.pdf (Accessed 20 December 2017).

HM Government (2017b) *Industrial Strategy: Building a Britain Fit for the Future* [Online], HMG. Available at www.gov.uk/government/publications/industrial-strategy-building-a-britain-fit-for-the-future (Accessed 20 December 2017).

HM Treasury (2015) *Fixing the Foundations: Creating a More Prosperous Nation*, Cm 9098 [Online], HMG. Available at www.gov.uk/government/uploads/system/uploads/attachment_data/file/443898/Productivity_Plan_web.pdf (Accessed 20 December 2017).

Holmes, C. and Mayhew, K. (2012) *The Changing Shape of the UK Job Market and Its Implications for the Bottom Half of Earners* [Online], The Resolution Foundation. Available at www.resolutionfoundation.org/app/uploads/2014/08/The-Changing-Shape-of-the-UK-Job-Market.pdf (Accessed 30 August 2017).

Jephcote, M. and Raby, R. L. (2012) 'A comparative view of colleges of further education (UK) and community colleges (US): Maintaining access in an era of financial constraint', *Research in Post-Compulsory Education*, vol. 17, no. 3, pp. 349–366.

Jørgensen, C. H. (2017) 'From apprenticeships to higher vocational education in Denmark: Building bridges while the gap is widening', *Journal of Vocational Education and Training*, vol. 69, no. 1, pp. 64–80.

Layer, G. (ed.) (2005a) *Closing the Equity Gap: The Impact of Widening Participation Strategies in the UK and the USA*, Leicester, National Institute of Adult Continuing Education.

Layer, G. (2005b) 'Closing the equity gap: Is it sustainable?', in Layer, G. (2005) (ed.), *Closing the Equity Gap: The Impact of Widening Participation Strategies in the UK and the USA*, Leicester, National Institute of Adult Continuing Education, pp. 199–203.

Marginson, S. (2016) 'The worldwide trend to high participation higher education: Dynamics of social stratification in inclusive systems', *Higher Education*, vol. 72, no. 4, pp. 4–25.

May, T. (2018) *PM: The Right Education for Everyone* [Online], Prime Minister's Office, 10 Downing Street. Available at www.gov.uk/government/speeches/pm-the-right-education-for-everyone (Accessed 19 February 2018).

Organisation for Economic Co-operation and Development (OECD) (2008) *OECD Thematic Review of Tertiary Education Synthesis Report*, Paris, OECD.

Organisation for Economic Co-operation and Development (OECD) (2012) *Post-Secondary Vocational Education and Training: Pathways and Partnerships*, Paris, OECD.

Organisation for Economic Co-operation and Development (OECD) (2014) *Skills beyond School: Synthesis Report*, OECD Reviews of Vocational Education and Training, Paris, OECD Publishing. http//dx.doi.org/10.1787/9789264214682-en

O'Malley, B. (2018, February 20) *Prime Minister Announces Review of Tertiary Education, University World News*, Issue 494 [Online]. Available at www.universityworldnews.com/article. php?story=2018022015081595 (Accessed 20 February 2018).

Osborne, J. (2005) 'Introduction', in Gallacher, J. and Osborne, M. (eds.), *A Contested Landscape: International Perspectives on Diversity in Mass Higher Education*, Leicester, National Institute of Adult Continuing Education, pp. 1–17.

Osborne, J., Gallacher, J., and Crossan, B. (2004) *Researching Widening Access to Lifelong Learning*, London, Routledge.

Piketty, T. (2014) *Capital in the Twenty-First Century*, Harvard, Harvard University Press.

Powell, J. W. and Solga, H. (2010) 'Analyzing the nexus of higher education and vocational training in Europe: A comparative-institutional framework', *Studies in Higher Education*, vol. 35, no. 6, pp. 705–721.

Pye Tait Consulting and Higher Education Funding Council for England (HEFCE) (2016) 'Employer demand for intermediate technical education in higher education', *Report to HEFCE, Bristol, Higher Education Funding Council for England* [Online]. Available at www. hefce.ac.uk/pubs/rereports/year/2016/techdemand/ (Accessed December 2016).

Saichaie, K. and Morphew, C. C. (2014) 'What college and university websites reveal about the purposes of higher education', *The Journal of Higher Education*, vol. 85, no. 4, pp. 499–530.

Scott, P. (1995) *The Meanings of Mass Higher Education*, Buckingham, Open University and Society for Research in Higher Education.

Sissons, P. (2011) *The Hourglass and the Escalator: Labour Market Change and Mobility*, London, The Work Foundation.

Teichler, U. (1988) *Changing Patterns of Higher Education Systems*, London, Jessica Kingsley Publishers.

Webb, S., Bathmaker, A. M., Gale, T., Hodge, S., Parker, S., and Rawolle, S. (2017) 'Higher vocational education and social mobility: Educational participation in Australia and England', *Journal of Vocational Education & Training*, vol. 69, no. 1, pp. 147–167.

Wheelahan, L. (2016) '"College for all" in Anglophone countries: Meritocracy or social inequality? An Australian example', *Research in Post-Compulsory Education*, vol. 21, no. 1–2, pp. 33–48.

Wolf, A. (2015) *Heading for the Precipice: Can Further and Higher Education Funding Policies Be Sustained?*, London, The Policy Institute at King's College London.

Wolf, A. (2016) *Remaking Tertiary Education: Can We Create a System That Is Fair and Fit for Purpose?*, London, Education Policy Institute at Kings' College London.

Chapter 13

Social justice and widening access to higher education in Scotland

The role of Scottish colleges

Sheila Riddell and Lucy Hunter Blackburn

Introduction

In the context of devolution, there has been growing interest in the extent to which social policy in the four UK nations appears to be converging or diverging (Greer, 2009; Mooney and Scott, 2012; Gallacher and Raffe, 2012; Riddell et al., 2016). Higher education has attracted particular interest because of the complex division of interests and responsibilities between the UK government and the devolved administrations. One of the main policy differences is the much greater use of further education colleges in the delivery of higher education in Scotland compared with the other nations, particularly England and Wales (Gallacher, 2014; Riddell et al., 2016). This chapter explores the pros and cons of the greater use of Higher National Certificate/Diploma (HNC/D) to degree articulation routes in Scotland in comparison with elsewhere in the UK, where the development of this type of provision has been much slower. As we demonstrate below, Scottish colleges have been far more successful than universities in attracting students from less advantaged backgrounds (Hunter Blackburn et al., 2016). At the same time, there continue to be concerns about the extent to which this expansion should be seen as introducing a further layer of differentiation into an already highly stratified higher education system (Boliver, 2011; Raffe and Croxford, 2015). In Scotland, the expansion of college-based higher education is generally seen as a success story. For example, the Final Report of the Commission on Widening Access (Scottish Government, 2016) stated:

> Articulation pathways, defined as progression from college to university where full credit is awarded for prior learning, is a distinctive and much admired feature of Scottish post-16 education. In our interim report, we identified the expansion of articulation pathways as a real success story of Scottish higher education and a powerful means of advancing access.
>
> (Scottish Government, 2016, p. 32)

However, there are also concerns that the disproportionate concentration of less advantaged students in colleges, as well as the concentration of students from advantaged backgrounds in older institutions, may indicate a form of social triage, with fewer economic, social and cultural advantages accruing to the former group (Bathmaker et al., 2008; Boliver, 2011; Gallacher, 2014).

In order to explore these issues, we begin with an overview of the literature on social justice, including the need for a renewed focus on outcomes, which, we argue, should be seen as the litmus test of fairness. We provide a brief summary of recent research on the provision of higher education in further education colleges in Scotland and England, highlighting the challenges which have been identified in both jurisdictions. This is followed by an overview of the Scottish and English policy context, describing the development of higher education in colleges and the thinking behind it. This is followed by an analysis of the social background of students in different types of institution, contrasting the social profile of colleges with that of post-92, pre-92 and ancient universities. We highlight the success of colleges in providing accessible courses in supportive learning environments for non-traditional students, while also drawing attention to the downsides of dealing with pent-up demand by diverting students from less advantaged backgrounds into a particular form of higher education. The paper concludes by questioning the Scottish Government's heavy reliance on the college sector as the principal driver of widening access, discussing the pros and cons of policy options that the Scottish Government might consider for the future.

Research informing this chapter

This chapter draws on research commissioned by the Sutton Trust (Hunter Blackburn et al., 2016) which focussed on access to higher education for students from less advantaged backgrounds in Scotland. The research used UCAS (Universities and Colleges Admissions Service), SFC (Scottish Funding Council) and HESA (Higher Education Statistics Agency) data to explore the following (1) applications, acceptances and entry rates by students from different social backgrounds across the UK; (2) higher education initial participation rates in the four UK nations; differences in participation rates by type of university and social background; the institutional composition of the university sectors in Scotland and England; and widening participation activities and debates. The report analysed the contribution of colleges to widening access in Scotland, which is the central focus of this paper. Throughout this chapter, while our main focus is on Scotland, we make comparisons between policy and outcomes across the UK, particularly with England. While it is important to avoid over-generalisation form cross-border comparative research, we believe that work of this type provides opportunities for policy learning because it throws into high relief the elements of specific systems which may not be apparent when viewed in isolation (Raffe and Byrne, 2005).

Social justice and the importance of outcomes

Although they are often implicit rather than explicit, competing theories of social justice and equality underpin widening access policies in higher education. Theoretical debates in this area have a long history, influenced by Rawls' *A Theory of Social Justice*, published in 1971. Drawing on Rawls' ideas, Miller (1999) suggested that social justice should be understood in terms of the under-pinning rationale of 'how the good and bad things in life should be distributed among the members of a human society' (Miller, 1999, p. 1). More recent thinking on this topic has been influenced by Fraser's tri-partite conceptualisation of social justice in terms of (re)distribution, recognition and participation (Fraser, 2005). Within the field of higher education, this suggests the need to examine the fairness of resource allocation and outcomes; the extent to which diversity and difference are respected; and the degree to which different groups of students are able to participate in institutional decision-making.

Phillips (2004) observes that a focus on equality of outcomes as a key element of a socially just society has come to be regarded as unsophisticated and outmoded. Critics point out that because people value different things, equalising resources may result in some people having an excess of what they regard as worthless, while other people are deprived of things they value. Rather, they argue, people should be empowered to make choices, which are likely to affect their future life chances but which should nonetheless be regarded as fair. In education, politicians and policymakers tend to adopt an equality of opportunity approach based on notions of merit and desert. For example, the Scottish government frequently claims that its system of higher education is available to 'all those with the ability to learn', unlike the English system which, it is claimed, depends on 'the ability to pay' (see, for example, the White Paper on Scottish independence (Scottish Government, 2013)). The importance of individual choice also seems to inform currently ascendant conceptualisations of equality, such as Amartya Sen's capability theory (Sen, 1992), which argues that policy should reflect and facilitate access to the social goods which people value, recognising the diversity of individual and group preferences. Phillips takes a different position, maintaining that the predominant equality of opportunity approach ignores the extent to which individual choices and therefore opportunities are socially structured. She questions the fairness of systems which base future life chances on choices which individuals make at a particular time and place. For example, a school leaver may decide to accept an apprenticeship or offer of employment rather than undertake further study, but cannot have any idea of the future economic and social consequences of this choice relative to others. Overall, Phillips rejects the idea that differences in outcome should be accepted as a justifiable consequence of individual choices. Linking equality of opportunity and outcomes, she maintains that whenever it is possible to detect disproportionalities in outcomes for specific social groups, we should assume systemic injustice and take action accordingly:

> It makes sense to start from the expectation that all groups would normally be distributed in roughly equal proportions along all measures of social activity: to expect, therefore, an equality of outcome, and to take any divergence from this as a reasonably safe indication that opportunities are not yet equal.
>
> (Phillips, 2004, p. 28)

This is the lens we adopt in examining patterns of participation in higher education in Scotland, focusing particularly on the role that colleges are expected to play.

The importance of college-based higher education in Scotland and England

In Scotland and Northern Ireland, and to a lesser extent in Wales and England, colleges play an important role as higher education providers. In Scotland, about 17 per cent of higher education, generally in the form of sub-degree programmes, takes place in the college sector, compared with 6 per cent in England and 1 per cent in Wales. In order to increase the proportion of the population with higher education qualifications, the Scottish Government has actively encouraged the expansion of the college-based higher education, placing no limits on the growth of student numbers in this sector. Colleges have been able to expand full-time HN provision because funding for this aspect of their work comes directly from the Scottish Funding Council. While university places have also increased in Scotland, student numbers continue to be centrally controlled, an approach which contrasts with the lifting of the cap on student numbers in England from 2016. College-based higher education in Scotland is cheaper than university-based provision, and relative cost is likely to be one factor driving its growth. Relative to population size, it is evident that Scotland has a smaller post-92 university sector compared with England and a higher proportion of high-tariff institutions, making it harder to gain a university place north of the Border (see Weedon's analysis of HESA benchmark data in Section 6, Hunter Blackburn et al., 2016).

The expansion of college-university articulation routes in Scotland has been supported by specific funding streams. For example, from 2007 onwards, articulation hubs have been supported. These generally involve the student spending the first two years of a four-year honours degree at college taking Higher National (HN) qualifications, followed by a move to a university for the final two years of an honours degree programme. In order to improve retention and completion rates, staff at college and university are encouraged to work together to design courses with a view to ensuring continuity in teaching methods and curriculum content. There is a new emphasis on associate student status, so that from the outset an HN student is registered at both the college and the university and has access to university facilities such as sports and information services.

Since the formation of the articulation hubs, there has been an increase in the number of students moving from college into the last two years of a university programme, increasing from 3,019 in 2011–12 to 3,469 in 2012–13 (Universities Scotland, 2014). However, it is clearly the case that the college/university pathway is far from smooth. According to SFC data, about 47 per cent of students taking Higher National qualifications at college progress to degree level study at university, and only 22 per cent are awarded full credit. Those receiving partial or no credit are required to repeat one or more years, leading to five or six year programmes of study to obtain an honours degree. This increases costs, even in the absence of tuition fees, and delays entry into the labour market. This is likely to be of particular significance to women, who may have less time to establish themselves in the workplace before taking maternity leave. Moving from a sub-degree programme in a college to a degree level programme at a university occurs much more frequently in some disciplinary areas and courses compared with others. For example, students studying for an HNC in beauty therapy at a college are less likely to progress to degree level study compared with computer studies students (Ingram and Gallacher, 2011).

In England, expansion of higher education over the past three decades has mainly occurred in the pre-and post-92 university sectors. While there has also been significant growth in higher education delivered in further education colleges, Parry (2009) argued that this provision has been neither coordinated nor protected, and further education colleges are often competing rather than collaborating with universities. In addition to HN qualifications, English further education colleges offer two-year Foundation Degrees, which may be topped up to a full honours degree through an additional year of study at university. Foundation Degrees may be studied at college or university and are normally awarded by a university. Recently, two English colleges (Newcastle College Group and Hartpury College) have been granted full degree-awarding powers, while others have been granted the power to award Foundation Degrees.

The expansion of higher education in English further education colleges was initially driven by the desire of the New Labour Government, following the Dearing Report of 1997, to achieve a target of 50 per cent participation in higher education in order to meet the expanding skills needs of a knowledge economy. However, as noted by Bathmaker (2016), the election of a Conservative-led Coalition government in 2010 led to a greater emphasis on the expansion of vocational rather than higher education. In a Statement to Parliament in 2010, Vince Cable, the Secretary of State for Business, innovation and Skills, stated that:

> The reality is that our best FE colleges and advanced apprenticeships are delivering vocational education every bit as valuable for their students and

the wider economy as the programmes provided by universities . . . There could be a law of diminishing returns in pushing more and more students through university.

(Cable, 2010)

While student numbers on college-based Foundation Degrees have continued to grow, English universities have tended to withdraw from foundation-level study, concentrating instead on the delivery of the traditional bachelor's programmes.

Experiences of higher education in colleges

Despite the recent expansion of articulation routes between colleges and universities in Scotland, there has been relatively little research on the impact of this change on student and institutional experience and identity, although Gallacher has documented policy developments and patterns of participation, as well as considering the significance of these changes (Gallacher, 2006, 2009, 2014). Ingram and Gallacher (2013) report on the findings of a qualitative study exploring the transition from college to university of students who entered Glasgow Caledonian University with HN qualifications in specific areas (Social Sciences; Business/Management Technology and Enterprise; Computing; and Engineering). While most of the respondents regarded their college qualifications as a useful preparation for degree level study, they also reported a number of difficulties in moving from college to university. For example, those moving into the second or third year of a degree programme found that the transition was challenging, involving a shift from small and supportive college learning community to a much more impersonal university environment where friendship groups had already formed. Furthermore, in particular subject areas, they found that they lacked specific skills, such as how to reference correctly, use software packages for data analysis and write discursive essays. Engineering students found that they needed to boost their mathematical skills and in general students reported that university assessment criteria were much more rigorous compared with the college regime. Christie et al. (2008) describe the tensions experienced by students with HN qualifications entering the first year of a degree programme at a Scottish ancient university. The students described a sense of loss and dislocation, as well as excitement and exhilaration, in coming to terms with an environment which felt alien in relation to their social class background and prior learning experiences. The studies discussed above all argue that institutions need to do much more to harmonise curriculum content and teaching styles. They also suggest that universities should do much more to support students' emotional and academic needs.

In England, Bathmaker and Thomas (2009) and Bathmaker et al. (2008) found wide variation in students' and lecturers' experiences of working across the FE/HE divide. In some cases, further education colleges provided effective bridging support between college and university level provision, helping students to adapt to the different teaching and learning demands of college and university study. By way of contrast, some students were confused by complex institutional boundaries between colleges and universities reflected in teaching and validation arrangements. Illustrating this point, a study by Parry and colleagues found that 17 per cent of students studying for a bachelor's degree at college thought they had applied to study at university (Parry, 2012). Bathmaker (2016) also found tensions between staff engaged in teaching at different levels within the same college. Some institutions maintained firm boundaries between different groups of staff in terms of workload and teaching space, leading to resentment.

In light of the expansion of college-based higher education principally in Scotland, and to a lesser extent in England, it is interesting that very little data is available on the economic returns of this type of provision. In Scotland, there appears to have been no recent research on the relative destinations and earnings of those undertaking HN qualifications at college compared with those following the traditional university route. Using Labour Force Survey data from 1999 to 2003, Gasteen and Houston (2007) found that HN-level and degree courses gave similar advantages in Scotland in terms of the probability of being in employment, but that the hourly earnings benefit for degrees was almost twice as great as for qualifications at HN-level, compared to having no qualifications. In England, more recent information is available. From 2008–09, annual surveys have been conducted of those undertaking higher education in further education colleges. Like the main DLHE (Destination of Leavers from Higher Education) survey, the HE in FE DLHE survey asks graduates a series of questions about their outcomes six months after leaving higher education. A report published by HEFCE in 2013 compared destinations and salaries of graduates from English further education colleges and universities. As shown in Figures 13.1 and 13.2, those obtaining higher education qualifications from a college who subsequently moved into employment earned significantly less than those graduating from university, irrespective of whether they graduated with an honours or foundation degree.

To summarise thus far, it would appear that in both Scotland and England the development of higher education in further education colleges has been somewhat ad hoc, although for a variety of reasons the Scottish government has been more consistent in its support of this sector. In both countries, it is clear that making the transition from college to university poses a particular set of challenges in adapting to a new learning environment halfway through a higher degree programme. College-based higher education programmes have typically evolved as training for specific occupations and continue to fulfil this function. At the same time, programmes in specific subject areas, such as computing, have morphed into transitional qualifications. Because of these dual functions, there are tensions in understandings of their underlying purpose, which are exacerbated by differences in college and university learning environments. Although

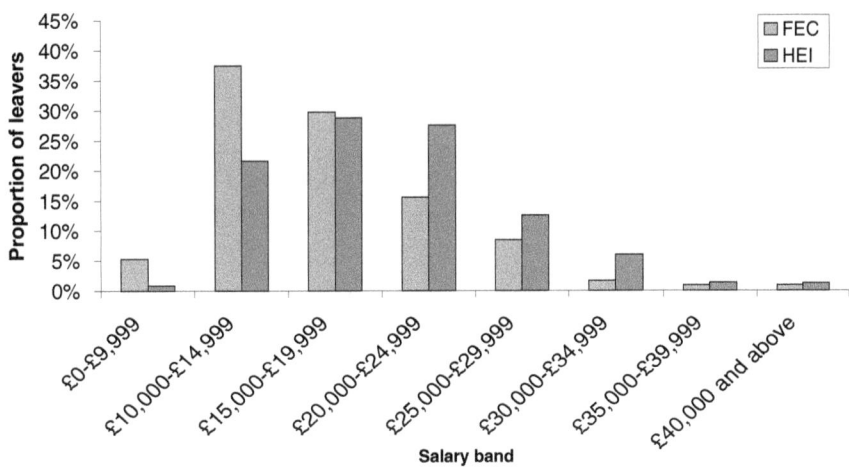

Figure 13.1 UK-domiciled full-time first-degree qualifiers from English HE providers in 2010–11 in full-time paid UK employment by salary band and institution type

Note: Salary reported six months after graduation

Source: BIS (2011)

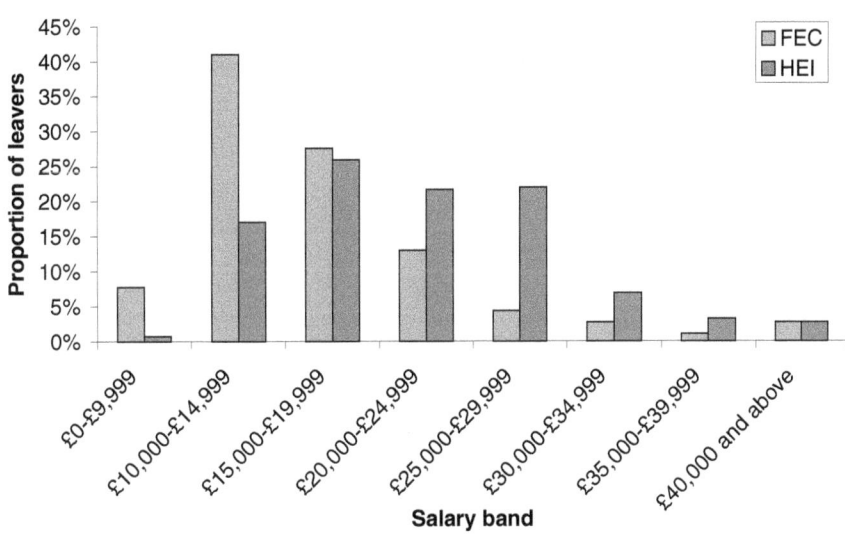

Figure 13.2 UK-domiciled full-time foundation degree qualifiers (from English HE providers in 2010–11) in full-time paid UK employment by salary band and institution type

Note: Salary reported six months after graduation

Source: BIS

the chances of being in employment are broadly similar for those with HN or degree level qualifications, evidence from England suggests that those with degrees are likely to have significantly higher earnings immediately after graduation (HEFCE, 2013) and over the course of a lifetime (BIS, 2011).

In the following sections, we explore patterns of participation in colleges and universities in Scotland and England by students from different social backgrounds, exploring the contribution made by colleges to widening participation.

Patterns of participation by type of institution in England and Scotland

In order to assess progress in drawing more students into higher education, there is often a focus on initial participation rates and in this section we contrast participation north and south of the border since it is often claimed that Scotland does particularly well in this regard. Comparisons of participation rates between the home nations adjust for changes over time in the size of the population. A number of participation rate measures are used in different parts the UK. The Higher Education Initial Participation Rate (HEIPR) is the only one which covers higher education participation in both college and university, in contrast to UCAS which only covers university. It is described as a suitable basis for UK comparisons by the SFC and is available for Scotland and England from 2006–07 to 2013–14. In effect, the HEIPR expresses how likely it is that a person will have entered higher education by the age of 30. By measuring participation in all forms of higher education and including those who do not enter immediately from school, it is a more inclusive measure than, say, UCAS age 18 entry rates.

Since 2015, the HEIPR has been published for Scotland only as a single headline figure, no longer providing a breakdown of how participation in HE varies by the type of institution (university or college) or level, treating Scottish Credit and Qualifications Framework (SCQF) levels 7 and 8 (Higher National and foundation degrees) identically to SCQF levels 9 and 10 (ordinary and honours degrees). Data are also not normally available by background. This chapter uses additional breakdowns of the Scottish figures provided by the SFC. Further breakdowns of the HEIPR for England were not available, but cross-referencing with other data allows some additional tentative comparisons.

Scotland has had higher levels of total participation in higher education than England for many years, long understood to be driven by the larger volume of activity at HNC/D level which takes place mainly in colleges. Very little degree level work is undertaken in Scottish colleges. Although the gap in the HEIPR between the two countries has narrowed since 2006, the HEIPR remains almost one-fifth higher for Scotland, standing at 55.0 per cent in 2013–14, compared to 46.6 per cent for England. Over the period, the HEIPR increased by 1.8 percentage points (3.4% proportionately) in Scotland and by 4.4 percentage points (10.4% proportionately) in England. The increase in HEIPR has not

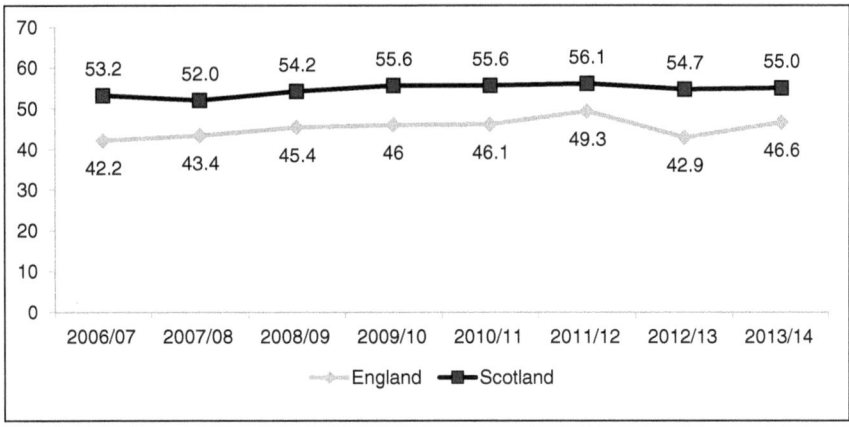

Figure 13.3 HEIPR 2006–07 to 2013–14, England and Scotland (2013–14 figure for England provisional)

Source: Hunter Blackburn et al. (2016)

been steady in either country. In Scotland, it peaked in 2011–12 and then fell back. In 2013–14, it remained below its 2009–10 value. The figure for England increased up to 2011–12, rising in that year, prior to a large increase in tuition fees. It fell sharply in 2012 and then in 2013 rose to a level slightly above its pre-2011 highest value (see Figure 13.3).

Initial participation rates by type of institution

To understand better the underlying trends, particularly for those from more disadvantaged backgrounds, further breakdowns of the HEIPR data have been obtained from the SFC (see Figure 13.4).

While the total HEIPR for Scotland is higher, initial entry to higher education institutions (HEIs) seems likely to be substantially higher in England. The HEIPR for universities and other HEIs in Scotland followed no steady trend. It was generally lower over the last four years of the period than the first and a little lower in 2013 than in 2006. Including entry into HEIs in other parts of the UK, the HEIPR for HEIs fell from 34.9 per cent to 34.1 per cent. By contrast, for colleges the HEIPR rose from 18.9 per cent to 20.3 per cent over the period. The figures for colleges showed a reasonably steady increase, although the highest figure was 21.8 per cent in 2011–12. Higher education provision in colleges therefore accounts for all the growth in the HEIPR for Scotland since 2006–07.

The HEIPR measures a student's initial point of entry and does not take into account that some of those who begin their higher education in a college will go on to undertake further undergraduate study in a university. Some

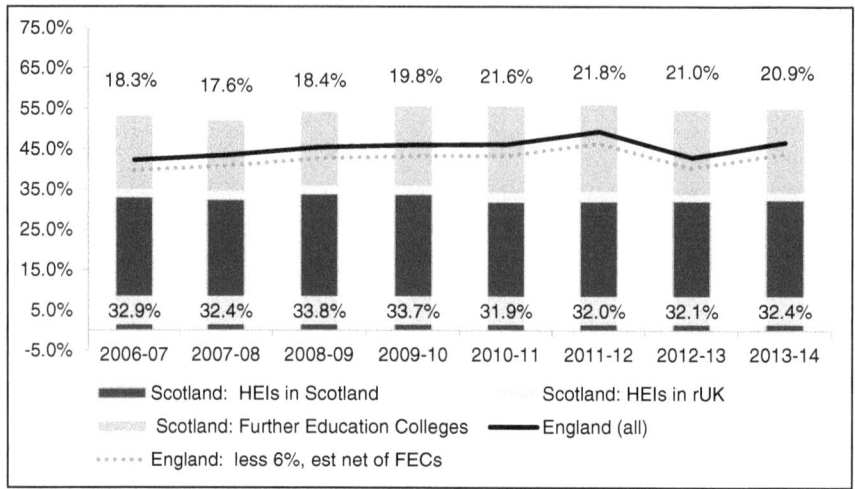

Figure 13.4 HEIPR in Scotland by institution type vs total HEIPR England (with estimate of effect of removing provision in English FECs)

Note: Labels added for HEIs and FECs in Scotland. The difference from the total shown above is accounted for by entry into HEIs in the rest of the UK.

Source: Hunter Blackburn et al. (2016)

students initially admitted to a college will eventually move to a university to do a degree. In 2013–14 there were around 17,500 successful HN completions, according to the SFC Infact database and just over 8,000 students who moved from a college to university.[1] Allowing for the fact that some students drop out between initial entry and successful HN completion, it might be expected that some 40 per cent of those initially entering a college course may move to university, probably enough to close the gap with England in degree level participation by age 30. However, students who do not get full credit – around 4,000 of the 8,000 – face one or more repeat years.

Social background and institutional type

Using further data provided by the SFC, for Scotland, it is possible to develop a more nuanced understanding of HEIPR, comparing attendance at different types of institution by students from different backgrounds. The participation pattern for the most and least deprived students is starkly different, with the former relying much more heavily on initial entry into a college than a university. The least deprived are almost three times more likely to enter a university than a college. Ninety per cent of the overall growth in the HEIPR for the most disadvantaged in Scotland since 2006 (6.3 percentage points) has been due to increased entry into college level higher education. Over the period 2006–2013, the difference in routes between the two groups has therefore become more pronounced. By 2013, 61 per cent of the most disadvantaged group initially entered HE via college, compared to 55 per cent in 2006 (see Figure 13.5).

The increase in the direct entry rate into HEIs by age 30 for the most disadvantaged has been relatively small, rising from 15.1 per cent in 2006 to 15.9 per cent in 2013, and not steady, ranging between 16.1 per cent (2008) and 14.4 per cent (2011). Once very low figures for entry into HEIs elsewhere in the UK are included, the figure for initial entry into HEIs rises from 15.6 per cent in 2006 to 16.3 per cent in 2013.

Overall, the HEIPR for the most disadvantaged in Scotland has increased over the period, though it was flat or falling slightly between 2010 and 2012. The HEIPR for the least disadvantaged 20 per cent in Scotland had no clear pattern: in 2013, it was much the same as in 2006, meaning that the gap between the most and least disadvantaged students had reduced. This mirrors the UCAS data. A small rise in college entry offsets a drop for HEIs. The figure for HEIs in the rest of the UK was the same at the end of the period as at the beginning.

The concentration of growth in college entry is likely to reflect the relatively tight capping of university places in Scotland at a time of rising demand. The Scottish Government fully funds places for Scottish (and EU) students and therefore restricts recruitment for these groups. Students from England, Wales and Northern Ireland pay fees and their numbers are uncapped. Colleges are funded on a

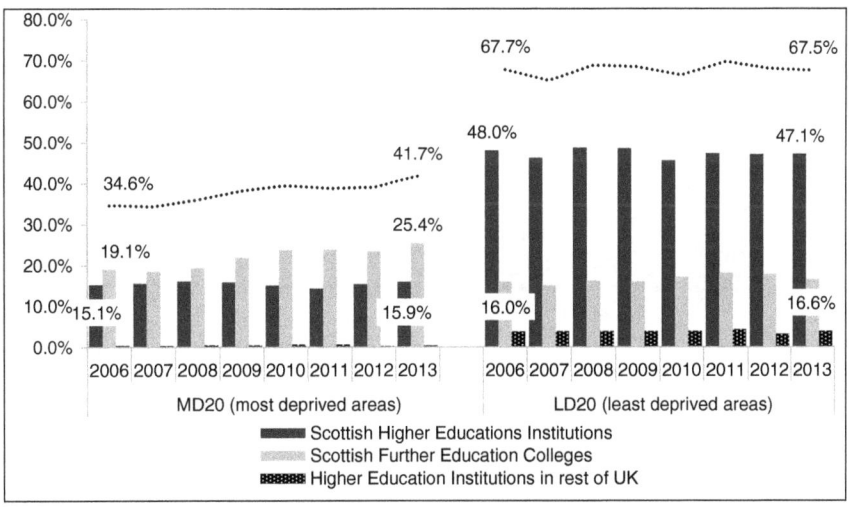

Figure 13.5 HEIPR in Scotland only, by SIMD MD20 (students from most deprived 20% of areas) and SIMD LD20 (students from least deprived 20% of areas) and institutional type

Source: Hunter Blackburn et al. (2016)

different model, which allocates less per place, and does not restrict recruitment so rigidly, so that colleges can be more responsive to demand. Since 2012, they have also been encouraged to shift their provision more towards younger full-time students studying for accredited qualifications. The figures here are consistent with the UCAS data showing signs of greater competition for university places over the period. As demand for entry into university has risen particularly quickly among this group, with government encouragement, it appears that that extra demand has in practice been met mainly by increasing HE provision in colleges.

Without equivalent data for England, it is not possible to estimate how much of the growth there in participation by more disadvantaged students may also have taken place in colleges (or other non-university providers, particularly private colleges). However, the smaller relative volume of provision in England outside HEIs makes it more difficult for these to account for so much of the change. The staged loosening and final lifting of the cap on university places in England also makes it less likely that demand has been displaced from universities into other providers.

Level of initial study

The SFC is also able to provide data on the split in the HEIPR between levels of study on initial entry (see Figure 13.6).

The strongest growth has been in HN-level entry and closely matches the increase in entry to colleges. The proportion entering direct into first degree courses has remained more or less static since 2008–09, excepting a peak in 2009–10.

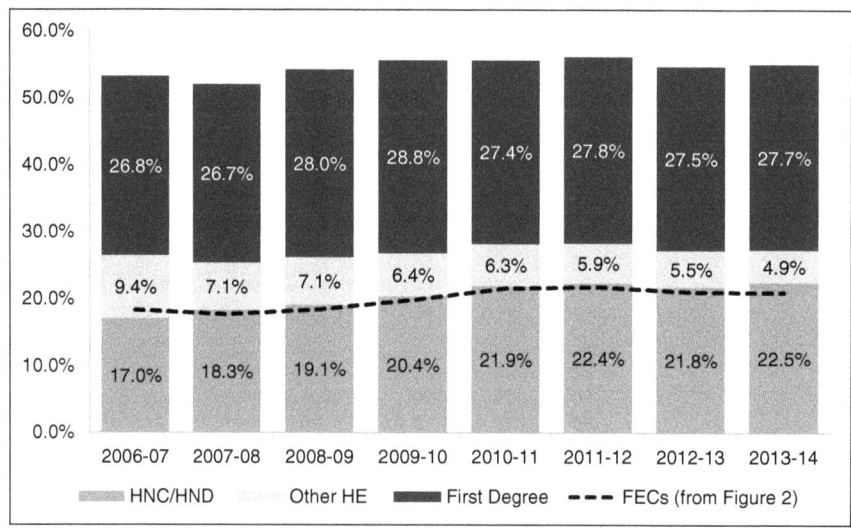

Figure 13.6 HEIPR by different types of course in Scotland

Source: Hunter Blackburn et al. (2016)

A further large change has been a near-halving of 'other HE' (mainly non-HN sub-degrees). This seems due in part to some of the switching to degree level provision at HEIs, although there may also have been some switching towards HNs in colleges. For this analysis, it was not possible to further separate this data by background, but the strong association of HN provision with colleges implies that the figures would look like those in Figure 4.4, with HN entry being much more significant to the most disadvantaged.

Again, the same figures are not currently available for England, but the relatively low level of sub-degree provision in universities, and small proportion of HE provided outside universities, suggests that the English figures are likely to show a higher HEIPR for first degrees.

To summarise, the increase in HEIPR has not been steady in either Scotland or England. In Scotland, in 2013–14 it remained below its 2009–10 value. The figure for England fell sharply in 2012 and then rose to a level slightly above its pre-2011 highest value. As demand for entry into university has risen, detailed analysis of the HEIPR reveals this was met by increasing HE provision in Scottish colleges. An increased level of entry into sub-degree programmes (HNCs and HNDs) in colleges accounts for all of the growth in the HEIPR for Scotland since 2006–07. In particular, entry to HN-level courses in colleges has been relied on to increase initial access to higher education for those from the most disadvantaged backgrounds. Ninety per cent of the overall growth in the HEIPR for the most disadvantaged in Scotland since 2006 (6.3 percentage points) has been due to increased entry into college level higher education. Rates of initial entry by age 30 directly into university have increased only slightly for the most disadvantaged. Since 2006, the difference in entry routes (direct entry to university from school, or entry to university via a sub-degree college programme) between the most and least disadvantaged has become more pronounced. The increased HEIPR in England may include some sub-degree growth, but this is likely to account for a small amount of the overall growth.

Levels of eventual entry into university-level higher education may be similar in Scotland to England, allowing for movement from HN and equivalent courses to university. However, students who progress from a two-year college HND programme to degree level study may take up to six years to complete an honours degree, incurring substantial additional time and cost. Given the high incidence of repeat years, for equal access on equal terms to the most competitive institutions, over-reliance on the HN to degree route is problematic, and it should not be simply assumed that this route makes up for initial differences in access, particularly to older universities.

Comparing patterns of participation between Scotland and England

Comparisons of participation between Scotland and England based on HEIPR tend to paint a positive picture of Scottish higher education. However, because increased participation in Scottish higher education by students from disadvantaged backgrounds has been in the college sector, it is important to consider the equivalence of college sub-degree programmes and university degrees. For the most disadvantaged, it seems likely that not only entry to university through sub-degree programmes but also some purely sub-degree provision would need to be regarded as equivalent to direct entry to university, to close the gap in participation rates between Scotland and England recorded by UCAS. Much discussion of higher education participation in different parts of the UK assumes equivalence between of colleges and universities. However, the data presented in this chapter suggests that we should be cautious in assuming such equivalence, as those articulating from college to university are disadvantaged in a number of ways. Overall, only half of those who enter a higher national college course subsequently move on to a university degree programme, and when they do it is usually in the post-92 sector. Of students who articulate, only half receive full credit. For students progressing into one of the ancient or pre-92 universities, this means that the process of obtaining a degree may take six years, with major implications in terms of loss of earnings. Women who subsequently take time out of the labour market to have children may experience a cumulative financial penalty, contributing to the persistent gender pay gap.

A further problem is that students who enter university with HN qualifications rather than a mixture of Highers and Advanced Highers are more likely than others to drop out, particularly from ancient universities (Kadar-Satat and Iannelli, 2016). As noted in our earlier review of the literature, this is likely to reflect a lack of alignment between the academic requirements of college HN courses and university degree programmes (Gallacher, 2014). For example, students on college courses are required to demonstrate the attainment of learning outcomes, which in some disciplinary areas, such as social care, may be practical rather than academic. Particularly in ancient universities, relatively little attention has been paid to supporting articulating college students once they are enrolled. Even for those who articulate with no credit (this group of students undertake a college HN course and then move into the first year of a university degree programme), there may be challenges. First-year teaching in some selective Scottish universities is at SCQF Level 8 (assuming attainment of Advanced Highers or A levels), so students entering these universities with Highers or HN qualifications are likely to find that there is a sudden increase in the level of academic work expected, with little additional support.

Quite apart from academic challenges, social barriers may also be encountered. Students entering the second or third year of a university programme after a college HN course may find that informal academic and social networks are already established. Breaking into these networks would be difficult for any student, but is likely to be particularly challenging for those from less advantaged backgrounds who may be the first in their family to attend university. Furthermore, because most articulation routes are from college to post-92 universities, the choice of degree subjects available to this group of students is limited. For example, to gain access to a higher paying job in the field of law or medicine, it is necessary to study at an older university.

Conclusion and future policy scenarios

College-based higher education has become an increasingly central part of the UK higher education system over time, particularly in Scotland, and its strengths in attracting students from less advantaged social backgrounds have often been emphasised. However, far less attention has been paid to its disadvantages. Almost half of students who embark on an HN course at a Scottish college do not progress to university-level study either because this was never their intention or because they encountered insurmountable hurdles along the way. Of those who do progress to degree level study, only half receive full credit for their earlier qualifications, resulting in up to six years of full-time study to obtain a bachelor's degree which would have taken three years in England. Drop-out rates are higher for those on 'two plus two' courses than for other students. Finally, those who graduate from colleges rather than universities appear to have significantly lower earning potential. These disadvantages accrue disproportionately to those from less advantaged backgrounds, and we should therefore be cautious in assuming equivalence between college and university higher education programmes.

In the light of these issues, in the following sections, we consider some of the future possibilities for college-based higher education in Scotland, returning to the need to ensure that the system of higher education system in Scotland is not only efficient, but also fair.

Improving articulation routes

The problem of poor articulation between college and university higher education is well recognised and is one of the principal areas being addressed by the recently appointed Commissioner for Fair Access in Scotland.[2] In light of the expansion of articulation routes between college and university, it has been argued that students with HN qualifications should always receive full accreditation, allowing them to progress to the second or third year of a university honours programme in the subject and institution of their choosing. As noted earlier, more selective universities may require students with HN qualifications to undertake a full degree programme. As a result, students who begin their higher education career in a college before moving to university may take six years to gain a degree. Issues, of course, arise with regard to the subject-specific knowledge that may be required by particular degree programmes and restrictions on student places in some areas such as medicine. However, if it were demonstrated that college-based higher education could provide a route into more selective universities, its status would almost certainly improve. Clearly, these issues will continue to be debated, but radical action is needed to address well-documented but unsolved problems of 'dependency and difficulty' (Bathmaker et al., 2008) in the relationship between colleges and universities, where colleges may be positioned as the 'poor relation'.

Responding directly to rising demand for university entry

The available evidence suggests that the growth in college entry has been due in part to an increase in the number of students wishing to gain entry to university, but who are unable to do so, with colleges relied on to absorb unmet demand for direct university entry, and for university level education more generally. College places are funded at a lower level, providing government with a strong incentive to allow the system to drift in this direction. In February 2017, after sustained questioning about the supply of university places by the Scottish Parliament's Public Audit and Post-Legislative Scrutiny Committee, John Swinney, the Cabinet Secretary of Education, conceded that it was likely that suitably qualified young people were failing to gain entry to university, saying that 'not everyone who wants to go to university is able to go to university'. However, this has never been clearly set out as a formal policy position and subject to scrutiny as such. The equity implications of a de facto policy of diverting young people from university to college requires far more attention. It carries a substantial risk of further stratifying the higher education experience, for as long as those entering the college sector are disproportionately from more disadvantaged backgrounds, compared to those gaining a university place. A detailed study of the current relationship between supply and demand for direct university entry, particularly among school leavers, at the national and sub-national levels is overdue. A plan to address any growing mismatch might include targeting additional university places towards parts of the country where there is persistent evidence of under-supply. Bathmaker (2016) has argued that colleges with a significant proportion of higher education provision should be recognised and valued as HE providers in their own right, rather than being seen as precursors to university provision. An alternative view is that colleges can successfully include a substantial higher education role without compromising their broader purpose, but only if it is for those for whom college entry is the preference. The more colleges are used as a substitute for direct university entry for those who want and are ready for it, the harder they may find it to maintain a distinctively valued identity.

Tackling disproportionalities within the higher education sector

We began this chapter by outlining of view of the criteria which should be used to judge the fairness of Scotland's higher education system. While acknowledging the multi-dimensional nature of social justice and equality, we emphasised that judgements of systemic fairness should be based on an analysis of the economic and social outcomes which are produced. In this chapter, we demonstrated the disproportionalities in participation by different social groups in different types of institution, noting that Scotland's fee-free regime continues to underpin a highly stratified system, where young people from socially advantaged backgrounds are concentrated in high status universities, while those from disadvantaged backgrounds are congregated in colleges. Colleges have been responsible for the vast majority of progress in relation to widening access, but students who find themselves on college courses face many additional barriers compared with their privileged peers. It is sometimes quite difficult to question the Scottish government's reliance on colleges to undertake the bulk of widening access work, since raising concerns of this nature may be interpreted as intellectual snobbery or a desire to protect the vested interests of universities. Throughout this chapter, we have acknowledged the work of both colleges and universities, but fairness will not be achieved until equal proportions of students from different social backgrounds are present in each type of institution. The Scottish government's widening access targets set out the expectation that by 2021 those from the most disadvantaged 20 per cent of backgrounds at least 10 per cent of entrants to every university, and, by 2026, 18 per cent of university entrants in total. By 2030, the government expects equal representation of different social groups in higher education overall. These targets still leave scope for institutional stratification. In order to monitor progress towards socially just patterns of participation, far better data are needed on 'who goes where and does what' (Reay, 1998), not just at college or university, but also in relation to later labour market outcomes.

Notes

1 Scottish Funding Council (2015). *Learning for all: Measures of Success*. Edinburgh: Scottish Funding Council, Table 12.
2 In December 2016, Professor Sir Peter Scott was appointed by the Scottish government as the first Commissioner for Fair Access following the publication of the report of the Commission on Widening Access.

References

Bathmaker, A.-M. (2016) 'Higher education in further education: The challenges of providing a distinctive contribution that contributes to widening participation', *Research in Post-Compulsory Education*, vol. 21, no. 1–2, pp. 20–32.

Bathmaker, A.-M., Brooks, G., Parry, G., and Smith, D. (2008) 'Dual-sector further and higher education: Policies, organisation and students in transition', *Research Papers in Education*, vol. 2, no. 2, pp. 125–137.

Bathmaker, A.-M. and Thomas, W. (2009) 'Positioning themselves: An exploration of the nature and meaning of transitions in the context of dual sector FE/HE institutions in England', *Journal of Further and Higher Education*, vol. 33, no. 2, pp. 119–130.

Boliver, V. (2011) 'Expansion, differentiation and the persistence of social class inequalities in British higher education', *Higher Education*, vol. 61, pp. 229–242.

Cable, V. (2010) *A New Era for Universities: Oral Statement to Parliament* [Online], DBIS. Available at www.gov.uk/government/speeches/a-new-era-for-universities (Accessed 24 March 2018).

Christie, H., Tett, L., Cree, V. E., Hounsell, J., and McCune, V. (2008) 'A real rollercoaster of confidence and emotions': Learning to be a university student', *Studies in Higher Education*, vol. 33, no. 5, pp. 567–581.

Department for Business, Innovation and Skills (BIS) (2011) *Returns to Higher Education Qualifications: BIS Research Paper* No. 45, London, BIS.

Fraser, N. (2005) 'Reframing justice in a globalized world', *New Left Review*, vol. 36, pp. 69–88.

Gallacher, J. (2006) 'Widening access or differentiation and stratification in higher education in Scotland', *Higher Education Quarterly*, vol. 60, no. 4, pp. 349–369.

Gallacher, J. (2009) 'Higher education in Scotland's colleges: A distinctive tradition', *Higher Education*, vol. 63, no. 4, pp. 384–401.

Gallacher, J. (2014) 'Higher education in Scotland: Differentiation and diversion? The impact of college-university progression links', *International Journal of Lifelong Education*, vol. 33, no. 1, pp. 96–107.

Gallacher, J. and Raffe, D. (2012) 'Higher education in post-devolution UK: More convergence than divergence?', *Journal of Education Policy*, vol. 27, no. 4, pp. 467–490.

Gasteen, A. and Houston, J. (2007) 'Employability and earnings returns to qualifications in Scotland', *Regional Studies*, vol. 41, pp. 443–451.

Greer, S. L. (ed.) (2009) *Devolution and Social Citizenship in the UK*, Bristol, Policy Press.

Higher Education Funding Council for England (HEFCE) (2013) *Destinations of Leavers from Higher Education in Further Education Colleges Key Findings: Leavers Up to Academic Year 2010–11*, Bristol, HEFCE.

Hunter Blackburn, S., Kadar-Satat, G., Riddell, S., and Weedon, E. (2016) *Access to Higher Education for People from Less Advantaged Backgrounds in Scotland*, London, The Sutton Trust.

Ingram, R. and Gallacher, J. (2011) *HN Tracking Study: Final Report*, Glasgow, Glasgow Caledonian University.

Ingram, R. and Gallacher, J. (2013) *Making the Transition for College to University: The Experiences of HN Students*, Glasgow, Glasgow Caledonian University.

Kadar-Satat, G. and Iannelli, C. (2016) *Beyond Access to Higher Education: Widening Access Initiatives and Student Retention in Scotland*, Edinburgh, AQMeN, University of Edinburgh.

Miller, D. (1999) *Principles of Social Justice*, Cambridge, MA & London, Harvard University Press.

Mooney, G. and Scott, G. (eds.) (2012) *Social Justice and Social Policy in Scotland*, Bristol, Policy Press.

Parry, G. (2009) 'Higher education, further education and the English experiment', *Higher Education Quarterly*, vol. 63, no. 4, pp. 322–342.

Parry, G. (2012) 'Higher education in further education colleges: A primer', *Perspective*, vol. 16, no. 4, pp. 118–122.

Phillips, A. (2004) *Defending Equality of Outcome* [Online], London, LSE Research Online. Available at http://eprints.lse.ac.uk/archive/00000533 (Accessed 24 March 2018).

Raffe, D. and Byrne, D. (2005) *Policy Learning from "Home International" Comparisons* [Online], CES Briefing No. 34. Edinburgh: Centre for Educational Sociology, University of Edinburgh. Available at www.ces.ed.ac.uk/PDF%20Files/Brief034.pdf (Accessed 16 October 2017).

Raffe, D. and Croxford, L. (2015) 'How stable is the stratification of higher education in England and Scotland?' *British Journal of Sociology of Education*, vol. 36, no. 2, pp. 313–335.

Rawls, J. (1971) *Theory of Justice*, Cambridge, MA, Harvard University Press.

Reay, D. (1998) '"Always knowing" and "never being sure": Familial and institutional habituses and higher education choice', *Journal of Education Policy*, vol. 1, no. 4, pp. 519–529.

Riddell, S., Weedon, E., and Minty, S. (2016) *Higher Education in Scotland and the UK: Diverging or Converging Systems?*, Edinburgh, Edinburgh University Press.

Scottish Government (2013) *Scotland's Future: Your Guide to an Independent Scotland*, Edinburgh, Scottish Government.

Scottish Government (2016) *A Blueprint for Fairness: Final Report of the Commission on Widening Access*, Edinburgh, Scottish Government.

Sen, A. (1992) *Inequality Re-Examined*, Oxford, Clarendon Press.

Universities Scotland (2014) *Delivering for Scotland: The Third Round of Outcome Agreements for Higher Education*, Edinburgh, Universities Scotland.

Chapter 14

The American community college

Complex missions, challenging reforms

Kevin J. Dougherty, Hana Lahr and Vanessa S. Morest[1]

Introduction

Community colleges – that is, publicly controlled colleges offering two-year degrees or less[2] – play a crucial role in higher education in the United States. In fall 2015, they numbered 920 (19.9 per cent of all degree-granting post-secondary institutions) and enrolled 6.2 million students (30.4 per cent of all students in degree-granting institutions) (U.S. National Center for Education Statistics, 2017, Tables 301.10, 303.25, 317.10). Moreover, these institutions are key providers of baccalaureate opportunities, occupational education, remedial and developmental education, and other educational services (Cohen et al., 2013). This central role of community colleges is reflected in the considerable attention they have received, particularly in the last ten years, from the US government and from leading foundations (Bill and Melinda Gates Foundation, 2017; Fain, 2015; Lumina Foundation, 2016; National Conference of State Legislatures, 2017; US Office of the President, 2010).

The attention community colleges have been receiving is highly warranted, because of their important and complex role in US society, the obstacles they face in adequately meeting that role and the difficulties in resolving those obstacles given the size and complexity of the community college sector. In the following, we describe the social missions of community colleges in the United States, analyse their complex impacts and challenges and describe and evaluate policy proposals that have been made to address those challenges.

The social role of US community colleges

In this section, we describe the social role of US community colleges. We describe their main credential offerings and the missions that they pursue.

Credentials

Community colleges offer a wide variety of credentials and programmes. They span traditional academic subjects and occupational (that is, career and technical) training. The credentials include certificates (requiring a year or less of training), two-year associate degrees in both applied and liberal arts fields and, in some states, four-year baccalaureate degrees (Cohen et al., 2013; Remington and Remington 2013).

In most community colleges, a majority of the credentials awarded are in occupational fields. In 2013, 67 per cent of associate degrees and certificates awarded by community colleges were in occupational education (U.S. National Center for Education Statistics, n.d., Table P152). The community college role in workforce preparation and economic development ranges from preparing students for their first job to retraining unemployed workers and welfare recipients, upgrading the skills of employed workers, assisting owners of small businesses and helping communities with economic development planning (Dougherty and Bakia, 2000; Cohen et al., 2013; Grubb, 1996; Jacobs and Dougherty, 2006).

However, baccalaureate preparation is also an important function of community colleges. Most community college students intend to get a bachelor's degree. Among first-time students who entered community colleges in 2003–04, 81.4 per cent aspired to ultimately complete a bachelor's degree or higher, and, by 2007–2008, 21.1 per cent had transferred to a four-year institution (Horn and Skomsvold, 2012, Tables 1-A and 3-A). Moreover, an increasing number of community colleges are offering baccalaureate degrees (Floyd et al., 2005; Remington and Remington, 2013).

Mission

The central mission of community college colleges is to be mass-access institutions, open to virtually the whole of a community. Hence, they offer a wide variety of programmes and credentials, charge lower tuitions than most other institutions, admit students even if they lack conventional college qualifications and operate in the evening and on weekends in dispersed locations as well as online. This breadth of mission is captured in the ethos of 'the open door college', which strongly differentiates community colleges from the more selective ethos of four-year colleges, particularly research universities (Bailey and Morest, 2006; Cohen et al., 2013; Handel and Williams, 2012).

In good part because of their broad mission and open door ethos, US community colleges tend to attract many more working class, minority and older students than do public and private universities. With regard to social class, 58 per cent of community college students in 2006 were in the bottom half of the socio-economic status (SES) distribution, while the comparable figure for students in 'competitive' public and private four-year colleges was 34 per cent (Carnevale and Strohl, 2010, Table 3.7). Meanwhile, in 2003–04, 40 per cent of community college students were non-white, while only 30 per cent of public four-year college students were students of colour (Provasnik and Planty, 2008, p. 40). Finally, 53 per cent of community college students in 2003–04 were age

24 or older, while the figure for public four-year colleges was only 19 per cent (Provasnik and Planty, 2008, p. 40).

In short, community colleges are assigned a key and very difficult role. They are expected to provide higher education opportunity and social mobility for less advantaged students. But this is to occur in a society with great social class and race inequality, where higher education access and completion are subject to powerful socio-political forces mobilised to preserve that inequality (Bastedo and Jaquette, 2011; Brint and Karabel, 1989; Dougherty, 1994; Karabel, 2005).

To a considerable degree, community colleges effectively address the complicated mission that they have been assigned. Several studies find that states and localities that are highly endowed with community colleges have significantly higher rates of college attendance than states and localities with a smaller community college presence (Dougherty, 1994; Leigh and Gill, 2003; Roksa, 2008; Rouse, 1998).

Community colleges also play a central role in supplying trained workers for 'middle level', 'semiprofessional' or 'technical' occupations such as nurses, computer operators and auto mechanics (Cohen et al., 2013; Grubb, 1996). In essence, community colleges play the role of the technical schools and apprenticeship systems found in other countries, and there is every reason to believe this role will expand with the growing call for more sub-baccalaureate education and a revival of apprenticeship training (Jacobs, 2015; Rosenbaum et al., 2017). Community colleges have experienced considerable success in their vocational training role. Career/technical graduates of community colleges receive substantial economic payoffs. For example, students earning a vocational associate's (two-year) degree from a community college on average earn 15 per cent to 30 per cent more in annual income than high school graduates of similar race and ethnicity, parental education, marital status and job experience (Belfield and Bailey, 2017; Grubb, 2002; Marcotte et al., 2005; Rosenbaum et al., 2017).

Challenges for USA community colleges

Despite their undoubted contributions, US community colleges have also been bedevilled by some major problems, particularly poor rates of credentials completion. We first document this problem and then analyse its causes.

Poor credentials completion

Many students entering the community college leave higher education without a degree (Rosenbaum et al., 2017). A national survey of students who entered a community college in fall 2010 found that six years later 45 per cent had left higher education without a degree of any kind. This figure contrasts strongly with that for students entering public four-year colleges and universities: 24 per cent (Shapiro et al., 2017).

Contributory factors

Several factors come together to produce the low rate of credentials completion described above. We will highlight both student and institutional factors.

Community college students are hampered by the fact that, on average, they are less well off financially than four-year college entrants. They also more often have family caregiving responsibilities. As a result, they more often need to take outside work, attend part-time and interrupt their studies. All this makes it more likely than they will eventually drop out (Goldrick-Rab, 2010; Seidman, 2005).

Another major source of the subpar results for many community college entrants is the fact that many enter higher education facing major academic obstacles to succeeding in higher education (Bailey et al., 2015; Goldrick-Rab, 2010). For example, among students entering higher education in fall 2004, straight out of high school, 53.2 per cent of those entering community college scored in the bottom half in tested math in the 12th grade, while the comparable figure for those entering public four-year colleges was 18.6 per cent (Provasnik and Planty, 2008, p. 54).

The organisation and operation of many community colleges and their subordinate place within a stratified system of higher education also has much to do with the inadequate outcomes for community college students (Bailey et al., 2015; Brint and Karabel, 1989; Dougherty, 1994, 2002; Handel and Williams, 2012; Rosenbaum et al., 2017). When we compare community college entrants and four-year college entrants with the same family background, academic preparation, and educational and occupational aspirations, community college entrants on average attain about 15 per cent *fewer* baccalaureate degrees than their four-year college peers. This baccalaureate gap holds even in quasi-experimental studies that systematically address issues of selection bias through instrumental-variables or propensity-score analysis (Doyle, 2008; Long and Kurlaender, 2009; Monaghan and Attewell, 2015; see also Dougherty, 1994; Jenkins and Fink, 2016). Similarly, community colleges differ significantly in their production of applied workforce credentials (certificates and associates of applied sciences) and the average earnings of their graduates, even when we control for the characteristics of their students (Clotfelter et al., 2013; Dunn and Kalleberg, 2016). This suggests the impact of institutional and systemic factors on student completion.

One of the central institutional obstacles that community college students encounter is that community colleges have great difficulty providing clear and consistent advice to students that will allow them to chart efficient paths through the institution, without getting lost, ending up in cul-de-sacs or taking too many courses. As many observers have noted, community colleges are typically organised like cafeterias, offering a plethora of courses and programmes but insufficient advice and structure on which ones to choose (Bailey et al., 2015; Karp, 2013; Rosenbaum et al., 2017).

Intake student advising at too many community colleges is poorly organised, with too many advisers who are part-time, not particularly expert and not able to spend much time with students (Bailey et al., 2015; Karp, 2013; Rosenbaum et al., 2017; Rosenbaum et al., 2006). Subsequent advising is often haphazard as well, with limited monitoring of student progress and guidance. Typically, detailed case management is largely missing, with colleges often unable to keep track of whether students are off track and provide personalised, developmental advising (Bailey et al., 2015; Rosenbaum et al., 2017).

Students needing academic and social support are also not well served by the organisational structure favoured by many community colleges. Student services often are scattered around the college and not well publicised. As a result, these student services may be hard to find and are accessed largely by students who are self-motivated and persistent (Bailey et al., 2015; Karp, 2013; Rosenbaum et al., 2006, 2017; Scott-Clayton, 2015).

Finally, developmental education is not working well in many community colleges. Developmental education is addressed to students who enter community college with academic skills – particularly in mathematics, reading or writing – that are judged as below college level (Cohen et al., 2013). Community colleges address these perceived skills gaps in a variety of ways (see below). National studies find that only 30 per cent of developmental students finish the developmental math courses in which they are enrolled (the figure for those in reading courses is 71 per cent) (Bailey, 2009, p. 13). And careful quantitative studies of the impact of conventional developmental education courses on course completion and later academic outcomes mainly find no impact, with positive impacts being rather rare and negative impacts not infrequent (Attewell et al., 2006; Bailey, 2009; Long and Boatman, 2013).

Promising directions of change

The difficulties community colleges encounter has produced a diverse array of policy and programmematic proposals. A number of strategies have crystallised out of these discussions: constructing clear pathways for students involving improved advising and instruction; restructuring occupational education; revamping transfer articulation; and restructuring developmental education.

Constructing clear pathways for students

The 'guided pathways' model has emerged as a particularly influential strategy for moving community colleges away from the 'cafeteria' model and toward a more integrated and cohesive model for student success in college (Bailey et al., 2015; Jenkins et al., 2017; see also Fein, 2012; Rosenbaum et al., 2006; Rosenbaum et al., 2017). This new approach has three central elements: systematically designing courses and programmes to facilitate transition to employment and further education; emphasising guided student choice of programmes and careers and creating a comprehensive educational plan for every student; and revamping advising structures and processes to ensure that students are making timely progress along their educational plan.

Systematic programme and course design

Under the guided pathways model, faculty and advisors should lay the ground-work for clearer pathways to further education and employment by mapping out programmes of study in consultation with employers and university part-ners. Degree maps should be constructed that chart which courses should be taken and in what sequence in order to complete credentials or to be ready for transfer to a university (Jenkins et al., 2017). A key principle of the new path-ways approach is that clear learning objectives (skills and knowledge) should be defined for each course and programme and each programme should prepare students for employment and further education in a given field. These pro-gramme objectives are supposed to provide a framework unifying curriculum, instruction, assessment, advising and course scheduling (Bailey et al., 2015).

Guided student exploration and choice

A second key element of the guided pathways approach is proactively reach-ing out to students to inform and structure their choices rather than letting them make poorly informed, often haphazard decisions (Bailey et al., 2015; Jenkins et al., 2017; Karp, 2013; Rosenbaum et al., 2006, 2017). This approach draws heavily on research in cognitive psychology and behavioural econom-ics (Kahneman, 2011; Scott-Clayton, 2015; Thaler and Sunstein, 2008; Thaler et al., 2013). This guided choice approach involves restricting the number of big choices students make so that they do not end up lunging at a choice with little information or making no choice at all because they are paralysed by the number of options available. One way of guiding student choice is to com-bine various discrete majors into 'meta majors' that students initially select and then within a meta major they make a later selection of a particular major. For example, St. Petersburg College in Florida has 10 'Career and Academic Com-munities'[3] and Northeast Wisconsin Technical College has 13 'Fields of Inter-est'.[4] Within these meta majors, students are helped to explore various degree and certificate options and more clearly see how these educational programmes lead to employment and careers. Some colleges are also developing a default curriculum for each meta major that provides exposure to the field of interest and lays the basis for later selecting a specific major (Bailey et al., 2015; Jenkins et al., 2017). Other colleges are designing, within each meta major, student suc-cess courses that provide advice to students on career planning, how to choose a major, study skills and so forth (Jenkins et al., 2017).

Revamped advising structures and processes

The revamped advising system in a guided pathways model would involve hir-ing more advisers, providing them with more training, attaching them more directly to the meta majors and using a case management approach (Bailey et al.,

2015; Jenkins et al., 2017; Karp, 2013; see also Rosenbaum et al., 2006, 2017). Degree audit systems should continuously track student progress on their education plan, provide suggestions on courses to take the following semester that are consonant with that plan, and prompt students and advisers to meet when the students hit certain cross points or have hit a course snag (Bailey et al., 2015; Jenkins et al., 2017; Rosenbaum et al., 2017; Wyner et al., 2016). Many colleges are considering how technology can be used to monitor how well students are progressing toward their goals and to facilitate advising processes and interactions that students might need (Kalamkarian et al., 2017; Karp, 2013). While advising will become more automated, it need not be at the expense of more personalised advising. The hope is that automating some tasks will allow for more personalised and in-person engagement.

Restructuring occupational education

The guided pathways model has great relevance to restructuring occupational education or career and technical education, in good part because it owes much of its origins to policy learning that occurred over several decades in the field of occupational education (Alssid et al., 2002; Fein, 2012). However, career pathways into the labour market have some specific features in addition to those general to the guided pathways model.

Because the focus of career pathways is on preparation for work (even if later education may be contemplated as well), those calling for such pathways argue that community colleges need to work closely with noneducational agencies to define skill requirements, determine labour demands and allocate training efforts. These noneducational agencies include employers, economic development and training agencies and organisations and community service organisations (Alssid et al., 2002; Bragg et al., 2012; Cleary et al., 2017; Fein, 2012; Jacobs, 2015; National Skills Coalition, 2017).[5] Moreover, because many occupational education students tend to be older and have multiple life obligations, career pathways will need to schedule courses at times that jibe with students' work schedules, attend to students' need for short-term as well as long-term credentials, address students' life circumstances (including child care, housing and transportation needs), efficiently integrate academic skills development (adult education and developmental education) with occupational education and general education and provide job-placement advising (Bragg et al., 2012; Fein, 2012; National Skills Coalition, 2017; Rosenbaum et al., 2017). Advocates of career pathways argue that attention to both short-term credentials (certificates taking a year or less) and long-term ones (two-year associates or four-year baccalaureate degrees) can be facilitated by constructing career pathways that allow for 'stackable' credentials, where short-term credentials lead into and can be credited toward longer-term ones. For example, a student might first graduate from a one year or less certificate programme leading to a job as an accounting clerk and subsequently add a two-year associate's degree leading to a job as a payroll clerk or a business assistant with accounting responsibilities (Bailey and Belfield, 2017; see also Alssid et al., 2002; Fein, 2012; Jacobs, 2015; McCarthy, 2015; Rosenbaum et al., 2017; Strawn, 2011). Such stacking leads to consideration of how to facilitate student movement between community colleges and four-year colleges.

Revamping transfer articulation between community colleges and universities

Most recent recommendations for revamping transfer articulation draw on the general effort to create guided student pathways (Jenkins et al., 2017). However, transfer-specific reform strategies have been proposed as well for both community colleges and universities.

Community college changes

Those proposing reforms in transfer articulation argue that a fundamental prelude to improving the community college role in transfer is to create a transfer-affirming culture that permeates the community colleges and is clearly reflected in their missions, organisation and public presentation (Handel and Williams, 2012; Wyner et al., 2016). More specifically, community colleges need to ensure that their instruction is on par with the requirements of receiving universities and four-year colleges (Morest, 2013; Wyner et al., 2016). Moreover, transfer aspirants should be strongly encouraged to leave the community college with an associate's degree in hand, since there is strong evidence that transfer students who are degree holders succeed better after transfer than those who leave the community college without a degree (Bailey et al., 2017; Jenkins and Fink, 2015). Finally, the quality of transfer advising should be improved by such means as pushing students to make an early selection of a major or meta major so that their advising can become more focused; providing transfer programme maps laying out courses, their prerequisites and recommended internships and other extracurricular activities; requiring students to take a college success course that includes rich transfer information; and advising students about how to finance their higher education over the full course of a baccalaureate degree (Bailey et al., 2017; Handel and Williams, 2012; Wyner et al., 2016).

Changes by universities and four-year colleges

A good part of transfer effectiveness lies in the hands not just of community colleges but also of four-year institutions and state governments. Four-year institutions decide how many transfer students they will accept, into which programmes and with which number of credits applied toward a baccalaureate degree.

Hence, policy researchers recommend that universities must join community colleges in creating a transfer-affirming culture. This would involve explicitly recognising how many transfer students they receive, how important they are to the university mission and how well they perform at university (Handel and Williams, 2012; Wyner et al., 2016). In order to increase the number and preparation of transfer students, universities are urged to set admission targets for transfer students; provide transfer aspirants with detailed information about university course requirements, funding availability, and transfer credit policies; and set aside funding for transfer students (Dougherty, 2002; Handel and Williams, 2012; Wyner et al., 2016). Finally, universities should aid their transfer students by improving their university advising through detailed degree maps and dedicated transfer advisers (Wyner et al., 2016).

Restructuring developmental education

The final set of policy recommendations for improving student outcomes in community colleges concern developmental education, that is, meeting the needs of students who enter community college with academic skills that are judged as below college level. Again, this effort is related to the guided pathways reforms, but there are additions specific to developmental education (Bailey et al., 2015; Jenkins et al., 2017; Morest, 2013; Rosenbaum et al., 2017).

Reducing the need for developmental education

Policy reformer argue that high schools and their students need to become more aware of where students' skills exiting high school do not align with college requirements through such means as early assessment and dual enrolment and make efforts to reduce that misalignment. For example, California has a programme in which students are tested during the 10th or 11th grades on their college proficiency so they get a sense of where they really stand. Those who score low are provided special math and English courses to improve their skills. An evaluation of the California Early Assessment Programme found that it reduces the need for remediation in college by 6.2 per cent in English and 4.3 per cent in math (Bailey et al., 2015; Long and Boatman, 2013). Another device for inculcating early awareness and remediation of skill deficiencies is dual enrolment, in which high school students take college-level courses while still in high school (Bailey et al., 2015; Morest, 2013).

Revamping student assessment at college entry

Research has found that scores on proficiency exams at the outset of community college are not highly predictive of who actually needs developmental education. Hence, policy researchers have strongly advocated efforts to revamp how entry assessment is done (Bailey et al., 2015; Morest, 2013; Rosenbaum et al., 2017). Colleges are developing placement tests that more closely align with college-level skills demands (Bailey et al., 2015). But even if colleges do not wish to put in this much effort, they have been urged not to rely on single test scores but rather use multiple measures. The predictive validity of assessment of student need for developmental education is considerably higher if colleges use both proficiency test scores and high school transcript data (grade point average and number of English and math courses completed). This reduces the incidence of students being placed in developmental education when it is likely they do not really need it (Bailey et al., 2015; Scott-Clayton et al., 2014).

Reshaping developmental education instruction

If students indeed need developmental education in community college, it becomes important to do it better, given the poor record of conventional developmental education (Attewell et al., 2006; Bailey, 2009; Long and Boatman, 2013). The typical form of developmental education has involved semester-long courses that meet 3–5 hours a week, focus on narrow skills in math and English rather than higher-order skills (e.g. assessing an argument or understanding statistical tables) and use a teacher-centred pedagogy relying on checklists and skill drilling (Bailey et al., 2015, pp. 120–121, 128–129; Grubb and associates, 1999, chapter 5). Various efforts are being made across the US to move beyond traditional developmental education by accelerating it and tying it more closely to college-level demands so students are less discouraged and less often drop out (Bailey et al., 2015; Jenkins et al., 2017; Long and Boatman, 2013; Morest, 2013; Rosenbaum et al., 2017). The popular 'co-requisite model' aims to place students in regular college-level courses – particularly students who need less developmental education – but provide extensive supplementary support (Bailey et al., 2015; Jenkins et al., 2017; Morest, 2013). Another emerging model is to contextualise developmental education with specific subject matter, often in vocational education, so that students can more readily grasp the utility of the math, reading, or writing skills they are acquiring in their developmental education course (Bailey et al., 2015; Long and Boatman, 2013; Morest, 2013). A final device is to compress developmental education courses and to tailor them to the specific skills students will need in introductory college level courses (Bailey et al., 2015). Evaluation studies have begun to accumulate indicating the fruitfulness of each of these approaches (Bailey et al., 2015).

Prospects for the reform programme

The reform programme described above – constructing clear pathways for students, reconstructing occupational education, revamping transfer articulation and restructuring developmental education – is clearly attractive. It is conceptually elegant and increasingly backed up empirically. Still, that reform programme faces daunting challenges. Let us review both the progress made by the reform programme and the challenges it faces.

Progress

The advocates of the reform programme have articulated a well conceptualised set of reforms that has attracted strong support from the Gates and other foundations, the federal and state governments, the American Association of Community Colleges, many community colleges and various policy and advocacy organisations (Jenkins et al., 2017). Moreover, early assessments of programmes taking the guided pathways approach find evidence that it is yielding significant benefits (Bragg et al., 2012; Strawn, 2011; Jenkins et al., 2017; Zeidenberg et al., 2010). For example, an early assessment of the performance of the 30 community colleges that are part of the AACC Pathways Project of the American Association of Community Colleges has found that almost all are making striking progress in implementing key aspects of the reform agenda (Jenkins et al., 2017). While most have not yet moved to full-scale implementation, all are moving steadily through initial planning to partial implementation of the many of the reforms discussed above.

Challenges

Despite the above, we are still a long way from determining whether these reform initiatives do indeed significantly boost the achievement and credential completion of community college students. Reason for caution comes from awareness of the important challenges – conceptual/empirical, financial and political – that the reform programme faces. Each is rather daunting, but by no means insurmountable.

Conceptual/empirical challenges

The reform programme has several different strands that may not always fit together smoothly. Will community colleges encounter tensions between constructing pathways to move students smoothly through the community college, restructuring training for the labour market, revamping preparation for transfer to university and reshaping developmental education? Historically, these various community college missions have proven to be rather contradictory, with community college effort in one area undercutting effort in other areas (Dougherty, 1994, 2002).

Furthermore, the reform programme has not yet specifically addressed how the proposed reforms will interact with differences among students, particularly by race, social class, gender and age. For example, is the quality of advising for female and minority students significantly affected by the racial and gender background and attitudes of their advisers? Moreover, more research is required to know whether these reforms will help address the persistent completion gaps for low-income and racial minority students in higher education.[6]

Another major conceptual/empirical challenge for the guided pathways programme concerns the determination of the skills requirements for occupational students. Employers and others have great difficulty forecasting what future skills requirements will be. They often state that skills demands are rising rapidly and that they are facing labour shortages, when in fact the evidence is quite ambiguous on both counts (Cappelli, 2014; Cleary et al., 2017, p. 586). Moreover, even if employers can effectively forecast their skills requirements, there remains the perennial problem that employers tend to focus on their own *immediate* skills needs, which may be at variance with their *long-term* skill needs and the need of workers to be prepared for lifelong learning (Cappelli, 2014; Cleary et al., 2017, p. 594).

But even if we do set these issues aside, there is still question about the empirical validity of the reform programme. As its advocates note, there is good evidence backing up this or that element of the programme but there is not much evidence on impact of the model as a whole. This lack is not easily remedied because it would be hard to do an experimental study on any model that requires institutional-level redesign (Bailey et al., 2015). That said, evaluations of the new Guttman Community College of the City University of New York – which has implemented many of the principles of the reform agenda – have found positive results (Bailey et al., 2015; Jenkins et al., 2017; Rosenbaum et al., 2017).

Financial challenges

A full-throttle pursuit of the guided pathways reform agenda will not be cheap. In fact, research indicates that the cost per entering student will go up, even if – because of higher completion rates – the cost *per graduate* will drop (Bailey et al., 2015; Jenkins et al., 2017). Given this, will guided pathways reforms suffer spending cuts in times of economic recession and cutbacks in government spending on higher education? This is particularly an issue for community colleges because of their greater dependence on state appropriations and the fact that they are already underfunded in comparison to public universities (Kahlenberg, 2015; Romano and Palmer, 2015). Moreover, most colleges that are implementing guided pathways are receiving little or no funding – either from state government or from philanthropy – to do this work. The one major exception is California, which appropriated $150 million to its community colleges implement pathways.

Political challenges

The financial challenges described above morph easily into political challenges that the guided pathways reform programme faces. The reforms proposed involve major changes in instruction and advising that touch very directly on the faculty role. While faculty may be broadly in sympathy with the goals of the guided pathways reform programme, they may be disquieted by specific elements. An indication of this possibility was the stiff faculty resistance within the City University of New York to the changes proposed under the Pathways programme (Bailey et al., 2015; Logue, 2017). Finally, the concept of guided choice faces a difficult challenge. There is a long-standing American tendency to decry efforts to guide student occupational choices as a 'socialist' restriction on choice (Schlafly, 1997). This opposition to any seeming restriction of choice is short-sighted because it ignores the restrictions of choice created by systems of social stratification and market forces (Dougherty, in press), but it remains a potent force as can be seen in the continuing American war over health care.

Summary and conclusions

This paper has analysed the organisation, social contributions, challenges and new reform directions of the American community college. Numbering nearly a thousand and enrolling nearly one-third of all students in American higher education, community colleges play a key role in college access, baccalaureate provision and job preparation. But this key role is marred by the fact that community colleges have inadequate rates of credentials completion. These problems are rooted to a great degree in institutional obstacles and systemic problems in American higher education. A powerful reform agenda has risen to address these problems, centred on charting clear student pathways into, though and out of the community college. This agenda provides a powerful roadmap for how to improve the community college. However, it also faces significant conceptual/empirical, financial and political challenges.

Notes

1 We wish to thank Davis Jenkins and Melinda Mechur Karp for their very helpful comments on an earlier draft of this paper. We also wish to thank Jim Jacobs for very useful leads on recent reforms in occupational education. All remaining errors are the authors' own.
2 In Florida and some other states, we would also have to include as community colleges formerly two-year institutions that now offer baccalaureate degrees as well (Floyd et al., 2005; Remington and Remington, 2013).
3 See The St. Petersburg College website, https://go.spcollege.edu/aos
4 See Northeast Wisconsin Technical College website, www.nwtc.edu/programs/fields-of-interest
5 See below for the challenges involved in working with employers and others to define labour market skills demands.
6 However, the Community College Research Center is launching a research programme to examine the impacts of guided pathways reforms on students of different racial and income backgrounds.

References

Alssid, J. L., Gruber, D., Jenkins, D., Mazzeo, C., Roberts, B., and Stanback-Stroud, R. (2002) *Building a Career Pathways System: Promising Practices in Community College-Centered Workforce Development*, New York, NY, Workforce Strategy Center.
Attewell, P., Lavin, D. E., Domina, T., and Levey, T. (2006) 'New evidence on college remediation', *Journal of Higher Education*, vol. 77, no. 5, pp. 886–924.

Bailey, T. (2009) 'Challenge and opportunity: Rethinking the role and function of developmental education in community college', in Harbour, C. P. and Farrell, P. L. (eds.), *Contemporary Issues in Institutional Ethics: New Directions for Community Colleges #148*, San Francisco, CA, Jossey-Bass, pp. 11–30.

Bailey, T. and Belfield, C. (2017) *Stackable Credentials: Awards for the Future?* [Online], CCRC Working Paper #92, New York, NY, Columbia University, Teachers College, Community College Research Center. Available at https://ccrc.tc.columbia.edu/publications/stackable-credentials-awards-for-future.html (Accessed 24 March 2018).

Bailey, T., Jaggars, S., and Jenkins, D. (2015) *Redesigning America's Community Colleges*, Cambridge, MA, Harvard University Press.

Bailey, T., Jenkins, J., Fink, J., Cullinane, J., and Schudde, L. (2017) *Policy Levers to Strengthen Community College Transfer Student Success in Texas* [Online], New York, NY, Columbia University, Teachers College, Community College Research Center. Available at http://ccrc.tc.columbia.edu/publications/policy-levers-to-strengthen-community-college-transfer-student-success-in-texas.html (Accessed 24 March 2018).

Bailey, T. and Morest, V. S. (eds.) (2006) *Defending the Community College Equity Agenda*, Baltimore, MD, Johns Hopkins University Press.

Barnett, E. A. and Bragg, D. D. (2006) 'Academic pathways and increased opportunities for underserved students: Crosscutting themes and lessons learned', *New Directions for Community Colleges*, no. 135, pp. 101–107.

Bastedo, M. and Jaquette, O. (2011) 'Running in place: Low-income students and the dynamics of higher education stratification', *Educational Evaluation and Policy Analysis*, vol. 33, no. 3, pp. 318–339.

Belfield, C. and Bailey, T. (2017) *The Labor Market Returns to Sub-Baccalaureate College: A Review*, New York, NY, Columbia University, Teachers College, Center for Analysis of Postsecondary Employment and Earnings.

Bill and Melinda Gates Foundation (BMGF) (2017) *Completion by Design* [Online], Bellevue, WA: Author. Available at http://postsecondary.gatesfoundation.org/areas-of-focus/networks/institutional-partnerships/completion-by-design (Accessed 24 March 2018).

Bragg, D., Dresser, L., and Smith, W. (2012) 'Leveraging workforce development and postsecondary education for low-skilled, low-income workers: Lessons from the Shifting Gears initiative', *New Directions for Community Colleges*, no. 157, pp. 53–77. https://doi.org/10.1002/cc.20006

Brint, S. G. and Karabel, J. B. (1989) *The Diverted Dream*, New York, NY, Oxford University Press.

Cappelli, P. (2014) 'Skill gaps, skill shortages, and skill mismatches: Evidence for the U.S.', *Working Paper* No. 20832, Cambridge, MA, National Bureau of Economic Research.

Carnevale, A. P. and Strohl, J. (2010) 'How increasing college access is increasing inequality, and what to do about it', in Kahlenberg, R. D. (ed.), *Rewarding Strivers: Helping Low-Income Students Succeed in College*, New York, NY, Century Foundation Press, pp. 71–190.

Cleary, J. L., Kerrigan, M. R., and Van Noy, M. (2017) 'Towards a new understanding of labour market alignment', in Paulsen, M. B. (ed.), *Higher Education: Handbook of Theory and Research*, New York, NY, Springer, pp. 577–629.

Clotfelter, C. T., Ladd, H. F., Muschkin, C. G., and Vigdor, J. L. (2013) 'Success in community college: Do institutions differ?', *Research in Higher Education*, vol. 54, no. 7, pp. 805–824.

Cohen, A. C., Brawer, F. B., and Kisker, C. (2013) *The American Community College*, 6th Edition, San Francisco, CA, Jossey-Bass.

Dougherty, K. J. (1994) *The Contradictory College: The Conflicting Origins, Impacts, and Futures of the Community College*, Albany, NY, State University of New York Press.

Dougherty, K. J. (2002) 'The evolving role of the community college: Policy issues and research questions', in Smart, J. and Tierney, W. (eds.), *Higher Education: Handbook of Theory and Research*, vol. 17, Dordrecht, Netherlands, Kluwer, pp. 295–348.

Dougherty, K. J. (in press). *Higher Education Choice Making in the United States: Freedom, Inequality, Legitimation*. London, UK, Centre for Global Higher Education, UCL Institution of Education, University of London.

Dougherty, K. J. and Bakia, M. F. (2000) 'Community colleges and contract training: Content, origins, and impacts', *Teachers College Record*, vol. 102, no. 1, pp. 198–244.

Doyle, W. R. (2008) 'The effect of community college enrollment on bachelor's degree completion', *Economics of Education Review*, vol. 28, no. 2, pp. 199–206.

Dunn, M. and Kalleberg, A. F. (2016) *Does College Focus Matter? Explaining Differences in Performance among Community Colleges in North Carolina*, New York, NY, Columbia University, Teachers College, Center for Analysis of Postsecondary Education and Employment.

Fain, P. (2015) 'Two years of free community college', *Inside Higher Education* [Online]. Available at www.insidehighered.com/news/2015/01/09/white-house-plans-take-tennessee-promise-national (Accessed 24 March 2018).

Fein, D. J. (2012) *Career Pathways as a Framework for Program Design and Evaluation: A Working Paper from the Innovative Strategies for Increasing Self-Sufficiency (ISIS) Project: OPRE Report # 2012–30* [Online], Washington, DC, Office of Planning, Research and Evaluation, Administration for Children and Families, Department of Health and Human Services. Available at www.acf.hhs.gov/sites/default/files/opre/inno_strategies.pdf (Accessed 24 March 2018).

Floyd, D. L., Skolnik, M., and Walker, K. (eds.) (2005) *The Community College Baccalaureate*, Sterling, VA, Stylus Press.

Goldrick-Rab, S. (2010) 'Challenges and opportunities for improving community college student success', *Review of Educational Research*, vol. 80, no. 3, pp. 437–469.

Grubb, W. N. (1996) *Working in the Middle*, San Francisco, CA, Jossey-Bass.

Grubb, W. N. (2002) 'Learning and earning in the middle, Part I: National studies of pre-baccalaureate education', *Economics of Education Review*, vol. 21, no. 4, pp. 299–321.

Grubb, W. N. and associates (1999) *Honored But Invisible: An Inside Look at Teaching in Community Colleges*, New York, NY, Routledge.

Handel, S. J. and Williams, R. A. (2012) *The Promise of the Transfer Pathway: Opportunity and Challenge for Community College Students Seeking the Baccalaureate Degree*, New York, NY, College Board.

Horn, L. and Skomsvold, P. (2012) *Community College Student Outcomes, 1994–2009* [Online], Washington, DC, National Center for Education Statistics. Available at https://nces.ed.gov/pubs2012/2012253.pdf (Accessed 24 March 2018).

Jacobs, J. (2015) 'Promising practices of community colleges in the new age of workforce development', in Van Horn, C., Edwards, T., and Green, T. (eds.), *Transforming U.S. Workforce Development Policies for the 21st Century*, Kalamazoo, MI, W.E. Upjohn Institute for Employment Research, pp. 305–314.

Jacobs, J. and Dougherty, K. J. (2006) 'The uncertain future of the workforce development mission of community colleges', in Townsend, B. T. and Dougherty, K. J. (eds.), *Community College Missions in the 21st Century: New Directions for Community Colleges No. 136*, San Francisco, CA, Jossey-Bass, pp. 53–62.

Jenkins, D. and Fink, J. (2015) *What We Know about Transfer* [Online], New York, NY, Columbia University, Teachers College, Community College Research Center. Available at http://ccrc.tc.columbia.edu/publications/what-we-know-about-transfer.html (Accessed 24 March 2018).

Jenkins, D. and Fink, J. (2016) *Tracking Transfer: New Measures of Institutional and State Effectiveness in Helping Community College Students Attain Bachelor's Degrees* [Online], New York, NY, Columbia University, Teachers College, Community College Research Center. Available at https://ccrc.tc.columbia.edu/publications/tracking-transfer-institutional-state-effectiveness.html (Accessed 24 March 2018).

Jenkins, D., Lahr, H., and Fink, J. (2017) *Implementing Guided Pathways: Early Insights from the AACC Pathways Colleges* [Online], New York, NY, Columbia University, Teachers College, Community College Research Center. Available at http://ccrc.tc.columbia.edu/publications/implementing-guided-pathways-aacc.html (Accessed 24 March 2018).

Kahlenberg, R. D. (2015) *How Higher Education Funding Shortchanges Community Colleges* [Online], New York, NY, Century Foundation. Available at https://tcf.org/content/report/how-higher-education-funding-shortchanges-community-colleges (Accessed 24 March 2018).

Kahneman, D. (2011) *Thinking, Fast and Slow*, New York, NY, Farrar, Straus, and Giroux.

Kalamkarian, H. S., Karp, M. M., and Ganga, E. (2017) *What We Know about Technology-Mediated Advising Reform* [Online], New York, NY, Columbia University, Teachers College, Community College Research Center. Available at http://ccrc.tc.columbia.edu/publications/what-we-know-technology-mediated-advising-reform.html (Accessed 24 March 2018).

Karabel, J. (2005) *The Chosen: The Hidden History of Admission and Exclusion at Harvard, Yale, and Princeton*, Boston, MA, Houghton-Mifflin.

Karp, M. M. (2013) *Entering a Program: Helping Students Make Academic and Career Decisions* [Online], New York, NY, Columbia University, Teachers College, Community College Research Center. Available at http://ccrc.tc.columbia.edu/publications/entering-a-programme-academic-and-career-decisions.html (Accessed 24 March 2018).

Leigh, D. E. and Gill, A. M. (2003) 'Do community colleges really divert students from earning bachelor's degrees?', *Economics of Education Review*, vol. 22, no. 1, pp. 23–30.

Logue, A. (2017) *Pathways to Reform: Credits and Conflict at the City University of New York*, Princeton, NJ, Princeton University Press.

Long, B. T. and Boatman, A. (2013) 'The role of remedial and development courses in access and persistence', in Perna, L. and Jones, A. (eds.), *The State of College Access and Completion*, New York, NY, Routledge, pp. 77–95.

Long, B. T. and Kurlaender, M. (2009) 'Do community colleges provide a viable pathway to a baccalaureate degree?', *Educational Evaluation and Policy Analysis*, vol. 31, no. 1, pp. 30–53.

Lumina Foundation (2016) *A Stronger Nation*, Indianapolis, IN, Author.

Marcotte, D. E., Bailey, T., Borkoski, C., and Kienzl, G. S. (2005) 'The returns of a community college education: Evidence from the National Education Longitudinal Survey', *Educational Evaluation and Policy Analysis*, vol. 27, no. 2, pp. 157–175.

McCarthy, M. A. (2015) *Flipping the Paradigm: Why We Need Training-Based Pathways to the Bachelor's Degree and How to Build Them*, Washington, DC, New America.

Monaghan, D. and Attewell, P. (2015) 'The community college route to the bachelor's degree', *Educational Evaluation and Policy Analysis*, vol. 37, no. 1, pp. 70–91.

Morest, V. S. (2013) *Community College Student Success: From Boardrooms to Classrooms*, New York, NY, Rowman and Littlefield Publishers, Inc.

National Conference of State Legislatures (2017) *Free Community College* [Online], Denver, CO, Author. Available at www.ncsl.org/research/education/free-community-college.aspx (Accessed 24 March 2018).

National Skills Coalition (2017) *Investing in Postsecondary Career Pathways* [Online], Washington, DC, Author. Available at www.nationalskillscoalition.org/resources/publications/investing-in-postsecondary-career-pathways (Accessed 24 March 2018).

Provasnik, S. and Planty, M. (2008) *Community Colleges: Special Supplement to the Condition of Education 2008: Statistical Analysis Report* [Online], Washington, DC, National Center for Education Statistics. Available at https://nces.ed.gov/pubsearch/pubsinfo.asp?pubid=2008033 (Accessed 24 March 2018).

Remington, N. and Remington, R. (2013) *Alternative Pathways to the Baccalaureate*, Sterling, VA, Stylus Press.

Roksa, J. (2008) 'Structuring access to higher education: The role of differentiation and privatization', *Research in Social Stratification and Mobility*, vol. 26, no. 1, pp. 57–75.

Romano, R. M. and Palmer, J. C. (2015) *Financing Community Colleges: Where We Are, Where We're Going*, Lanham, MD, Rowman and Littlefield.

Rosenbaum, J. E., Ahearn, C. E., and Rosenbaum, J. E. (2017) *Bridging the Gaps: College Pathways to Career Success*, New York, NY, Russell Sage Foundation.

Rosenbaum, J. E., Deil-Amen, R., and Person, A. E. (2006) *After Admission: From College Access to College Success*, New York, NY, Russell Sage Foundation.

Rouse, C. E. (1998) 'Do two-year colleges increase overall educational attainment? Evidence from the states', *Journal of Policy Analysis and Management*, vol. 17, no. 4, pp. 595–620.

Schlafly, P. (1997) 'School-to-work and Goals 2000', *The Phyllis Schlafly Report* No. 30 (9) [Online], Alton, IL, Eagle Forum. Available at http://eagleforum.org/psr/1997/apr97/psrapr97.html (Accessed 24 March 2018).

Scott-Clayton, J. (2015) 'The shapeless river: Does a lack of structure inhibit students' progress at community colleges?', in Castleman, B. L., Schwartz, S., and Baum, S. (eds.), *Decision Making for Student Success: Behavioral Insights to Improve College Access and Persistence*, New York, NY, Routledge, pp. 102–123.

Scott-Clayton, J., Crosta, P. M., and Belfield, C. R. (2014) 'Improving the targeting of treatment: Evidence from college remediation', *Educational Evaluation and Policy Analysis*, vol. 36, no. 3, pp. 371–393.

Seidman, A. (ed.) (2005) *College Student Retention*, Westport, CT, Praeger.

Shapiro, D., Dundar, A., Huie, F., Wakhungu, P., Yuan, X., Nathan, A., and Hwang, Y. A. (2017) 'A national view of student attainment rates by race and ethnicity–Fall 2010 cohort', *Signature Report* No. 12b, Herndon, VA, National Student Clearinghouse Research Center.

Strawn, J. (2011) *Farther Faster: Six Promising Programs Show How Career Pathway Bridges Help Basic Skills Students Earn Credentials That Matter*, Washington, DC, Center for Law and Social Policy.

Thaler, R. H. and Sunstein, C. R. (2008) *Nudge: Improving Decisions about Health, Wealth, and Happiness*, New Haven, CT, Yale University Press.

Thaler, R. H., Sunstein, C. R., and Balz, J. P. (2013) 'Choice architecture', in Shafir, E. (ed.), *Behavioral Foundations of Public Policy*, Princeton, NJ, Princeton University Press, pp. 429–439.

U.S. National Center for Education Statistics (2017) *Digest of Education Statistics* [Online], Washington, DC, Author. Available at https://nces.ed.gov/programmes/digest/current_tables.asp (Accessed 24 March 2018).

U.S. National Center for Education Statistics (n.d.) *Total Number of Credentials Awarded by Title IV Postsecondary Institutions, Overall and in Occupational Education, by Credential Level, Control, and Level of Institution: United States, 2013* [Online], Washington, DC, Author. Available at https://nces.ed.gov/surveys/ctes/tables/P152.asp (Accessed 24 March 2018).

U.S. Office of the President (2010) *Building American Skills through Community Colleges* [Online], Washington, DC, Author. Available at https://obamawhitehouse.archives.gov/issues/educa tion/higher-education/building-american-skills-through-community-colleges (Accessed 24 March 2018).

Wyner, J., Deane, K. C., Jenkins, D., and Fink, J. (2016) *The Transfer Playbook: Essential Practices for Two-and Four-Year Colleges* [Online], New York, NY, Columbia University, Teachers College, Community College Research Center. Available at http://ccrc.tc.columbia.edu/ publications/transfer-playbook-essential-practices.html (Accessed 24 March 2018).

Zeidenberg, M., Cho, S. W., and Jenkins, D. (2010) *Washington State's Integrated Basic Education and Skills Training Program (I-BEST): New Evidence of Effectiveness*, New York, NY, Columbia University, Teachers College, Community College Research Center.

Conclusions

Chapter 15

Challenges for college education

Reflections and some conclusions

Jim Gallacher and Fiona Reeve

In our introductory chapter, we identified three roles or missions for colleges which can be identified in many countries across the world, although the form and emphasis may vary between countries. These are: the provision of vocational education and training (VET); the promotion of social inclusion; and the provision of higher education, and links with the higher education institutions. Many further education colleges in the UK, Ireland and community colleges in the USA and Canada now attempt to pursue all of these missions. While the chapters in this book have demonstrated the multi-faceted contributions which colleges are now making to education and training, they have also shown that there can be conflict between these missions, and this can weaken the contribution which colleges are making. In this respect, Keep notes that 'English FE finds itself torn between delivering a social inclusion, second chance agenda and trying to upgrade the status of its traditional vocational E&T offering'. In this concluding chapter, we will begin by considering some of the challenges which colleges face as they seek to reconcile these potentially conflicting missions, before going on to consider some of the opportunities for colleges which are emerging.

Challenges for colleges

In our introductory chapter, we discussed two major changes in the economy and in society which have weakened the position of colleges in many countries. The first of these has been changes in the nature of work, including the impact of de-industrialisation, the decline of apprenticeship training and the continuing impact of automation and globalisation, which have arguably resulted in a 'hollowing out' of the labour market, with a greater emphasis of jobs which require higher levels of skills and a relative decline in jobs at the intermediate level. The second has been the 'surge' in participation in mass higher education across the world (Marginson, 2016) and the tendency for many young people to proceed to university and degree education rather than part-time vocational education in colleges alongside employment. The impact of these changes has been to weaken the position of colleges as providers of vocational education as traditional training markets have diminished, and universities have increasingly been recognised as the providers of education for occupations involving higher level skills. In this respect, Keep notes that in the UK Industrial Strategy published in 2017, colleges get only a 'walk-on part', while the main focus is on scientific research and R&D (DBEIS, 2017). Associated with this has been a decline in the strength of links with employers. Keep emphasises the importance of employers and the choices which they make with respect to training but the relatively low level of demand from employers in the UK and the limited levels of training which they themselves provide. We have also noted in the introductory chapter that the limited linkages between employers and the education and training system in the Anglophone countries can be contrasted with the much more highly integrated systems which exist in Germany and other European societies (Deissinger in this volume and Wheelahan and Moodie, 2017). One impact of this more limited level of engagement between colleges and employers can be seen in the relatively marginal role which colleges now have in the direct provision of apprenticeships in the UK, which is noted in Reeve and Gallacher's chapter. By contrast independent training providers have been more successful in responding the needs of employers and now have a major role in apprenticeship training (Hupkau and Ventura, 2017).

Associated with this diminishing role with respect to VET has been an increasing emphasis on the social inclusion agenda, and the provision of 'second chance' learning opportunities for both young people and adults. The wider social inclusion role of colleges has only been discussed relatively briefly in this book, reflecting the limited research on this issue. However, the role of colleges in widening access to higher education has received greater attention. Dougherty et al. indicate the continuing importance of this role for community colleges in the USA in their chapter, and it has become increasingly important for colleges in other Anglophone countries, including the UK, Ireland and Australia. Linked to this is the third mission we have identified, the provision of higher education, and opportunities for transfer to degree courses in universities, or the provision of access or bridging courses which create second chance opportunities for entry to bachelor's degrees. While the chapters by Dougherty et al., Riddell and Hunter Blackburn, and Bergin et al. indicate the success which colleges have in promoting social inclusion, and widening access to higher education, they also document some of the limitations of this work, and some of the conflicts in mission it can give rise to. A particularly significant issue in this respect is the evidence from the work of Riddell and Hunter Blackburn that students from the most disadvantaged groups are more likely to find opportunities in the colleges and the less prestigious post-92 universities in Scotland, while students from the more advantaged family backgrounds are more likely to enter the higher-status, 'ancient' universities. Bergin et al. also report that students from the Irish colleges were more likely to gain entry to the less prestigious Institutes of Technology rather than the universities. A further problem is one of relatively low completion rates in community colleges and disappointing progression rates to four-year degree programmes, reported by Dougherty et al. All of this confirms the concerns of Brint and Karabel that colleges could have a potential 'cooling out' role as a result of which students are 'diverted' from four-year bachelor programmes in universities (Brint and Karabel, 1989). This then indicates a possible conflict between these two closely related missions for the colleges; the measures to provide new routes into higher education may in fact be at odds with a focus on social inclusion. Bathmaker in her chapter also discusses a further range of difficulties colleges face in 'seeking distinction and addressing equity' which emerge from their ambiguous location at the 'nexus of higher education and VET'.

Bergin et al.'s discussion of the issue of access to higher education also highlights another important problem which colleges must address. They note that, with the growth of a system of mass higher education in Ireland, many young people now see this as their goal and see entry to college and progression through this route as an unsatisfactory second best. This reflects the greater prestige accorded to academic rather than vocational qualifications in many countries, and particularly those in the Anglophone tradition. This is often contrasted to the high status of vocational routes in German speaking countries, although it can be noted that even in Germany, there are now more young people who are entering higher education than the dual system, which has been so dominant in vocational training (Deissinger's chapter). This problem of a lack of status for vocational education training has been reflected in policy in many countries. Paul Little comments on the emphasis which there has been on higher education in the UK, and Keep has noted the weakness of the college sector in the policy agenda. This has then contributed to weaker funding streams for the college sector, which in turn make it more difficult to provide high quality provision, especially for subject areas such as STEM which are increasingly seen as policy priorities (Keep and also Reeve and Gallacher in this volume).

It is clear from much which has been written in this book, and in other research and policy documents, that colleges, despite rhetoric about their continuing importance for VET and wider skills agendas, now lack status in many countries throughout the world, and there is a lack of clarity about their purposes and priorities. If they are to establish positions of greater significance in systems of education and training these problems much be clearly recognised and addressed, as Little argues in his chapter. We will now consider some options which may open opportunities to take this agenda forward.

Opportunities for colleges

At a policy level, the importance of colleges continues to be acknowledged, and indeed, as some of our contributors have suggested, it has been re-emphasised as politicians recognise the value of effective skills policies. For example, the UK politician Vince Cable's recognition of the value of investment in a dual mandate for colleges, which involves both vocational education and social inclusion, as an alternative to further expansion of the higher education sector has been widely quoted (see, for example, Doel and Little in this volume). However, too much of this policy has been at the level of rhetoric rather than leading to initiatives which make a real difference. In this respect, Cher Pong's outline of a comprehensive skills policy in Singapore is interesting. This recognises the role of the three main stakeholders: employers; individuals (including their representative organisations); and colleges and other training providers. It also recognises the need to address the predominance of the academic at the expense of the vocational, and the importance of work-based learning alongside college-based learning and begins to outline policies which are being implemented to address these issues. More generally, there have been some interesting developments in a number of countries which have moved beyond rhetoric and could create opportunities for colleges.

The renewed interest in apprenticeships in a number of countries is potentially important. Ryan discusses the initiative in the UK, which has set a target of three million new starts in England, and suggests that colleges could have a key role in providing the off-the-job training for many apprenticeship programmes. Cher Pong also refers to a programme in Singapore which is similar to apprenticeships and is termed the Earn and Learn Programme (ELP), but is targeted at graduates from polytechnics and the Institutes for Technical Education (ITE). Tang and Yuan also report a new interest in apprenticeships in China since 2010. In this case they note that a range of different types of pilots have been established to identify the most suitable model for different environments. Similarly, in the UK, we have also seen the development of several different types of apprenticeships, Higher and Degree, in England, and Foundation and Graduate in Scotland to sit alongside those at lower and intermediate levels. Those at the higher and degree/graduate levels are designed to produce new, higher level vocational qualifications to address skills gaps at that level. All of these developments suggest the possibilities of new opportunities for colleges to re-establish a role in this type of vocational education and training. However, there will be obstacles which must be overcome.

The first of these relates to the quality of apprenticeships in some cases. Ryan notes that there have been significant problems with the quality of much of what has been developed in England, and colleges may need to work with employers and the agencies responsible for the development of apprenticeships to ensure that programmes exist which provide the opportunity for high quality training. However, this leads to another problem in that we have noted that colleges in the UK now have limited involvement in apprenticeship training and with employers. Furthermore, employers' demands for training and their commitment to it have been low. It can be noted that this issue has also been recognised in China, and Tang and Yuan have outlined a range of national policy initiatives which have been designed to tackle this problem and establish closer integration between colleges and workplace enterprises.

All of this underlines the central importance of the links between colleges and employers if the role of colleges in vocational education and training is to be improved and re-established as a more central element in their missions. This point is underlined by Deissinger's discussion of the marginal role which full-time college education continues to have within the German VET system, associated with their limited engagement with employers and work-based training. However, Doel in his chapter suggests that professional and technical education and training (PTET) should be the defining role for colleges and at the core of what they do. His chapter is also helpful in attempting to define what is distinctive about technical education. However, it is clear that attempting to re-establish this central role for PTET, and the relationships with employers which will be required, will not be easy and new strategies will be required. One interesting proposal in this respect has emerged from the work of Hodgson and Spours and their associates in East London, where they have been developing new approaches to partnership, working with colleges and employers to create local High Progression and Skills Ecosystems (HPSE) (Hodgson et al., 2017). However, Keep in this volume has noted that international research suggests that while ecosystem approaches show considerable promise, implementing them will not be easy and will be resource intensive.

A related area of interest is the perceived lack of higher level vocational qualifications in many countries in a context where university-based degree education has become so dominant. Associated with this is the problem of graduate underemployment, which Little and Reeve and Gallacher refer to in their chapters. It has been noted that this is now around 30 per cent (Green and Henseke, 2017), and Alison Wolf has emphasised the importance of responding to this issue in a number of her recent publications (Wolf, 2016). In their chapter on higher level qualifications, Reeve and Gallacher suggest that there may be opportunities for colleges to build on their roles within the local or regional environments in which they operate and to identify the sectors in which there would be the greatest potential. Deissinger's discussion of the role of colleges in providing training for occupations in the health sector in Germany is an interesting example in this respect. This will again require careful work with employers to identify the best opportunities and to present options to students that they will see as being potentially rewarding. Developments of this kind may be best undertaken in colleges which already have a significant proportion of higher level courses, and they may wish to build on this to establish themselves as more specialist institutions. There may even be value in some colleges being re-designated with some suitable title such as institutes of technology or polytechnics. Cher Pong has noted that in Singapore the institutional architecture has been designed to create opportunities for students to progress to applied studies as alternatives to the academic route, while Deissinger notes that similar opportunities now exist in Germany through the universities of applied science (Fachhochschulreife). Bathmaker also comments on government initiatives in England to establish National Colleges and Institutes of Technology. Moodie et al. in their chapter outline another approach to establishing new qualifications of this type in their discussion of applied degrees in some of the community colleges in Ontario. They identify four characteristics of applied degrees:'the curriculum is specific to an occupation rather than a general preparation for work, life or further education; the pedagogy includes more practical work, often at a workplace, than non-applied degrees; the curriculum and pedagogy integrate knowledge fundamental to the practice of an occupation; and the outcome is a qualification relevant to the labour market'. It is suggested that in applied degrees, disciplinary knowledge will be recontextualised for the field of practice, and the field's established rules and practices will be restructured and systematised for teaching. As Moodie et al. suggest, this 'opens a distinctive role for colleges in codifying, restructuring and systematising rules and procedures of practice'. Further work around the idea of developing applied degrees in colleges could create interesting opportunities for the development of these higher level vocational qualifications. This would again involve developing close relationships with employers and employees.

If we move beyond the opportunities to strengthen the vocational mission of colleges, we can consider measures which might strengthen the work they do in widening access to higher education, which is discussed in several chapters in this volume. In this context, Dougherty et al. note the attention that the community college sector in the USA has received in the last ten years from the US government and foundations such as the Bill and Melinda Gates Foundation, reflecting the important but challenging role which these institutions have in American society. In a similar way, Riddell and Hunter Blackburn note that improving the articulation links between colleges and universities in Scotland will be an important issue for the Scottish Government's Commissioner for Fair Access, and this has indeed featured in his first annual report (Commissioner for Fair Access, 2017). In the case of the US community colleges, the focus has been on developing and implementing a reform programme designed to improve credential completion. In the case of Scotland, the focus is on measures to ensure that college students do not encounter unnecessary obstacles in making the transition from college to university, that they receive full credit for their college qualifications and that they are not restricted in the choice of institution or subject area. What is perhaps important to note when reflecting on what can be done to address these issues is that it will require change, not just in the colleges, but in national policy and relationships with other stakeholders, and particularly the universities. Dougherty, when commenting on the challenges which colleges face in implementing programmes to improve completion rates, notes the financial constraints which colleges have to work within, and Little has noted the more favourable policy and financial climate that the higher education institutions have worked within for many years. Riddell and Hunter Blackburn have commented on the uneven playing field which continues to exist between universities and colleges, making it difficult for colleges to negotiate partnership agreements with the universities as equals. Dougherty also comments on challenges from the universities which colleges face when seeking to implement change. We have noted in our introductory chapter that a lack of status is a problem which colleges face in many countries, reflecting the status of the academic route when compared with the vocational one. We have suggested that there has been policy rhetoric which emphasises the contributions which the college sectors make, but this seldom has resulted in policy and funding initiatives which result in any real change.

The importance of the policy frameworks within which colleges operate has been a theme which has emerged in a number of the contributions to this volume. Keep has contrasted differing approaches to skills policy, which shape the relationships between employers and colleges, Cher Pong has outlined a comprehensive policy framework in Singapore, and Bathmaker has discussed the impact of the changing policy landscape in England. It is clearly difficult for colleges themselves to change these policy agendas, but it seems crucial that more should be done to create alliances between national bodies which represent the colleges, employers and students to consider the most effective ways of having a voice in these policy debates. This could help to create a space in which colleges could make a more effective contribution in the field of vocational education and more widely to tertiary education. A related issue is the relative lack of research relating to the work of colleges, which makes it more difficult to develop evidence-based policy. We hope that one outcome of this book will be to encourage more research on the work of colleges which will inform future debates on policy and practice.

Concluding comments

In this concluding chapter, we have sought to bring together some of the key issues which have emerged from the various contributions to this book. In our final comments, we would like to highlight two questions for those involved in college education. The first is whether there is a need for colleges to focus more clearly on their key objectives. We have suggested that colleges may have three main functions or missions, but there can be tensions between them. The pursuit of one may conflict with the successful achievement of another, and at times those responsible for colleges may be insufficiently aware of this tension. The interviews with principals in the Irish colleges reported in Bergin et al.'s chapter would seem to indicate this. It is also clear that colleges can be driven by national policy priorities which can change too frequently and by funding models over which they have little control. However, there may be opportunities for colleges to identify more clearly what their key objectives should be within the range of functions they can perform and to develop strategies which enable them to pursue these objectives more effectively at the expense of others.

The second question is: what are the opportunities for 'policy learning' which may be helpful in establishing successful strategies for the future? David Raffe made the distinction between 'policy learning' and 'policy borrowing', and this continues to be very helpful in considering how we can learn from successful policies and initiatives in other countries (Raffe and Byrne, 2005). In his work, he emphasised the dangers of policy borrowing, in which policymakers identify interesting and successful initiatives in other countries, and seek to import them into their own countries. A common example of this would be the German dual apprenticeship system, which has been widely admired throughout the world, but cannot easily be transposed into other contexts, where there has been a very different history of relationships between employers, workers and providers of VET. By contrast, Raffe suggests we can learn from other countries by considering what is working and why and what opportunities there may be to adapt our own policy and practice in the light of this learning. There are several examples of attempts to engage in policy learning outlined by a number of our contributors (see, for example, Cher Pong and Tang and Yuan), and we hope that this book may encourage more work of this kind.

References

Brint, S. G. and Karabel, J. (1989) *The Diverted Dream: Community Colleges and the Promise of Educational Opportunity in America 1900–1985*, Oxford, Oxford University Press.

Commissioner for Fair Access (2017) *Laying the Foundations for Fair Access: Annual Report 2017* [Online], Edinburgh, The Scottish Government. Available at www.gov.scot/Publications/2017/12/2659/downloads#res529104 (Accessed 17 December 2017).

Department for Business, Energy and Industrial Strategy (2017) *Industrial Strategy: Building a Britain Fit for the Future*, Cm 9528, London, DBEIS/HMSO.

Green, F. and Henseke, G. (2017) *Graduates and "Graduate Jobs" in Europe: A Picture of Growth and Diversification, Centre for Global Higher Education*, London, UCL Institute of Education.

Hodgson, A., Spours, K., Jeanes, J., Smith, D., Vine-Morris, M., Vihriala, R., Bollam, J., Cook, B., Clendenning, D., Harris, M., and Kazempour, T. (2017) 'Education, skills and employment in East London: An ecosystem analysis', *ELVET Programme Research Briefing No. 1*, London, UCL Institute of Education, Centre for Post-14 Education and Work.

Hupkau, C. and Ventura, G. (2017) *Further Education in England: Learners and Institutions* [Online], Briefing Note 001, LSE, Centre for Vocational education Research. Available at http://cver.lse.ac.uk/textonly/cver/pubs/cverbrf001.pdf (Accessed 15 November 2017).

Marginson, S. (2016) 'High participation systems of higher education', *The Journal of Higher Education*, vol. 87, no. 2, pp. 243–270.

Raffe, D. and Byrne, D. (2005) *Policy Learning from "Home International" Comparisons* [Online], CES briefing No. 34, Edinburgh, Centre for Educational Sociology, University of Edinburgh. Available at www.ces.ed.ac.uk/PDF%20Files/Brief034.pdf (Accessed 30 September 2016).

Wheelahan, L. and Moodie, G. (2017) 'Vocational education qualifications' roles in pathways to work in liberal market economies', *Journal of Vocational Education & Training*, vol. 69, no. 1, pp. 10–27.

Wolf, A. (2016) *Remaking Tertiary Education: Can We Create a System That Is Fair and Fit for Purpose?*, London, Education Policy Institute.

Index

Note: Page numbers in italic indicate figures; those in bold indicate tables.

Lightning Source UK Ltd.
Milton Keynes UK
UKHW020629150622
404452UK00015B/248